The Edge

of

Everest

A WOMAN CHALLENGES THE MOUNTAIN

Sue Cobb

STACKPOLE
BOOKS

Published by
STACKPOLE BOOKS
Cameron and Kelker Streets
P.O. Box 1831
Harrisburg, PA 17105

Printed in the United States of America

10 9 8 7 6 5 4 3 2 1

First Edition

Library of Congress Cataloging-in-Publication Data

Cobb, Sue.
     The edge of Everest : a woman challenges the mountain / Sue Cobb.
     —1st ed.
          p.   cm.
     ISBN 0-8117-1681-3
     1. Cobb, Sue. 2. Mountaineers—United States—Biography.
3. Mountaineering—Everest, Mount (China and Nepal) 4. Everest,
Mount (China and Nepal)—Description and travel.   I. Title.
GV199.92.C6A3   1989
796.5'22'092—dc20
     [B]   89-11385
                                                                              CIP

The Edge of Everest

To Chuck, Chris, and Toby,
to the Cowboys, and
to all those with the Cowboy spirit

CONTENTS

FOREWORD

When my close friend Sue Cobb first said "Aconcagua," I patted her politely and said, "Great," trying hard not to be condescending. But a year later, when she said "Everest," I could only barely conceal my wonderment, doubt, and above all, worry. It became worse when I started getting biweekly reports from Base Camp.

But whatever unhappy emotions she fostered when she first said "Everest" to me, it is all forgiven as I put down the last pages of this book. I read it nonstop in about as much time as a strong climber (not me) can negotiate the Khumbu Icefall. And it is every bit as exhilarating.

Even more—it's dead honest. With great economy of style, being direct and to the point (as she is in every part of her life), Sue has recounted one of the most remarkable stories of the mountains I have ever read, and for one single reason: by style and total objectivity, she captures the sheer agony of an Everest expedition in a way that is neither overdone nor exaggerated. It's real—every line of it—and should stand as the primer for years to come on the incredible hardships of it all. Sue Cobb will not be forgotten by anyone who reads this book.

—Frank Wells, President, The Walt Disney Company,
and coauthor of *Seven Summits*

In a remarkable combination of human effort and narration, Sue Cobb clearly and incisively shares the gamut of experiences, emotions, and personal insights one gains on this intense and unforgiving learning curve that is called an Everest climb.

—Dick Bass, developer of Snowbird Ski and Summer Resort,
oldest person to summit Everest (at age 55),
and coauthor of *Seven Summits*

ACKNOWLEDGMENTS

George McCown—chairman of the board of governors of the Wyoming Centennial Everest Expedition, venture banker, world traveler, civic leader, and philanthropist—gave magnanimously of his time, resources, and leadership skills, for which the team is extraordinarily grateful. On behalf of the Cowboys, I convey many thanks to Larry Parker and the other members of the WCEE board and to the WCEE's board of advisers and honorary board of governors.

We greatly appreciated the support and involvement of Wyoming Governor Mike Sullivan, United States senators Malcolm Wallop and Alan K. Simpson, Representative Dick Cheney (now Secretary of Defense), and the people of the state of Wyoming.

We are indebted to our many corporate sponsors, and to all of those individuals throughout the country who caught the Cowboy spirit and donated both time and money.

We thank Mary Skinner for her tireless work on behalf of the expedition, and the other Skinner family members who made so many sacrifices for the expedition. We thank Steve Zuckerman for his behind-the-scenes efforts.

To the 187 Tactical Airlift Squad of the Wyoming Air National Guard and particularly to the crew of MAC FLIGHT 1954-01, members of the 75th MAS, United States Air Force: many thanks, you are the greatest.

I thank my colleagues at Greenberg, Traurig, Hoffman, Lipoff, Rosen & Quentel, P.A., Miami, for their encouragement and support.

I am extremely grateful to personal friends of the Cobb family who gave funds so generously and who continued throughout the three months of the expedition to convey their support through calls, letters, and prayers. And, of course, my family. Thank you for making me feel like the most valuable human being in the world.

AUTHOR'S NOTE

This is not a hard-core climbing book. It is not even the definitive account of the remarkable saga of the Cowboys on Everest. It is a personal journey.

I am well aware that each of my teammates had a completely different experience on Everest than I did. I wish I could bring them all to life on these pages, so that the reader could hear their stories as well. But life's experiences are inevitably observed through the tinted glasses of the individual viewer. There are a myriad of stories to be told.

This is how I remember the Cowboy expedition.

Sue McCourt Cobb
April 1989

PROLOGUE

The evening of September 16, 1988, was one of the worst of my
life. For nine days I had carried back-breaking loads up the miserable
moraine of the East Rongbuk Glacier, which flows out of Everest's
north side into the high plateau of Tibet. Finally, I was resting at our
Advanced Base Camp at 21,120 feet. On my arrival there I had my first
opportunity to study carefully the most critical, most technical, and
most dangerous portion of our route: the North Col. Prone to avalanche, laced with crevasses, dotted with giant ice seracs that crash
down unexpectedly, this deadly 2,000-foot vertical wall of ice and
snow has stopped many teams in their tracks.

Bob and Courtney Skinner, the leaders of the Wyoming Centennial Everest Expedition, who had invited me to join them on Everest,
both had acute high-altitude sickness and were at our Base Camp
several thousand feet below. In the Advanced Base Camp were twenty
of my teammates, not one of whom thought that I could climb the
North Col, much less reach the top of Mount Everest. I was exhausted, lonely, and depressed, with no moral support and little prospect of gaining any. Now it was time to start up the North Col and into
Everest's Death Zone. I didn't know if I could find the inner strength
to carry on.

Thirteen thousand miles away, my husband, Chuck, was in Detroit with several other members of the University of Miami board of
trustees to see the Miami football team play Michigan. Chuck was
riding in a taxicab with Jim McLamore and Mel Greenberg, explaining
to those two friends what was happening on my trip to Everest. As he
was describing our climb, the cabbie slowed the car, turned, and

asked, "Are you talking about that group of Cowboys from the United States that are trying to climb Mount Everest?"

Chuck answered, "Yes."

The driver, with some excitement, responded not with a question but with a statement: "That woman's not your wife!"

"Yes, she is," said Chuck. For a moment there was silence.

"I've been following that team since they left the States," the cabbie said. "I think it's fantastic—what they're doing." He paused in thought. "You know they're just ordinary people . . . ordinary people trying to climb the highest mountain in the world. Someday I'm going to do something like that."

And that is exactly what Courtney Skinner wanted to accomplish, to show a cab driver in Detroit—and perhaps a few others—that ordinary people can do extraordinary things.

Everyone has an Everest inside.
It may not be a mountain peak, or a raging river,
or a deep ocean, but we all have our challenges.
It is reaching beyond our grasp,
striving to go further than we ever thought we could,
that makes life worthwhile.

Courtney J. Skinner

CHAPTER I

International Incident

JULY 30, 1988. SAN FRANCISCO. I remember the moment it hit me that I would be spending three months away from home in a hostile world of rock, ice, and snow. One Sunday in mid-July, Chuck and I were on the bridge of a boat anchored in the harbor off Martha's Vineyard, enjoying the gourmet lunch our good friends Frank and Dale Loy had brought aboard. It was a luscious day—clear and warm, with a soft breeze. Sitting in our bathing suits, with glasses of white wine in hand, we toasted our health and our blessings. Suddenly there flashed through my mind a vision of the base camp below the East Rongbuk Glacier, the starting point of our route to the top of the world—Mount Everest, 29,028 feet high. The model for this vision was the base camp of Aconcagua in the Argentine Andes, the highest peak in the Western Hemisphere. It is bleak and dirty. Trash and waste from people, dogs, and mules defile the vegetationless plateau. Remnants of previous expeditions litter that rocky wasteland. There is not one inviting thing about it. The contrast between that vision and my present reality was jolting.

While playing on the grass courts at the International Tennis Hall of Fame in Newport, Rhode Island, that same July weekend, I was reminded that the game of tennis, one of my life-long hobbies, was founded on gentility. It is a very civil ritual. My mind turned to the upcoming venture—just about as far away from civilization and gentility as one can get.

I like these stark contrasts, black and white, the extremes. It seems to me that contemplating the extremes, experiencing the extremes, puts more life into the middle ground where most of us live most of the time.

In two days I leave for China. This afternoon my friend Shari DuBois treated me to lunch. She asked, as all my friends do, what this upcoming trip is all about. The Wyoming Centennial Everest Expedition is a bold venture. It is one of Wyoming's first official centennial events. The cowboy symbol is meant to represent the Wyoming—and American—spirit of independence, free enterprise, and love of challenge. The Cowboys, as we call ourselves, intend to climb Mount Everest via the difficult Northeast Ridge route in the classical siege style: fixed ropes, oxygen, and a chain of preestablished camps. The thirty-five members of the all-American team were selected by leaders Courtney and Bob Skinner after a series of interviews and training climbs. One of the goals is to provide Himalayan climbing experience for young American climbers. Another goal, which has devolved on nearly every American team in the last few years, is to put the first woman from the United States on the summit of Mount Everest.

Climbing the mountain is not our only purpose. Members of the expedition will participate in valuable scientific programs, including geological research pertaining to the uplift history of the Everest region, glacial geology for age-dating, and structural geology indicating extension of the known normal fault to the high summits. The team will take atmospheric samples for chemical analysis, and will participate in demonstrating a real-time weather-forecasting model in conjunction with the meteorology department at Penn State University. Perhaps of greatest impact will be the medical research, the focus of which is the testing and use of portable hyperbaric chambers for medical emergencies. The inclusion of educators and artists on the team ensures that on our return, our experiences will be shared with others.

The expedition is ambitious, and the personnel are diverse and talented. In addition to research capabilities, the team, collectively, has the ability to cook, sew, repair, and make any needed items from bibs to headlamps to radios. Members must splice ropes, repair stoves, dig snow caves, build igloos, put in ropes and ladders, modify oxygen regulators and masks, climb and sleep in subzero weather at high altitudes, and not incidentally, sustain their equilibrium over three long months away from home. The Cowboys have no Sherpas and no porters. Except for low-altitude yak support, all tasks, including all carrying of gear, fixing camps, cooking, and cleaning, will be done by team members.

JULY 31, 1988. I'm en route to Travis Air Force Base to meet the Wyoming Air National Guard C-130 transport plane, which is bringing most of the climbers to the West Coast from team headquarters in Pinedale, Wyoming. We had bad news this morning. The Chinese have refused to allow our United States military plane to land in China. We are now being told that we must go to Okinawa. About 17,000 pounds of equipment and supplies has already been sent to Beijing by freighter, but how will we get into China the 12,000 pounds that we are carrying? How will we get the total of 29,000 pounds from Beijing to Base Camp? How will we arrange and pay for commercial flights for our people? Serious problems. I contacted the United States embassy in Beijing today and others are making calls to try to resolve the problem.

The team arrives in a few minutes. We will all be together tonight for the first time for a press conference at the Top of the Mark. I am curious about these people with whom I'll be living for the next three months.

AUGUST 1, 1988. TRAVIS AIR FORCE BASE. 2:30 A.M. Our C-5, the largest airplane in the world, leaves at 9:30 for Dover, Delaware, the first leg of our trip. We will stay overnight in Dover so that a helicopter can be loaded aboard. My 24-year-old son, Tobin, has been able to join me for the flight to China. Chuck and our 25-year-old son, Christian, will meet us in Beijing.

EN ROUTE TO DOVER. Toby and I have settled into our seats for the first leg. Most everyone is sleeping—a good time to get accustomed to talking to my tape recorder, which will be my high-tech diary.

This flight really began years ago on the wings of a dream in the mind of Courtney J. Skinner, mountaineer, educator, and unabashed romantic. Court and his five brothers grew up in the shadows of the wild and beautiful Wind River Mountains of Wyoming. In the below-zero Wyoming winters, they learned survival as a way of life. Later, the Skinner brothers would work together at their Wilderness School in Pinedale to pass on their knowledge to thousands of students and young adults who spend summers hiking, fishing, climbing, horse-back riding, and rafting under their tutelage.

Bob Skinner, with us now as director of mountaineering, was a world-class rock climber and skier who later taught survival for the Air Force. Now Bob runs the Skinner Brothers' elk- and deer-hunting operations. Bob is the John Wayne of the outfit: strong, quiet, espous-ing the fundamental values of the Old West, leading by example, expecting the most from each person, and doing the most himself. Over six feet tall and close to 200 pounds, with a no-nonsense atti-tude, he is also known as the Enforcer. Paradoxically, Bob is also a fabulous cook and a talented seamstress. He has developed, de-signed, and sewn many innovative mountain products, such as a cold-weather survival suit and a chimney-topped, spindrift-proof tent. Bob could have made someone a dandy wife.

If Bob is John Wayne, Courtney is Gene Autrey. Smaller in stature, less obviously the cowboy, obviously the dreamer. And Courtney has big dreams: Take a large, self-sustained, all-American team across China and Tibet to follow in the footsteps of British climbers George Leigh Mallory and Andrew Irvine, with a siege-style assault on Mount Everest. Take students and teachers and artists and scientists. Open the Himalayas to young American climbers and senior citizens. Cele-brate the cowboy spirit that opened the West! Celebrate Wyoming! Celebrate America!

Courtney is the expedition leader. He is a geologist by training and an explorer by nature. He spent five years at the South Pole with the United States Antarctic Research Program. Though he has never led an expedition to the Himalayas, he has led expeditions in many other parts of the world. "There's an Everest in everyone," he says, and he believes that given the opportunity, people will not only suc-ceed, but excel.

I like Court's philosophy and I like his deputy leader, Fred Ried-man. Fred saved my life once, on a training climb in South America. Fred is 30 years old and lives in Salt Lake City. A climber, skier, and biker, he is solid in body and spirit, gentle and even-keeled, but his quiet nature belies his resolve. Fred's extensive mountaineering back-ground adds depth to our team.

I have climbed with a few other members of the team, but most I am meeting for the first time.

As for me, I'm one of the senior citizens, a 50-year-old wife, mother, and attorney on leave of absence from my law firm, with a lifelong love of the mountains but limited big-mountain climbing experience.

Before we left the States, I was often asked, "How long have you been in training for this venture?" The answer is, all my life. I grew up on a ranch in Southern California in a quiet and protected environment. My brother Peter and I honed some of the same instincts for independence and self-sufficiency that the Skinners were perfecting in Wyoming. I could fish, hunt, ride, and calf-rope before I was 10. I attended a small public school, where I was a good student and a good athlete. Before I outgrew loving my horse more than any human, I found myself enrolled at Stanford University. My pastoral life changed forever.

When I was a sophomore at Stanford, I met a lanky, crew-cut student-athlete who had his eyes set on the Olympics and who trained, studied, and played with more intensity than anyone I'd ever known. Before he made the 1960 United States Olympic team as an alternate in the 110-meter high hurdles, we were married. I was 21. He was 22. With both of us working, we scraped together $60 a month to pay rent on a weather-beaten one-bedroom wooden house behind the Stanford campus. Chuck graduated, served as an officer in the Navy, got an M.B.A. at Stanford, then focused with his accustomed intensity on business and, not surprisingly, met with considerable success.

Along the way I taught at a private girls' school, became mother of two sons, and pursued my athletic interests by taking up alpine skiing at the resorts near our home in San Francisco. In 1971, I felt I was sufficiently skilled to enter some races and at age 34 I ran my first downhill. I thought I'd found my calling in life! I spent the ski season weekends racing on the veteran's circuit with ex-collegiate and Olympic stars and had some very satisfying results. After the national championships I was ranked number two in the nation by the United States Ski Association in veteran skiing. That year I also won the United States National NASTAR championships in Aspen. For my first season of racing I was having phenomenal success and I loved it. Then Chuck was offered an exciting new business opportunity, to be the chief executive officer of Arvida Corporation. In the summer of 1972 we moved to Miami. My ski racing career was over.

In Florida, tennis replaced skiing, and with my normal attentiveness to the subject at hand, I practiced several hours every day: a hundred forehands down the line, a hundred backhands down the line, then cross-courts, volleys, serves, overheads; play through a specific point, do it again, again, and again. Boring. But I won my share of tournaments and had an enjoyable tennis business on Key Biscayne with my good friends Donna Floyd Fales and Andy Garcia.

By 1974 Chris and Toby had reached junior high school and began to stay after school for sports. Family constraints no longer defined my free time. Tennis was obviously not taking me to Wimbledon. In fact, my friends said that with my forehand, I wasn't going *anywhere*. I began thinking about a part-time job, but even with a B.A. from Stanford, I wasn't qualified to do much. Nor did I have any marketable talents.

Then one day I formulated a plan to go back to school and get an advanced degree. I just didn't know what discipline I should try. The University of Miami in Coral Gables was close by—what was their best graduate school? I'd heard about the new woman dean at the law school, Soia Mentschikoff. Why not law? The law school application material reminded me that there was an entrance exam, the L.S.A.T. I hadn't been in school for fifteen years; I didn't know whether I had the right mind for law or not; I was afraid I'd fail the test. Maybe I'd just take it and see if the results showed any aptitude for law. If I was a total failure, I'd look elsewhere. I didn't want anyone to know, so I didn't even tell Chuck—I just slipped out and took the exam. Somewhat to my surprise, in 1975, at age 38, I found myself entering the University of Miami School of Law.

Not without difficulty, I balanced the roles of wife, mother, and student, studied hard, and upon graduation was offered a job in one of Florida's most prestigious firms. For almost five years I practiced in the civil litigation section, handling a variety of commercial matters. I received sufficient encouragement to feel that I was on track to become a partner in the firm in June 1984, at the end of my sixth year. Then in May 1983 the senior partners approached me about switching to the corporate department and learning the field of municipal finance. They wanted to start a bond department and asked me to help lead the effort. I was interested in the new challenge, having grown weary of the cynical and constantly adversarial world of a trial attorney. But there were no assurances that the firm could be successful in the bond field (few firms outside New York had been), and I was worried about my partnership track. "Sorry, Sue, no assurances on that, either," said a senior partner. "Do you want this new job or not?"

It was time for a leap of faith. I said yes and entered into the steepest learning curve of my life. Along with my years of service on the Federal Reserve Bank board of directors in Miami, my exposure to the financial markets and the sophisticated practice of municipal finance opened another new world. Because we enticed several brilliant and experienced bond attorneys from northern firms to come join us, we grew rapidly. I worked hard those years, often twelve- to fifteen-hour days, with many all-nighters to meet the intransigent financial deadlines. Chuck, then the chief operating officer of Penn Central Corporation, lived during the week at the Carlyle Hotel in New York. On weekends we'd meet in Miami, New York, or someplace else where either of our businesses might send us. Eventually Chuck orchestrated a leveraged buyout of Arvida and moved back to Miami. And yes, I did make partner in June of 1984.

I was jostled out of my thoughts by the bustle of activity in preparation for landing.

DOVER, DELAWARE. **6** *P.M.* Elevation: 28 feet. As we landed, Steve Gardiner cracked: "Only 29,000 feet to go!"

We were assigned rooms, some in barracks and some in officers' quarters. I was assigned a two-bed room in the barracks already occupied by an enlisted woman. That was fine until I got there and found the room saturated with smoke. I think she'd been smoking nonstop for days. I found Julie Cheney and Sibylle Hechtel's room and slept on their floor. We were an odd lot: the 30-year-old blonde mountain guide and medical researcher; the 37-year-old German-American ice climber and Ph.D.; and me, the 50-year-old amateur climber and lawyer. We stumbled over each other and tried to be polite.

AUGUST 2, 1988. Up at 6 A.M., organizing gear, having breakfast, preparing for an 8 A.M. press conference. During the night I slept fitfully. I thought about my chances on Everest. I know that more people have traveled in space than have reached the top of Everest. I know that only about one of every six teams is successful. I know that no American team has been successful on our route, and that only one American has ever climbed Everest from the north side. I also know that historically, the death rate on Everest is almost 10 percent. Which three members of the Cowboy team will not be on the plane home? As a designated summiter, I can't help but think about the fact that for every person who reaches the summit, one dies trying. Pleasant dreams, Sue!

The morning press conference was interrupted by messages relating to the Chinese refusal to allow the team to land in Beijing. Saturday morning, before we left, we had received the Fax from our military contact in Washington, D.C., sent by the Chinese authorities: the Air Force C-5 and the helicopter were welcome in Beijing, but to protect the civilian airline authority of China (CAAC), the climbing team would have to enter Beijing via commercial aircraft. We were shocked and not prepared to respond quickly, since on Saturday all team members were in various stages of transit. No business could be conducted on Sunday, nor on Monday, a holiday in China. It appeared to be by design that the message was not relayed until Saturday morning, Pacific Standard Time, when we were literally up in the air. We had few alternatives and no time to bring pressure to bear on the CAAC or the Chinese Foreign Ministry. We decided to proceed as planned on the C-5.

With the support of the White House Science Office, which had been favorably impressed with the type and amount of research being done by the Cowboys, we became a Presidential Mission, eligible for space-available travel on a scheduled government flight to China. It was our good fortune that a United States Air Force C-5 was scheduled to fly to Lhasa, Tibet, in early August. The Wyoming Air National Guard agreed to transport the team to Travis Air Force Base on one of their training missions. Columnist Jack Anderson, in a nationally syndicated column, criticized the team's air support, but rightly pointed out that there had been no additional cost to the government or taxpayers, since the flight had previously been scheduled in conjunction with the Boeing company's helicopter demonstration in Tibet and was being paid for by Boeing.

I had been surprised that the United States Air Force could fly into, over, and around China, but when I asked about that one day at the Pentagon I was told, "It is not a problem." That has turned out to be inaccurate information as far as our team is concerned. Our chances of landing in Beijing do not sound good, now that our embassy in Beijing has told me that not even Queen Elizabeth had been allowed to enter China on her own plane. Thirty-five team members, eight Cowboy supporters (going only to Lhasa), and six tons of food and climbing gear are winging into the unknown.

We are now en route from Dover to Elmendorf Air Force Base in Anchorage, Alaska, and the issue has still not been resolved. We have in-flight communication with both Washington and Okinawa, but we do not know whether we will be able to get into China. MAC Flight 1954-01 continues under military orders to deliver us to Lhasa, Tibet. Through diplomatic channels, we have asked the CAAC to at least let all of our cargo (the 12,000 pounds aboard the plane and the 17,000 pounds in Beijing) go on the Air Force plane to Lhasa. The team may end up scattering and taking any commercial flights available, or we may have to charter a flight from Okinawa, Hong Kong, Tokyo, or Beijing. Our biggest concern is the security of our equipment. Our second biggest concern is the delay. Then there's the money. It's rather unsettling.

The C-5 aircraft is extraordinary. It is the largest airplane in the world. It can carry 350,000 pounds and has a cargo hold of 36,000 square feet. We sit above the cargo hold in a configuration that is similar to a commercial 747. There are, however, no windows and only about seventy seats, all facing backward. There is a crew of eighteen, including four pilots, two navigators, and a flight surgeon. We are sharing the ride with seventeen Boeing aircraft company employees who are accompanying the helicopter to Lhasa. The colonel in command gave every passenger a chance to see the cockpit and watch the crew in action—fun even for the most jaded traveler.

AUGUST 4, 1988. KADENA AIR FORCE BASE, OKINAWA, JAPAN. 7:30 P.M. We are billeted at the Shogun Inn, the distinguished visitors' quarters for Pacific Air Force, 313th Air Division. The weather here in Kadena is about the same as Dover: 98 degrees, 98 percent humidity. There is, however, a refreshing breeze.

Upon our arrival, the base commander boarded our plane and advised us that although the airwaves had been hot among Kadena, Washington, and Beijing, we did not have clearance to fly into China. We were taken to customs and were discussing our alternatives when a message arrived from the United States ambassador to China, Winston Lord. If we agree to certain conditions, we will be cleared into Beijing.

The CAAC is going to exact its pound of flesh by charging a $24,000 landing fee. We are delighted to be able to fly in on the C-5, but it's unlikely that the Chinese will let the team go with the Air Force to Lhasa. We will probably have to charter a CAAC plane. It's a pain in the rear. And will cost. We still hope to be able to send all our cargo to Lhasa on the C-5.

The change of heart on the part of the Chinese had not been happily forthcoming. By pure coincidence, my husband, then serving as undersecretary of commerce for travel and tourism for the United States, had a long-scheduled meeting with Director General Hu, the head of the CAAC, on the very day the Cowboys were winging to Kadena. Chuck was arguing for concessions for the Cowboys when a strongly worded telegram arrived from the White House. The telegram message was the product of telephone meetings and communiqués between the White House Science Office, Wyoming's two senators, Malcolm Wallop and Alan Simpson (both of whom served on the expedition's honorary board of governors), United States Ambassador Winston Lord and the Chinese ambassador to the United States, Han Xu. That combination has done the trick. We are going to be allowed to land in Beijing on the C-5. The Chinese will save face by exacting the landing fee, payable *before* we touch down. Fortunately, Chuck is on hand to advance the money.

AUGUST 5, 1988. The flight to Beijing was not uneventful. First we were told we couldn't take off because of weather. Then we took off, but had to turn around. Before we got back to Kadena we were again cleared to Beijing, this time to an auxiliary airport. As we approached Beijing, our crew was nervous. The weather was bad and the delays caused us to be uncomfortably low on fuel. Some of our knuckles turned white, but we had a smooth landing on a short, rain-slick runway. When the plane touched down, a spontaneous cheer went up from the team members. We had landed in China. We felt that we had made it. Yet we have a whole continent still to travel.

CHAPTER II

Chinese Checkers

AUGUST 6, 1988. BEIJING. Most of the team has scattered to see this strange and marvelous city. Courtney and Fred and I have been trying to figure out how we are going to move our people and gear from Beijing to Lhasa. The CAAC has unequivocally said that the C-5 cannot take us or our freight. We must book CAAC flights. Our gear will have to go overland by truck. Courtney and Fred were still negotiating with the Chinese when I left with Chris, Chuck, and Toby to go to Xi'an for a day. We expect to meet the team in Lhasa.

AUGUST 7, 1988. CHENGDU, SZECHWAN PROVINCE. My family and I spent a day in Xi'an seeing the terra-cotta warriors, fired and buried in the third century B.C. by the last emperor of the Qin Dynasty. To date some 6,000 warriors in battle formation have been excavated. We departed for the Xi'an airport at 10 P.M. to get our flight to Chengdu, only to be informed that our CAAC flight would be delayed for several hours. We were learning what many others already knew: CAAC stands for China Airlines Always Cancels. We finally arrived at the airport at midnight. In a crush and mad rush (because everyone knows there may never be another flight) we got on the plane.

At the Chengdu airport we were greeted by some tired Chinese tourism officials, who took us to the Jin Jiang Hotel. It was 3 A.M. We would have a 5:45 A.M. wake-up call to be back at the airport for a 7 A.M. CAAC flight to Lhasa. With an hour and a half of sleep we again hit the muddy road to the Chengdu airport, only to learn— guess what—that the CAAC flight to Lhasa had been canceled. Toby, Chris, and Chuck all began to panic about how they were going to get out of China to meet their various commitments. They asked the tourism official who was escorting us back to the hotel to try to ar- range a flight for all three of them to Canton the following day. I began to panic about where I was going to meet the team, since I did not know whether they had gotten out of Beijing. Overhearing us, our English-speaking van driver commented on having seen two buses around 3 A.M., on the airport road, carrying a lot of Anglos. At the hotel, I learned that the Cowboys were, indeed, in Chengdu, asleep. I left messages for Courtney and Fred and went back to bed. But sleep has not come.

This is where I part company with my family. In the recesses of my mind is the thought that anything can happen. Certainly I will be exposed on this expedition. I worry about the other terrible prospect— that a tragedy could befall a member of my family while I am away and so out of touch as to be useless. I could barely talk to Chuck all day because every time I looked at him, I was reminded that it will be well over two months before I see him again—if I get back alive.

3 P.M. After our disorganized night, we slept until midday. I located my teammates and went with Julie Cheney, Sibylle Hechtel and Jeb Schenck to do some Coors Light beer photographs in the marketplace in Chengdu. We think that the team will be able to depart at 7 A.M. tomorrow for Lhasa (unless the CAAC cancels its flight, of course). The gear that was left in Beijing is to be transported by five trucks and is to meet us in Xegar, one day's drive from the Everest Base Camp. With the drivers changing off and driving night and day, it is expected to arrive on August 13, only two days behind our scheduled arrival of August 11. I am skeptical. It is important, however, for the team to be in Lhasa for two or three days anyway, for acclimatization, so we will do our best to get there and *hope* that our gear will meet us in Xegar. The C-5 is in Chengdu and, according to the United States Air Force, is still available to us if the CAAC destroys our plans again. At this point, however, it appears unlikely that the Chinese will help us expe- dite our travel. They're making too much money off us. There are those members of the team who call it extortion.

Since rejoining the team in Chengdu, the best story I've heard is an account of Dave Frawley's adventure in the Forbidden City in Beijing, the day I was in Xi'an. "It seems," Fred Riedman, Sr., says, "rest rooms were in short supply, and after two hours with bladder bursting, Dave barely made it into a public rest room. Dave crowded into a place along the fully occupied men's urinal. As Dave was relieving himself with great satisfaction, his most valuable possession, his passport, dropped into the urinal and was swiftly floating down the yellow river toward the cesspool. Dave, while continuing to relieve himself, knocked down a number of Chinese men and retrieved the passport at a modest depth." I understand he was chased out of the rest room by a gang of wet and angry men.

On a more serious note, Dan Pryor related that Courtney had announced in Beijing that since the expedition had suddenly incurred expenses for hotel rooms and cargo transport, each team member would have to contribute additional money. For some members, the news landed like a small bomb. They felt victimized. To others, it was not an unexpected twist.

AUGUST 8, 1988. Our wake-up call came at 5:30 A.M. for the bus ride from the hotel to the airport for the ever-questionable CAAC flight, scheduled out at 7:40. Amazingly, the plane left around 8, but only after twenty-six members of our team were bumped. I made the cut and am en route from Chengdu to Lhasa, no longer with family support.

Chuck decided, because of his schedule of meetings in Hong Kong and the Philippines, that the CAAC's propensity to cancel flights made it too risky for him to try to go on to Lhasa. Chris wanted to get to Hong Kong in time to take part in the wedding of a friend who works in his architectural office in Coral Gables. Toby was ready to go home. So all three were booked on a plane from Chengdu to Canton. I have no idea whether their plane actually left.

My family has been solicitous of my adventure. Chuck is concerned, I know, and many times has suggested that I not push too hard. He even asked Courtney to see that I didn't go beyond my limits (an intrusion that I both appreciate and resent). Chris and I had a good laugh because, as we discussed our thoughts, it was clear to me that he was thinking of things from my perspective—why was I doing it, what were the rewards, what were the risks; while I was thinking of it from his perspective—how would you feel about your mother going off to climb Everest, how much danger is there, will she be back? There's nothing quite like your oldest son! Toby, from the beginning, has been my biggest cheerleader. His final words each day throughout the trip have been, "Go for it, Mom. Go for it." There's nothing quite like your youngest son!

The flight was a normal CAAC flight, which is to say, it wasn't great. We landed in Lhasa at 9:30 A.M. on a dismal day in what looked to be massive flooding. Steve Marts, who has flown into Lhasa several times, said it was the wettest that he had seen it. We heard that the British expedition, now in the base camp we are soon to occupy, has abandoned all summit attempts because the late monsoon weather has caused unusually heavy snow on Everest, resulting in extreme avalanche danger. Also, we heard there were major landslides on the Kathmandu-Lhasa road, and the road is out. That will affect the Georgia team, which we met at the Chengdu airport. Among the members of the Georgia trekking team is Dr. Henry King Stanford, a long-time family friend, former president of the University of Miami, interim president of the University of Georgia, world traveler, and renowned scholar. The Georgia team is attempting the Kangshung Face, a difficult route. Henry will trek to their base camp.

We boarded a bus for the two-hour drive from Gonkar Airport to the town of Lhasa and booked into the Lhasa Hotel, where we have special room arrangements courtesy of Holiday Inn, which manages the hotel. When we stepped off the bus, our team members who had already reached Lhasa were there to greet us. David Padwa has been here for two weeks. He is familiar with the city, has learned some Tibetan, and acts as our guide. Alexandra Hildebrandt and Ethan Goldings are also in town.

We had lunch and ventured downtown to the Bokhar, the old marketplace, to view the wares and kibitz with the Tibetans, even though we don't know each other's language. We did not see any overt signs of uprisings by the Tibetans against the Chinese, but we know that unrest is just below the surface. The Chinese invaded Tibet in 1950 and overthrew the Buddhist theocracy. Nine years later the Chinese army brutally suppressed a widespread rebellion, and the Dalai Lama, Tibet's spiritual leader, fled to India with thousands of followers. Tibet has since been rocked by periodic independence demonstrations, during which many Tibetans have been killed. Monks have been told that if they participate in a demonstration, they will be executed or imprisoned for life. Although Tibet is culturally, linguistically, and racially different, the Chinese have shown no intention of loosening their grip on this vast territory. To Beijing, Tibet is a strategic region, bordering on a potentially hostile India.

Lhasa, Tibet's capital, is a segregated city. An estimated 70 percent of the city's more than 100,000 people are ethnic Chinese who have come from other parts of the country to work here for hardship pay. The Chinese section, built since the Chinese invasion in 1950, looks much like any other Chinese city, with gray concrete office buildings and apartments. The Lhasa Hotel is in this "new" Chinese section. The Tibetan part of the city takes the visitor back several hundred years in history. In the center sits the Jokhang Temple, the holiest site in Tibet. It is surrounded by the Bokhar, the circular marketplace. Standing on a hill between the Lhasa Hotel and the Jokhang Temple is the 1,000-room Potala Palace, for centuries the home of the Dalai Lama and his entourage. Immediately next to the hotel is Norbu Lingka Palace, formerly the summer residence of the Dalai Lama. It is now the People's Park.

There is great poverty. We were advised to change our 10-yuan notes (the equivalent of about $3) to smaller bills to accommodate any purchases, as 10-yuan notes are too big for most Tibetans to change. The majority of Tibetans wrap themselves in layers of black cloth, mostly ragged and well used, but some dress in clothing that designates the region from which they come. Such garments are enlivened with bright red and blue embroidery.

The front of Jokhang Square is a gathering place for beggars and the infirm, seeking to engage the sympathy of each tourist who passes by. In the Bokhar, which circles the temple, Buddhist pilgrims prostrate themselves and move clockwise, one body length at a time, while merchants attempt to hawk their wares—handmade jewelry, cloth, yak butter, and prayer flags. Growing accustomed to foreign travelers, these entrepreneurs now have a few words of English, such as "last price," "change," and "money." Everything is negotiable. The Tibetans are so eager to sell their goods that they tirelessly follow any prospective buyer. It is difficult to say no. From our observations, Mack Ellerby couldn't. I last saw Mack earlier today walking across the square laden with necklaces and other trinkets, followed by a large entourage of vendors. The Pied Piper of the Bokhar. He seemed to be enjoying himself immensely.

All around the marketplace and on every hill and high point, multicolored prayer flags—worn by weather—flutter in the breeze. We will purchase prayer flags to put in our camps and white offering flags for our yaks. Maroon-robed monks sit patiently and beat drums while reading from prayer cards. Prayers spin off prayer wheels and chants blend harmoniously in the background. *Om mani padme hum. Om mani padme hum.* "Greetings, thou jewel of the lotus." The smell of incense is omnipresent. The buildings are mostly dull, white-washed limestone, one or two stories high. On the second floor of some, the window frames are painted in bright greens and blues and reds, giving the strange appearance of a decaying Austrian village. The streets have a significant amount of mud, but on the whole, Lhasa seems cleaner to me than Chengdu.

AUGUST 9, 1988. LHASA, TIBET. Elevation: 12,500 feet. I am rooming with Julie Cheney, our other designated woman summiter. She is a warm and sensitive individual, yet I know that she has a will of steel. I remember my reaction on the Mount Rainier training climb, when I first met Julie: "She's smart," I thought. "She has a great sense of humor. She sparkles—and she can bristle!" I like her a lot.

Although Julie has been climbing for only four or five years, she has dedicated herself to the sport. As a guide, she has made it her full-time profession. She seems to have the same ability to focus on and work tenaciously at a challenge that characterizes successful individuals in both sports and business. She also seems to be realistic in her expectations with regard to the mountain. I asked her what she expects to find on the high, exposed ridges that lead to the Everest summit. "I think it'll be very windy," she said. "So windy it sucks the air right out of your mouth. That's disconcerting and I'll feel a little panicked." She thought for a moment. "It's going to be a struggle, probably seven to eight breaths per step. It's going to be a struggle mentally and physically. But if you can put your head down and go, you can make it. Weather permitting, of course." I like her attitude.

AUGUST 10, 1988. Julie got up early and went with Dave McNally, Mack Ellerby, and Brian McLean to climb one of the small peaks nearby. I slept in (which I call "pacing myself"). I decided on a thirty-minute run and headed off towards the Norbu Lingka Palace. The 12,000-foot elevation slowed my running, but I felt good. I stopped by the Nepalese consulate to arrange for a visa, just in case we exit through Nepal.

The environment here is stimulating, with the bright blue sky and green-brown hills. The Tibetans smile and make us feel welcome. The Chinese, however, seem uncomfortable with Americans. They probably know that I am reading Peter Avedon's book, *In Exile from the Land of the Snows*, a disturbing account of the Chinese takeover of Tibet.

Our delayed team members arrived today from Chengdu. We are now missing only Brian Shoemaker and our liaison officer, known as the LO, who represents our host unit, the Chinese Mountaineering Association, or CMA. Every group that visits China must have a host. The LO of the host stays with the group throughout its trip, acting as both guide and observer. He checks us into hotels; he checks us out of hotels; he checks on our baggage; and he checks on us. We have also been assigned two interpreters, a jeep driver, and two aides. A year ago, Courtney and Fred flew to Beijing to negotiate our protocol with the CMA and fix our schedule, permits, hotels, transportation, and costs in China. It seemed like a contract to us, but now we see it is simply the basis for continuing negotiation.

After dinner last night the team gathered in the second-floor lounge of the Lhasa Hotel to meet a Buddhist lama, visiting from the Dalai Lama's retreat in India, with whom David Padwa has struck up a friendship. David asked the lama to discuss Tibetan-Chinese relations and give the team a Buddhist blessing. Our lama is 44 years old and on a year-long pilgrimage to Tibet. One of the many monks who fled with the Dalai Lama across the Himalayas into India in 1959, he has stayed in the exile Tibetan community in India, working with the Dalai Lama, building schools and keeping the Tibetan religion alive. His flowing purple robes commanded immediate respect and his soft but firm voice caused all of us to lean forward in eager anticipation to hear his comments. The blessing of the team was particularly moving. The lama presented Fred Riedman, as deputy leader, a traditional white offering scarf and a picture blessed by the Dalai Lama.

Next came a meeting with Ambassador Winston Lord and his wife, Betty Lord, author of *Spring Moon*. The Lords have been the United States representatives in China for the last three and a half years. The ambassador was helpful in mediating our problems with the CAAC, and I had invited him and Mrs. Lord to join us. Ambassador Lord was gracious in his comments and insatiably inquisitive about mountain climbing.

AUGUST 11, 1988. In the coffee shop today I met with the assistant manager of the Lhasa Hotel, who explained the hotel business in China. It seems that Holiday Inn was forced to manage the Lhasa Hotel in order to do business in the rest of China. Clearly, it is a frustrating job. The hotel is state owned, and employees are allocated here, as they are to all other jobs, by the party. No matter what the job, all employees are paid the same amount. Thus there is no incentive for anyone to excel. Some promotions are possible but bring a raise of only 3 yuan (approximately $1 U.S.) per month. Additionally, employees are not allowed the three-hour midday break that all other Tibetans and Chinese take. They are pushed hard and work longer hours than other locals, but the rewards are not commensurate. When there is a need for more employees, the personnel manager, who is a party member, assigns the next people on his list (without any hotel training, of course) to fill the jobs. In an attempt to provide entertainment to the European and American guests, the management purchased a hundred video tapes. Eighty of them, including *The Sound of Music*, were confiscated by the party.

While waiting for Brian and the LO to arrive, and for the CMA to arrange our transportation to Base Camp, we occupy much of our time with team meetings. The Cowboys are divided into five subteams. Team One is the Base Camp crew, led by Dan Pryor. Team Two, headed by Ted Handwerk, is the research and climbing support team whose primary duties will be to put in the low-altitude camps (Camps I, II, and III). Teams Three and Four, led by Jeb Schenck and Brian McLean, respectively, each have six high-altitude support climbers. They are responsible for the camps at 23,000 feet and above. The six designated summit team members—Jim Burnett, Julie Cheney, Orion Skinner, Fred Riedman, Jr., Bob Bohus, and I—make up the fifth subgroup.

Our meetings last night were productive. The four team leaders, Jeb, Brian, Ted, and Dan, met with the two Skinners and the summit team members to analyze the route maps, identify camp locations, and define each team's role on the mountain. We are fortunate that we have the benefit of enlarged sections of Bradford Washburn's new contour maps of Everest, scheduled for publication in the November 1988 *National Geographic*, which give us details never before available. Though the exact elevation of the top of Mount Everest seems to be the subject of continuing measurements, as of August 1988, 29,028 feet is accurate.

In Lhasa, we were able to observe the annual **tonka** *ceremony at the Drepung monastery. Opera troops in regional attire mix with the thousands of Tibetans who come to watch.* PHOTO BY JEB SCHENCK.

AUGUST 12, 1988. Today is the day we were scheduled to arrive in Base Camp. We're still in Lhasa. We hope that Brian Shoemaker and the LO will arrive today so that we can leave tomorrow.

We got up at 6:30 this morning to go to a ceremony at the Drepung Monastery, the center of four universities in Tibet before the Chinese takeover in 1950. In 1959 the Chinese bombed much of the monastery, and its population of 10,000 was reduced to about 200. The annual ceremony, rarely witnessed by foreigners, centers on the *tonka,* a tapestry about forty-five yards long. With the *tonka* on their shoulders, rolled up like a carpet on a showroom floor, the 200 monks ascend a hill beside the monastery. About 5,000 Tibetans, who have gathered from around the country for the occasion, line the route, throw white blessing flags onto the *tonka,* and join the procession. At the top of the hill, the monks let the *tonka* unroll itself downhill, revealing a colorful picture of Buddha. Thereafter, opera troops composed of men from outlying districts of Tibet begin an hour of chanting and dancing.

I hitchhiked a ride back to the Lhasa Hotel for yet another team meeting. For the last two days we have been uncertain about who will continue on the trip and who will be sent home. In Chengdu,

Courtney had apparently been told by the CMA that there were not enough trucks to get all forty-one of us (thirty-five Cowboys and six Chinese) and our fifteen tons of gear from Lhasa to Base Camp. When Courtney arrived with the second contingent of Cowboys on August 10, he immediately made that announcement. All of us were upset, but those who were the latest to join the team (or who had put in the least work or raised the least money) were especially uneasy. Then Courtney retired to his room for two days and refused to discuss the matter. He did not emerge even for the team's Buddhist blessing.

There have been so many uncertainties in this process of taking so many people and so much gear across China and Tibet that we are all frustrated. Team members feel like marbles manipulated by the Chinese in a nightmare game of Chinese Checkers. Courtney and Bob both appear exhausted from the months of anxiety and effort leading to our departure. Sometimes they're not communicative and sometimes the communication is unclear. I can understand the mental strain they've been under, but we need strong and decisive, not divisive, leadership. I'm discouraged. Perhaps after Courtney has rested a couple of days, he will be back in the proper frame of mind to lead this team forward. Meanwhile, small anti-Skinner groups are forming. Those most fearful of being sent home are angry and upset. Those of us who feel some degree of security recognize that we need everyone if we are to climb Everest. I'm not saying anything, but if any of my teammates are sent home, my inclination is to go with them. Today's meetings solved nothing.

We've been in Lhasa five days now. Every time I walk around this small city and its temples, I think about Chris because I know how much he would enjoy it. He loves to go off and mingle with people. He always returns with wonderful photographs of the faces of the local inhabitants, of their architecture, of their produce and wares. Actually, I try not to think about Chris and Toby and Chuck, because it makes me sad that they're not here. The four of us have traveled extensively together and it has always been an enormous pleasure. I miss Chris's quiet, contemplative style and unexpected, sudden streaks of humor. I miss Toby's unlimited and unbelievable energy and exuberance. I miss Chuck's presence. I even miss Chuck's incessant questioning, in every country, of every person who speaks English (and some who don't) with his insatiable thirst to learn more about their history, their religion, and their culture. I miss my family.

AUGUST 13, 1988. 9 A.M. We learned late yesterday that we're *all* going. We are waiting now for the trucks. Last night I took a long hot shower and wondered how long it would be before I had such comfort again. Ten weeks? Brian and the LO had arrived in the middle of the day and everything's on "go." There may yet be hitches with our gear, en route from Beijing. Washouts and mudslides are blocking the road, and the trucks are experiencing delays. Since we may have to stay in Xegar more than one day, Bob Skinner and his troops have gone out to purchase food and cooking utensils, so that we can take care of ourselves if necessary.

Courtney has now agreed, after initially refusing to let the team get split up again, that we should use the one Nissan wagon assigned to our team to send an advance party to Base Camp to meet with Sir Lowell Guinness and the leaders of the Everest '88 British Expedition. They have been occupying our Base Camp but are scheduled to leave any day now. They can instruct us on the use of our communications setup, which Guinness leased from COMSAT, Inc., of Washington, D.C. A transportable communications system, this TCS-9000 operates through the INMARSAT Indian Ocean satellite and gains access to the world via the coastal earth stations at Elk, Norway; Singapore; and Yamaguchi, Japan. Courtney and David Padwa arranged with Guinness for the Cowboys to pick up the TCS-9000 lease. U.S. West has agreed to cover some of our transmission costs. We will be the first United States team ever to dial directly home from Everest. With David Padwa's lap-top computer, we will be able, via the satellite, to access electronic mailboxes in the United States for expedition business and for our weather lifeline to Penn State. We also need to learn as much as we can from the Brits about the habits and condition of the mountain.

We have said our good-byes to Mary and Kelly Skinner. Mary, Courtney's wife, is our expedition coordinator. She must return to Pinedale to handle the phones and the paperwork blizzard. Kelly was one of the first alternates for the two high school scholarship positions on the expedition. She was able to accompany us to Lhasa but now must return to start her freshman year of college. Luke Omohundro and Mike Jauregui, the two scholarship winners, will continue to Base Camp with us.

Everybody is really hyper. We will hit the road this morning for Xigatse.

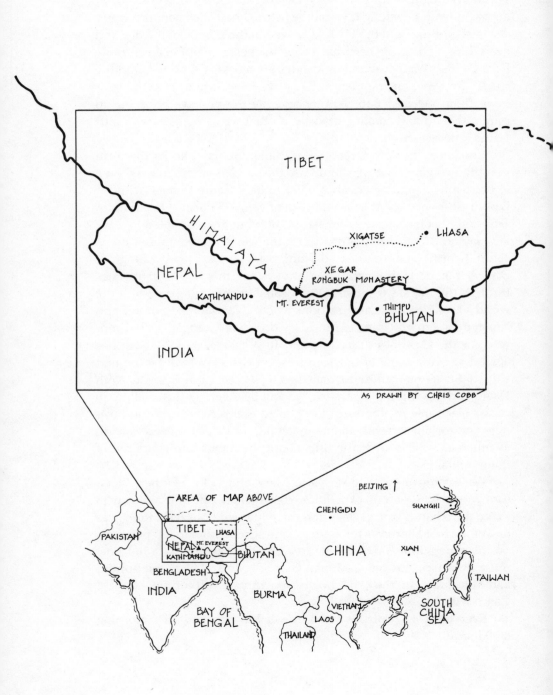

TIBET

HIMALAYA

NEPAL

XIGATSE • LHASA

XE GAR
RONGBUK MONASTERY

KATHMANDU •

MT. EVEREST

• THIMPU
BHUTAN

INDIA

AS DRAWN BY CHRIS COBB

AREA OF MAP ABOVE

BEIJING ↑

CHENGDU •

SHANGHI •

TIBET
LHASA

NEPAL
MT. EVEREST
KATHMANDU

BHUTAN

CHINA

XIAN •

PAKISTAN

BENGLADESH

TAIWAN

INDIA

BURMA

VIETNAM

SOUTH
CHINA
SEA

BAY OF
BENGAL

LAOS

THAILAND

CHAPTER III

Beyond Civilization

AUGUST 13, 1988. En route from Lhasa to Xigatse. We left the Lhasa Hotel in an ancient bus and a 1941-vintage Chinese lorry stuffed with gear bags. Jim Burnett and Quintin Barney are riding in the lorry. We loaded the excess gear on top of the team bus and piled in. This bus is an authentic relic. Some windows work, some don't. All the seats are wet, some are mildewed. Our driver is Tibetan and mean-tempered.

Civilization, as we know it, is behind us. We cross the Tsangpo River and follow a narrow, bumpy road north. In about fifty miles, we turn west toward Xigatse. Our little caravan includes the relic bus, the Mitsubishi gear truck, a blue Toyota Landcruiser carrying our six Chinese handlers, and a white Nissan Patrol vehicle with the team leaders. Thirty of us are in the bus. Our first stop is not twenty miles outside Lhasa. The bus is pulled over by a Chinese army truck because the load on top has hit some telephone wires. The Chinese appear to be furious, but let us go . . . temporarily. Around the next bend in the road three oncoming Chinese army jeeps screech to a halt and block our path. A dozen green-clad army personnel leap out, guns in hand. We are taken to a Chinese military compound where we park next to a bullet-pocked wall, which we're told is used for executions. After forty minutes of intense negotiation, we're allowed to

Our relic bus needed to be pushed and cajoled through field, stream, and worst of all, mud. PHOTO BY JEB SCHENCK.

leave. Our Tibetan driver has had his license revoked permanently for hitting the telephone wires. He has a ten-day license to take us to Xegar. This does not improve his disposition. We're on our way again . . . temporarily.

Another hour down the road, our antique bus comes to a huffing, wheezing halt. Two more hours are wasted. Finally, the driver gets the bus going. But it is *slow* going. Unfortunately, it is still monsoon season. Again, Steve Marts says the roads are the worst he's ever seen. We bounce, bump, and plod along in our springless excuse for a vehicle. We ford rivers, cross creeks, bounce off rocks, drive into fields. Periodically, our bus gets stuck and all thirty of us get out and push.

The terrain is spectacular. Steep, shale-covered mountains herd us toward a pass. We cross Okamea Pass (15,728 feet) and Karo Pass (16,437 feet). We drop into lovely green valleys, with distinct plots of barley, wheat, and mustard. We climb up switchback dirt roads and reach terrain that is unforgiving, rocky, bleak. Some places are so steep that I can look out the bus window and peer straight down for 2,000 feet. Generally the land is arid, but the rain has caused muddy roads and monumental erosion. Our bus slips and slides perilously. We follow the road, up, then down, then back up. We're never below 13,000 feet. Our moody Tibetan driver, who has just lost his only means of livelihood, turns out to be a skillful bus wrangler.

Many of my teammates are sick: flu, colds, altitude sickness, nausea, motion sickness. I feel fine. The guys with long legs are in agony. The tiny Chinese bus seats are not made for six-foot-three Americans. We have many pit stops and many mud stops to either push or unload all passengers so that the unweighted bus can make yet another impossible maneuver. But we have no food stops—and no food. The gear truck has outpaced us since the bus breakdown, and all our food and warm gear went with it. I have been cold all day because the passenger door immediately in front of my seat doesn't close all the way, admitting a constant breeze of 38 degrees F. At one mud stop when I tried to help push our bus free, I sank into mud to my ankles. Now I am both cold and muddy. My tennis shoes are not a pretty sight.

How privileged I am to be traveling across China, even in the oldest bus known to mankind. Having this kind of an adventure when 240 million of my fellow Americans remain at home is still of some awe to me. It's been a rough trip—Steve Marts keeps saying he has never seen anything like this—but there are humorous points along the way. At every stop, Tibetans materialize out of nowhere and show enormous interest in the strange foreigners and their variety of gadgets, cameras, recorders, Walkmans. When the bus broke down and was disabled for two hours, several young women (I would guess their ages to be 13 to 15) got into animated sign-language conversations with some of the fellows on the team. As the guys reentered the bus to leave, the girls were standing at the door to bid each one goodbye with a riveting and well-directed goose, very much to the surprise of each recipient.

As we pull into Xigatse, we have been jolting across Tibet for fifteen hours. I have loved every minute of it.

AUGUST 15, 1988. XIGATSE. Elevation: 12,800 feet. After we finally arrived at the hotel in Xigatse, I was the first to step out. I sank into a full two feet of flowing mud—and quickly reboarded the bus. With some maneuvering through the flooded parking lot, our wonder-driver deposited us by an elevated cement porch and we all scrambled into the hotel.

Today I woke up with the premonition that once again we won't be going anywhere. Have I dreamt it? No, Julie confirms the bad news: after I had gone to sleep last night, someone came by with word that a massive mudslide sixty miles southwest of here has blocked the road. That's the direction we're headed. Nothing can get through. No cars. No trucks. No buses.

Mack Ellerby reminds us that one of the virtues of a true mountaineer is patience. "If we are on the mountain and we have bad weather," he says, "there is nothing to do but to sit it out, be patient, and wait. Precipitous movement can cause accidents or death. So we might as well start practicing our patience now, right here in Xigatse." That's a difficult lesson for me.

Everyone's humor has stayed pretty much intact, making the hardships of the trip bearable. I was even accused by Brian McLean this morning of being entirely too upbeat. I promised that I would try to tone down my generally positive nature. It may happen anyway because being in Xigatse is not the highlight of anyone's life.

Xigatse is Tibet's second largest city. I am sitting in the sun on the porch of the foreigners' hotel, with the sounds of Xigatse ringing in my head. The Tibetans who have sufficient funds purchase three-wheeled tractors. They remind me of the long powerboats on the Chao Phya River in Bangkok—loud and fast. The habit of the Tibetan drivers, whether they are in a jeep or a truck or a bus or any other vehicle, is to honk the horn at all times. Happily, most people can't afford motorized transportation. I can also hear the bells of bicycles and carts drawn by donkeys. The donkeys are small, perhaps three to four hands high, but they pull fully loaded carts twice their size.

This is still a completely agrarian economy. Farmers bring their produce into the market daily. We visited the market yesterday after-noon and found it much like Lhasa's, though smaller. There is a section for foreigners to barter and a separate section for goods and produce that the locals and the nomads sell among themselves. En route to Xigatse we saw a number of nomad tents and yak trains typical of the Tibetan high plateau. With their long hair and curved horns, the yaks are impressive. They are also, I am told, very individ-ual in their personalities, and some are very aggressive. I plan to stay out of their way. The animals that I love are the long-haired goats. They are smaller than our domestic goats—about the size of a small Airedale—with curly horns and silky hair several inches long. They spring along in that light but stiff-legged fashion of the deer family, with hair bouncing up and down like a 13-year-old girl's page-boy haircut.

When we arrived in Xigatse, we were so exhausted we just scraped off the mud and tumbled into bed. I share a room with Alex-andra, who has a terrible cold, and Julie. We have three beds, a toilet that flushes (but apparently doesn't accomplish anything, it is so malodorous), a faucet for cold water, and the ubiquitous Chinese Thermos bottle of hot water, which we are told is sterilized. I am leery of the water and use iodine tablets. Despite being tired, I felt great yesterday. I was eager to continue our journey, reasoning that any delay might provide even more time for the rain to dissolve the roads. I also think that the higher we can get, the more time we will have to acclimatize. We are now only a little bit higher than Lhasa. So, feeling good and wanting to keep rolling, I was agitating for that program at breakfast. But a few people had taken a beating on the bus ride and simply didn't feel well enough to travel. By 11 A.M. Courtney still wasn't up. Bob "John Wayne" Skinner, Dan Pryor, and our LO were wandering around trying to figure out where our five gear trucks were between Beijing and Xigatse. We also seemed to be having a money problem with the hotel. There was so much confusion, it became clear to me that we weren't going anywhere for another day.

Around 2 P.M. yesterday our advance team—Courtney, Dan Pryor, David Padwa, and Matt Ellenthal—left Xigatse with a Chinese driver in the white Nissan, heading for Xegar and on to Base Camp, to meet the British. Dan, the Base Camp manager, wants to begin to organize and build the camp. David, our research director and communications officer, helped in the negotiations with the British on the TCS-9000 and needs to learn the operations. Matt is assigned to communica-tions and is one of our professional photographers. The rest of us settled in for another day in Xigatse. Those who were not feeling well slept and the rest of us walked to the center of town to the market. Our best purchase was a dozen high-top, black rubber boots, the kind dairy farmers wear, for $5 U.S. each. Size was not an issue—they were either large or small. Several of us, like me, each had only one pair of now wet and muddy sneakers. David Frawley had only thongs. Now our feet are fortified to push the bus all the way across Tibet.

After shopping, we gathered at the hotel for dinner. Chinese dining rooms in hotels assigned to tourists have a section for foreigners and a section for the Chinese, divided by movable screens. The food is marginal, to be generous. Mostly we don't know what we're eating. There seem to be a lot of vegetables fried in yak butter. We try to eat only things that are cooked, but our digestive systems are getting used to a variety of unidentifiable objects. The ingredients of last night's dinner were not important, however, because many quart bottles of Chinese beer graced our tables and everybody got pretty relaxed.

During dinner Fred Riedman, Sr., enticed by his son to accompany the team to Base Camp, commented on the water shortage at the hotel, which alternates among occasional warm water, cold water only, and no water at all. "I've been waiting a day and a half for warm water for a shower," Fred said. "I was checking at half-hour intervals. At the first cry that the warm water was on, I raced from my room and luxuriated in the warm water, lathering myself fully from head to toe. Just when I was ready to rinse, all the water pressure ceased." He finished by attempting to towel off the soap.

The LO related today that our trucks are in Lhasa and that our gear is being shifted from big trucks to smaller trucks, which will be able to negotiate the worsening road between Lhasa and Xigatse. We are suspicious that these smaller trucks are yet another way to charge more money. It is true, though, that since we arrived, many trucks have failed to make it to Xigatse from Lhasa because of the road conditions. We are basically stuck between two giant mudslides.

We also received a handwritten message from Courtney, delivered by a man he'd met south of Xigatse. The message says, "Nissan made it through slides—bus can, too. Push." Looks like we're going to try tomorrow.

Meanwhile we are caught in a financial argument with the Chinese Mountaineering Association and the Tibetan Sports Council. As I understand it, the CMA requires 100 percent prepayment for all anticipated costs and expenses of an expedition in China, as set forth in the protocol. The CMA, upon receiving payment, books the trucks and the hotels and other services and pays for those items. In Tibet, some of the money goes to the Tibetan Sports Council. We sent the CMA copious amounts of money but, as it turns out, only about 80 percent of what they say we will actually spend. We got off to a pretty bad start with the Chinese government and the CMA by arriving on the C-5, thus cutting out the CAAC and CMA portions of the airline transportation fee. Hence the $24,000 landing fee. Next, they were upset because we had made our own arrangements through Holiday Inn of America to stay at the Lhasa Hotel, again denying the CMA its fee. The CMA expected to charge us something like 300 yuan per person per night to stay at the Lhasa Hotel; they would have paid the Lhasa Hotel 150 yuan and split the difference with the Tibetan Sports Council. We have the most miserable, rotten, oldest bus available because they were mad at us for making our own arrangements.

Today the CMA is telling us that it is the Tibetan Sports Council that is angry, that they canceled our hotel reservations in Xigatse, where we are now, and in Xegar, where we intend to go tomorrow, because of the Holiday Inn business. The Xigatse hotel is saying that we owe them approximately $4,000 U.S. because we're an independent group, and we didn't have reservations. We say, we paid the CMA. The CMA says that they paid the Tibetan Sports Council and it's the Tibetan Sports Council that hasn't paid the hotel. So we're going around in circles (all through translators) and no one's happy. It's almost unbelievable that it's August 15. The Cowboys left the United States on August 1 and we're not to Base Camp yet.

I wish there were some way to communicate with Chuck. It's strange to be isolated here and have no means of communication. Telephone and telex service from Xigatse is out because of the storms. We will not be able to communicate until we are in Base Camp and have access to the INMARSAT system.

I guess Chuck is now in New Orleans at the Republican National Convention. He's been working hard for George Bush's campaign. Just the week before I left Washington, when the polls were at the worst from a Republican perspective, Chuck and I were at the Vice President's house. Chuck mentioned to Vice President and Mrs. Bush that I was leaving in a few days to climb Everest. Like many people, they reacted with surprise. When we left that evening, the Vice President said, "Good luck, Sue. You and I both have huge mountains to climb."

"It is our great good fortune, Mr. Vice President," I responded,

*On the trip between Xigatse and Xegar, our gear truck seemed to be contin-
ually stuck on rocks and in mud. Freeing it often required the efforts of the
entire team.* PHOTO BY JEB SCHENCK.

"that the safety of the free world doesn't depend on my getting to the
top of Mount Everest."

AUGUST 16, 1988. 4 P.M. On the road again. About sixty miles from
Xigatse we ran into numerous areas where the road had washed away.
We have had to drive through deep erosion channels and over unstable, rocky terrain. Several times all members of the team have had
to get out and push the bus, often using shovels to move earth and
rocks. It is laborious progress. Always the Tibetans appear out of
nowhere to watch. Occasionally they help. Our one gear truck, which
this time is staying close to the bus, also keeps getting hung up on
rocks and needs to be pushed and pulled till it's free. Sometimes

Chinese trucks are stuck, too, but nobody helps them. Our mean-tempered driver has mellowed while exercising his not inconsiderable skill. He seems to relish our loud applause as he gets us out of ditches and mudslides.

We've just finished a lunch of hard rolls and canned Spam (purchased in Lhasa) and are traveling over a pass at 14,700 feet. At every high point prayer flags, tattered bits of cloth on reed poles, reach out of piles of rocks toward the Tibetan gods. This particular pass is higher than any mountain peak in the contiguous forty-eight states. Still the mountains are rising all around. A river runs beside us, sometimes at road level, sometimes falling into a deep gorge. The road is decent here: much of the drainage is beneath us and there are green shrubs and alpine flowers to help stay the erosion. At lower elevations the erosion makes the water muddy red and sometimes wholly brown, but here the river water is clean.

We cross broad plateaus with mile after mile of barley and wheat fields, deep green and absolutely beautiful; small adobe-like villages of Tibetans spring up here and there. Then we go into rocky terrain; then through areas of massive, unchecked erosion. Tibetan women work the rock hills with picks, digging out scrub brush to burn in the winter. Barefoot children herd goats and sheep and collect yak dung for fuel. The dung cakes are stacked neatly on their sides on top of the walls surrounding the stucco houses, as fuel is a precious thing.

This road, known as the Friendship Highway, connects Lhasa and Kathmandu. The travel is harsher than anything I have ever seen in the United States, including Black Bear Pass in Colorado (the worst that I can think of): more difficult conditions, much steeper and much longer drops, a great deal more instability due to erosion, and of course, much higher altitudes. My altimeter is now showing 15,100 feet. Mountains rise up fifty yards across the river gorge still 3,000 to 4,000 feet higher. On the mountain face we see, periodically, the meditation caves of the devoutly religious Tibetans.

Despite everything I have read about expeditions across China, I couldn't have imagined the variety, the beauty, and the remoteness of this area. I am not alone in this regard. "A connected narrative of our wanderings in this amazing country could hardly be true to its disconnected character. The White Rabbit himself would have been bewildered here," wrote Lieutenant Colonel C.K. Howard-Bury in *Mount Everest, The Reconnaissance*, in 1921.

Many times, as I look out the window of the bus, I am quite certain that the rear wheels, over which I am sitting, will slide right down a ravine. There is so much erosion that as we approach each curve in the road, I can see where the embankment has lost its fill and been severely undermined—as much as three feet under the roadbed. Roads and bridges hang in space. "Tibetan bridges are so constructed as to offer the passenger ample opportunities of experiencing the sensation of insecurity and contemplating the possibilities of disaster," wrote the Colonel. It hasn't changed since 1921.

In addition to reading about the early British expeditions, I have been listening on my Walkman to the book recording of *The Prophet*. So many things to learn, so many things to see. I just finished that and gave it to Fred Riedman, Sr., who rewarded me with a candy bar. In honor of Fred's fifty-eighth birthday last night, David Frawley organized dinner at a one-room Tibetan restaurant in Xigatse. Seventeen of us went; other team members were too queasy about the local restaurants. It was a perfectly delicious meal. For less than a dollar each we had an enormous bowl of broth, followed by chicken with celery and black mushrooms, tiny snails with mustard greens, thin slices of broiled lamb, yellow and green beans in soy sauce, and wonderful fried potatoes. The highlight was a dish of peanuts and mutton cooked in yak butter with scallions and green peppers. We drank quart-size bottles of Chinese beer to help our intonation as we sang choruses of "Happy Birthday." Westerners (particularly weird ones who sing loudly off-key) are still enough of a curiosity that we attracted quite a crowd. Many Tibetans peered at us through the open windows and doors and begged for food. The owner chased the beggars away, but as we left, we saw that he had put out the platters of our leftover food.

On the way back to the hotel, David Frawley, Michael Jauregui, Brian Shoemaker, and I ran into the Tibetan who had sold David a much-needed pair of shoes earlier in the day in the marketplace. By sign language the Tibetan invited us to his home. It was one room, about twelve feet square, and quite dark. A third of the room was occupied by a platform built up about three feet, on which four people of varying ages were already lying or sleeping. There were two women tending pots of food, with four young children underfoot. This one room was adjacent to a patio, about ten feet square, that had many carefully tended pots of blooming flowers. All the doors and windows were decorated in brilliant blues, reds, and yellows. Without being able to communicate orally, the Tibetans were gracious hosts, smiling and bowing to us four curious Westerners.

We are now at the Jia Tsuo La (*la* means pass), 145 miles from Xigatse, at a height of 17,122 feet. Only a few more hours to Xegar. Shortly after we leave Xegar, we will turn off the Friendship Highway toward the Rongbuk Valley. Then we'll cross one more 17,000-foot pass and have our first view of Mount Everest.

CHAPTER IV

Dogtown

AUGUST 17, 1988. XEGAR. Elevation: 14,000 feet. We arrived at 8:30 last night. Xegar, it seems, has a large and socially active population of dogs. In fact, the British expedition refers to Xegar as Dogtown.

Our hotel was once a military compound. Almost all expeditions going to the Rongbuk Valley stay here. Julie tells me that previous expeditions have reported bedbugs. We are in a wing that, as far as I can tell, does not have any of the little creatures. By Cobb standards, though, I can only say that the accommodations are grim. The room is about ten by twelve. It is dirty. We have two bed platforms with quarter-inch pads for mattresses, and two small chairs. I am sharing this luxury suite with Brian McLean. The bathroom facilities down the hall consist of three holes in the cement. Foul smell. One simply squats and aims for the hole. No showers. No plumbing. We are awakened in the morning by a loudspeaker echoing across this small valley from a Chinese military compound, reciting the propaganda of the day.

We had dinner last night in the hotel dining room, another huge hall divided by movable Chinese panels and dotted with round tables that seat eight or ten people. In addition to some of the same foods we had in Xigatse, we have tiny peeled tomatoes coated with sugar crystals, small bowls of roasted peanuts, raw dough rolls the size of oranges, and occasionally meat (which may explain why they keep so many dogs here). The three physicians on our expedition have recommended that we not eat anything raw, but since many of the Chinese dishes are well cooked in yak butter, we've been pretty well fed—even if not exactly to our tastes. Sometimes the food just isn't appealing to my Western appetite and I can't bring myself to eat it. I've already lost about five pounds. We must consume liters of fluids so as not to become dehydrated, and we use anything that's bottled and capped: beer, orange soda, mineral water. Several people are down, two or three of whom have been very sick: some flu, some colds, some gastrointestinal problems, some high-altitude sickness. I've felt good the whole way. I have been extremely careful in my hygiene. I carry a small plastic bottle of liquid soap, so that if I touch something questionable, I can whip out the soap and resanitize myself.

Spirits are holding up pretty well despite what has become an unexpectedly arduous journey, with roadblocks ranging from mudslides to uncooperative Chinese bureaucrats. It is August 17, and we thought we'd be in Base Camp on August 12. I suspect Chuck and the boys have an image of me up at Base Camp, but here I sit in Dogtown.

We left Bob and Orion Skinner in Xigatse to await the arrival of the five trucks from Beijing. According to the LO, four have made it to Lhasa and the fifth is on its way. I hope he's right. The extra day of holding is good in some ways, because now that we're at 14,000 feet, we can all use a day or two of acclimatization. It is clear from the history of Everest climbs that the more slowly one gains elevation and the longer one stays in the neighborhood of 14,000 feet, the better the chances of good health and success on the mountain.

Courtney is at Base Camp with our three teammates, only twelve or fourteen hours away. According to a message from him, delivered by a departing British climber whom we passed on the road, things are in good order. Court has purchased forty-six cylinders of oxygen from the British and also some tents and food. Knowing Courtney, he's probably sitting at Base Camp right now, revising the team's schedule for the umpteenth time.

I first met Courtney Skinner in 1984 when he came to Miami to visit the private school of which I was a trustee. He was doing a road show for the Skinner Brothers Wilderness School, where many people from the East Coast send their children during the summertime, and promoting other Skinner-led mountaineering trips. The Skinner expeditions reminded me of the trips that I took for many years with my father and brother in the High Sierra. My father was an avid fly fisherman, and every summer we would pack into the mountains by mule, set up camp for three or four weeks in some remote location, and climb to the high lakes to fish for golden trout. Courtney's spirit reminded me of my father's spirit, too. So I asked him to put me on the mailing list, thinking maybe I'd be free to take a trip someday.

The following year, 1985, was the biggest bond year in the history of municipal finance, and as the year rolled toward an end, when all our transactions had to be closed because of January 1 changes in the tax laws, we were virtually killing ourselves in the bond department at my office. I was strung out. Then a flyer arrived from the Skinner Brothers, saying they were leading a group to Aconcagua in Argentina in late January. Something clicked. January and February are always slow in the bond business, and the firm now had numerous capable bond attorneys, so a three-week trip suddenly seemed like a possibility. Though I had done little mountain climbing of a technical nature, and no expeditionary climbing, that did not mean to me that I wasn't fully capable of climbing the highest mountain in the Western Hemisphere. I simply had to convince the Skinners that I was capable, and then maybe fake it a little. My biggest concern was how to tell Chuck that I wanted to take three weeks and climb a 23,000-foot peak in South America. Of course, I suggested he go with me, even though I knew his interest wouldn't be strong enough to pry him away from his job. It was going to be something that I would be doing alone, unlike everything else in our relationship. After we were married in 1959, and until I left for South America, I don't think we'd ever spent more than four or five days apart. Chuck has, however, always supported me in things I decide to do, though sometimes resignedly. In January 1986, I showed up at the Miami International Airport and met my new teammates for the flight to Buenos Aires.

There were sixteen of us on that trip, including Courtney and Bob Skinner, Orion Skinner, Fred Riedman, and Brad Werntz, all now on this expedition. Despite a bout with hypothermia, I felt good about the climb in Argentina and harbored the thought that maybe some other year I would do something similar. The Skinners invited me to join their Memorial Day climb of Mount Rainier, but that was the weekend my son Christian was graduating from the Tulane University School of Architecture. So the rest of 1986 went by with no climbing other than a couple of "fourteeners" in Colorado. I didn't forget about Rainier, though, and in May 1987, I joined the Skinners for the Rainier climb.

After we summitted Rainier, Courtney asked me whether I would consider going to Everest, for which the Chinese had granted him a postmonsoon 1988 permit. I didn't see how it was possible, but I said that I would keep it in mind. Shortly thereafter Courtney asked me to join his team as part of the board of governors. I was pleased to do that, thinking that somehow or other I could be a part of the Everest experience. I began to get more involved. In August 1987 I met with the board of governors in Jackson, Wyoming, and became excited about what was going on. I immediately had confidence in the chairman of the board, George McCown. I began talking to Chuck about going to Everest and trying to get some encouragement, or at least acquiescence. When Courtney broached the subject to me of being a summiter, I was ready to commit—at least mentally. There were many things to come in between.

AUGUST 18, 1988. My fifty-first birthday. Yesterday afternoon Bob Skinner arrived from Xigatse with the LO and reported no news whatsoever on our trucks. There is no way we can move out of Dogtown without our equipment.

To kill time, Sheri King and I climbed up to the ruins of an old monastery, perched on the edge of a cliff, a thousand feet above town. From the peak we saw lush, green valleys running off in different directions, as if the peak were the hub of a wheel and the valleys the spokes. In the distance were a number of mountains with snow-capped tops. Sheri and I descended to the stone houses, crowded together at the base of the cliff, that constitute the town of Xegar. These small homes, connected by earthen walls, have communal yards filled with dogs, goats, and children whose noses seem to run unceasingly. We wandered through the labyrinth and reached the Xegar monastery for the obligatory tour. On the way back to the hotel, we stopped at several roadside stands. Sheri purchased a roll of toilet paper for my birthday, a very thoughtful and useful gift.

My mind skipped back to a year ago, when I turned 50. I told Chuck that if we had to do something to celebrate, the only thing that interested me would be to relax in Telluride, or to be with a couple of

Bob "John Wayne" Skinner looks in vain for our five missing lorries. PHOTO BY
ORION SKINNER.

close friends at home. In his inimitable way he accomplished both. He
called dozens of dear friends of mine from high school, college, and
postcollege days and gathered them in Colorado for an absolutely
smashing weekend. What a contrast to be in Dogtown! On the East
Coast of the United States it's 3 A.M. In another four or five hours my
family will wake up and remember it is August 18. They'll be wishing
me a happy birthday about the time I go to sleep tonight. They know I
am in Dogtown. We had a message that the advance team has the
TCS-9000 working and has been in contact with the United States.

My companion today, Dr. Sheri King, is a 33-year-old emergency
room physician from Pueblo, Colorado. She's attractive, smart, fun,
and just a kick to be with. Her quick sense of humor keeps me on my
toes. Her conscientiousness as a physician has already evidenced
itself on a number of occasions as we've slogged across China. She's a
great addition to our team. Most Tibetans have never seen a black,
though, so she draws curious stares as we walk through the streets.
She's great with the children who always follow us around—much
more patient and communicative than I.

In the time I've spent hanging around with Sheri in Xegar, I've tried to learn as much as I can about the various altitude sicknesses. I have no medical training, but as I understand it, the illnesses fall into a wide range of ailments, referred to generally as acute mountain sickness, or AMS. People who rapidly ascend to high altitudes are subject to such symptoms as headaches, nausea, shortness of breath, loss of appetite, insomnia, dehydration, disorientation, clumsiness, and often, short-term memory loss. There are two advanced stages of AMS: high-altitude pulmonary edema (HAPE) and high-altitude cerebral edema (HACE). High-altitude retinal hemorrhaging, not usually seen below about 17,000 feet, is another manifestation of oxygen deprivation. Additionally, at high altitudes, injuries and infections do not heal normally because of the low pressure of oxygen in the tissues. Frostbite of appendages is also a greater danger because the body directs more oxygen to the vital organs.

Both pulmonary and cerebral edema are terminal, sometimes within hours, unless the afflicted individual descends to a lower altitude, with the concomitant increase in air pressure. Pulmonary edema involves the transfer of fluid forced through capillaries into the lungs, resulting in a condition of rales or gurgles, coughing, and drowning in one's own fluids. In cerebral edema, injury to the brain tissue from lack of oxygen results in swelling of the brain, unconsciousness, and death.

The culprit in the medical problems at high altitude is not lack of oxygen per se (the percentage of oxygen in the air does not change) but the decrease in atmospheric pressure, which leads to a decrease in the oxygen partial pressure in the lungs and thus to a decrease in the oxygen transferred to the blood. At 21,000 feet the average barometric pressure is about 330 millimeters of mercury (mm Hg), compared with 760 mm Hg at sea level, or less than half the sea level value. At 24,000 feet oxygen in the system is less than one-third what it is at sea level, and at 29,000 feet it is closer to one-quarter. It is said that the average person transported from sea level to the summit of Everest would lose consciousness in sixty seconds. The human body does, however, adapt to the lower pressure of oxygen if ascent is gradual. That is acclimatization. As evidenced by inhabited villages, 17,000 feet is the maximum height at which humans can acclimatize and live for extended periods.

Other than my climb with Sheri, the main thing that I accomplished today was to wash my hair and some clothes. That might seem easy, but consider that we have no hot water and no running water. We do have a plastic wash bowl in our room. I took that to the well for fresh, cold water, drawn with an old bucket. I washed the clothes and two or three more times drew water to rinse them. I used the same process to wash my hair and take something of a Navy shower. The clothes are now hung out on bushes to dry.

Bob Skinner, Ethan Goldings, and our LO took off this morning to look for the trucks. We're hoping they will show up tonight or that we'll get word of a sighting, but we're without any telecommunications. Absent somebody driving up with a note in hand, we have no contact with the outside world.

In my reading today I came across a good explanation of the contingencies that can keep climbers from reaching the summit: "Anything like a breakdown of the transport will be fatal; soft snow on the mountain will be an impregnable defense; a big wind will send back the strongest; even so small a matter as a boot fitting a shade too tight, may endanger one man's foot and involve the whole party in retreat. The climbers must have above all things, if they are to win, good fortune, and the greatest good fortune of all for mountaineers, some constant spirit of kindness in Mount Everest itself, the forgetfulness for long enough of its more cruel moods; for we must remember that the highest of mountains is capable of severity, a severity so awful and so fatal that the wiser sort of men do well to think and tremble even on the threshold of their highest endeavor." So wrote George Leigh Mallory in *The Reconnaissance of the Mountain*, 1921.

10:30 P.M. I had a surprise birthday party. We are still in this former military compound that is below the standards of any hotel that anyone I've ever known has stayed in. However, the Tibetans are trying hard to make our stay pleasant, within their means, and the place is not without certain charms. Tonight our team had four tables on the foreign side of the big dining hall. Toward the conclusion of dinner, Jim Robinson and David Frawley announced that it was my birthday and time to celebrate. After distributing bottles of the local gooseberry wine, the boys gave me a variety of gifts that represent the very best Xegar has to offer. First a huge bow with a safety pin on the back. It's lacy, obviously handmade, and very fetching on my stained sweatshirt. Next, some exotic cosmetic cream with directions in Chinese. I have no idea what it is or where to use it. That was followed by five large, thick-skinned balloons and an excruciatingly ugly pink stocking hat of some synthetic fiber. Naturally I had on both my bow and my hat, with balloons in hand, as the party progressed. My birthday cake arrived. It was another roll of toilet paper with a candle stuck in the middle, which everyone deemed a most practical gift.

"Speech! Speech!" the Cowboys shouted. So I told the story of how the Tibetans came to inhabit this land. "They are descendants of the early mountaineers, the climbers who came even before the time of Mallory and the great British expeditions of the early Twenties. Those expeditions," I said, "were brought into Xegar by the CMA and left here without trucks and without any of their gear. After some time the mountaineers were forced to adapt. They were in the sun all day, so they got very darkly tanned. They needed food, so they started an agrarian economy. Their grandchildren now cultivate the land around Xegar."

During a rousing chorus of "Happy Birthday," Carl Coy set off a round of firecrackers, which I was sure was going to bring the entire Chinese army. The inflated balloons, being batted from table to table, inspired a volleyball game, with tables 1 and 2 against tables 3 and 4. Obviously the Chinese cloth screens dividing the room were the perfect net. The Tibetans watched in amazement at our spirited game until one of the Cowboys crashed through a screen. We were promptly thrown out.

AUGUST 19, 1988. XEGAR. Good morning, Comrades! We've heard the morning propaganda and are ready for another day in Dogtown. Four happy campers are defecting early this morning. Our two high school scholarship students, Luke Omohundro and Mike Jauregui, leave with Fred Riedman, Sr. and Brian Shoemaker on a truck bound for Base Camp. That arrangement has been made, not without difficulty, because those four have to start back to the United States in four days. After a statewide competition in Wyoming, Mike and Luke emerged as winners of the Wyoming Outdoor Council–expedition scholarships, with passage to the Everest Base Camp. Immediately upon returning to the United States, Mike will be attending Gonzaga University in Spokane, and Luke, Georgetown University in the District of Columbia. Fred Riedman, Sr., an attorney, must go home soon for business; Captain Brian Shoemaker, a March 1988 retiree from the United States Navy, will return as a civilian to the Antarctic, where he had served in the military.

The students have been extremely eager to see Base Camp and get a glimpse of the mountain. Luke told me that when the expedition leaders began to talk about sending people home to save money, he and Mike figured they'd be first to go. "We realize that no matter what, we're still having an incredible experience," Luke said. "And we've been warned all along not to have unrealistic expectations."

"But here you are," I said, "so close. I imagine it's impossible not to set your sights on getting to Everest."

"It's different for you team members. I mean, you're all concerned about making it up the mountain. We two students will be content just to see it. Like when Courtney threatened to send people back, we tried to lay low, to avoid him, so as not to remind him that we were still tagging along. Every second of every hour of every day, we've heard the clock ticking."

"And now you're going?"

"You bet! Just when it appeared that our options had run out!" Luke was flush with the excitement. "At your birthday party, the guys at my table decided to sneak us, Mr. Riedman, and Captain Shoe-maker onto a cargo truck going to Base Camp. It's happening—we're finally going to Mount Everest!"

He ran off to finish throwing his gear into a bag. No sooner were they all ready than the driver changed his mind, not once, but several times. He is not supposed to carry passengers, and he will have to go through a military checkpoint. Naturally enough, he fears he will lose his license. But at 3 A.M. he changed his mind for the last time: he would go in two more hours. The four stowaways trudged across the muddy courtyard with their gear and concealed themselves in the back of the truck. We checked their camouflage—tarps, abetted by cover of darkness and fog—and hoped the driver would slip inconspicuously through the checkpoint on his way to Everest.

AUGUST 20, 1988. We're stuck. The Chinese have an inertia about their way of life. Perhaps it is because of their thousands of years of history. The mountains will always be here for them. But our permit runs only so long. How can we get them to accommodate our sense of urgency? Each region has different rules and different little political kingpins that make life difficult.

We have learned, however, that one thing that does motivate the Chinese is hard currency. Everything for foreigners is at least double, if not triple. All the stalls and the delays are in the end rectified by more cash. From the Chinese perspective, it seems to be business as usual. From our perspective, it's extortion—and infuriating.

Before he left Xigatse with the advance team, Dan Pryor said to me over dinner, "You know, Sue, in China we're far enough away to see America. The successes tower over the clouds, and the failures, which certainly have girth, appear diminutive in comparison to the Chinese landscape." Dan might have mixed a few metaphors there, but the thought was right.

We have some hope, despite all evidence to the contrary, that our trucks will arrive late today so that we can move on. In the meantime, what shall we do? After rejecting Sheri King's idea of lolling around the pool or going to the art gallery (because neither exists), we have decided to climb a rather steep peak just in back of our hotel. For the first time I've been feeling pretty lethargic, but I want to get out for acclimatization purposes. If the gear does come today, we'll be going to Base Camp at 16,700 feet, so best to get out and climb a little.

9 P.M. I'm sitting in my room with half a loaf of three-week-old San Francisco sourdough bread that has somehow survived in the bottom of my pack. I just couldn't take another meal in the dining hall. I was excruciatingly slow on the climb today. I felt really bum. By the time I got back to the hotel, I was sagging. I'm not sure whether it's from the altitude, although in the past I've acclimatized easily, or from one of the illnesses running around among the team. I don't know which to hope for, but I will try to hark back to the days when I was tutored in Christian Science and be well in the morning. I'll have to see if it works in China. Ethan Goldings came by with a steamed roll, and Bob Skinner just popped in with some hot tea. Nice of them. That will be dinner. It's been a pretty rotten, bum, Dogtown day as far as I'm concerned.

AUGUST 21, 1988. We had a major earthquake last night. I was lying in bed and felt the tremors, but having grown up in California, I was waiting for something really monstrous before I moved. Roomie Brian was not equipped with such earthquake experience. He started yelling, "Anne! Anne! We've got to get out of here!" Since he then raced straight to the door, I didn't have the immediate opportunity to tell him who he was rooming with. I took no offense. He is not the first to switch Anne Stroock and me. I wonder whether he'll be that excitable on the mountain.

The earthquake, we learned this morning, was indeed a major

one, causing extensive damage and scores of deaths in India, Nepal, and China. We wonder what it did at Base Camp.

AUGUST 22, 1988. The roof of the world, as the Himalayas are known, seems to be caving in. With the monsoon we've had torrential rains, floods, mudslides, earthquakes, and roads washed out. With so much gear and so many people, the whole process has been a logistical nightmare. Today we have a new delay.

Late in the morning we decided to use our one lorry to send twenty climbers to Base Camp, even though our five gear trucks have not arrived. We gathered enough sleeping bags, pads, and warm clothing from the whole team to ensure that twenty people could sleep warmly at Base Camp. Even if there aren't tents, they can huddle in the mess tent and the White House, the British communications hut that we have acquired. I was not one of the twenty selected to go because I've not been well. So we remaining eleven waved good-bye to the fortunate twenty, and off went the lorry toward Base Camp. I felt let down, like I'd been left behind. Which I was. I returned to my cubicle and had been reading for over an hour when I heard some noise outside and looked down from my second-story window to see our truck pull up. About six miles out of Xegar on the road to Base Camp, the sole bridge over the Phung Chu River was washed out. There is no way around it.

With the new delay, I decided to take another conditioning hike. The rest of the team was either consumed in a game of hearts or had already gone on a hike, so I struck off by myself toward one of the mountains a couple of miles away. I chose a route toward the top that looked fairly simple, and it was, until I saw three goat herders in my path less than a hundred yards ahead. In the morning, I had been reading Fox Butterfield's extraordinary book, *China: Alive in the Bitter Sea,* and I'm in a section where he tells about all the rapes during the Cultural Revolution. The power of suggestion overcame me. I was leery of being by myself in this isolated area with three rough-looking nomads, who each had a long dagger strapped to his waist. They motioned for me to come toward them, but I indicated, by pointing, that I was headed in a different direction. The different direction was toward the other side of a nearby spur of the mountain, where I would be out of their view as I climbed to the peak. I started a gradual ascent. The minute I was out of their sight, however, my new route became steep, hand-over-hand climbing on crumbly rock and shale—difficult, because it so readily gave way under hand and foot. I was tense. None of my teammates knew where I'd gone. I could be in serious trouble if I fell. But *tense* wasn't as persuasive as *afraid*. I took a deep breath and up I scrambled, hand over hand, 300 feet to the top.

After reaching the top, which I judged to be about 16,500 feet, I met two Tibetan children who had been tending sheep in a high pasture. They must have laughed as they watched me struggle up from below when there was an easy route nearby to hike up. They clearly hadn't read Butterfield's book! A girl, about 10 years old, and cute as she could possibly be, and a boy of 11 or 12 greeted me with ear-to-ear smiles. I gave them some candy. They showed me how to sling a missile, used to control sheep and dogs, by doubling an eight-foot rope so that it cradled a rock in its fold. Swung properly, the stone hurls toward its target. The boy could hit a lone sheep at fifty yards. When I tried it, my rock always went backward. They got a real kick out of that and giggled as I tried several times. Good thing my livelihood doesn't depend on that skill. They showed me the easiest route back down to Xegar and I returned in time for dinner and good news.

We learned from some Brits, just in from Xigatse, that our five-lorry convoy is negotiating its way through the terrible mudslides this side of Xigatse. So we know that they are getting close. Now our problem is the bridge washout. Bob Skinner has suggested that thirty-one of us put enough rocks into the river to build a roadbed. Others who looked at the washout are not convinced, but we'll try. Terrific timing: the bridge goes out August 22, the trucks arrive August 23.

CHAPTER V

Escape from Xegar

AUGUST 23, 1988. XEGAR. 11:55 P.M. About twenty of us went to the Phung Chu River to see whether we could do something about the bridge. The earthquake had caused a huge mudslide upstream, which changed the water flow in such a manner that almost the entire force of the river hit the supporting structure of the bridge. Gradually it gave way, and a ten-yard width of road caved in, leaving only a twelve-inch strip of roadbed connecting the two ends of the bridge. There were probably 150 Tibetans milling around on one side of the river or the other, and a few Chinese drivers standing by their trucks. Nobody was doing a thing to fix the bridge, so we thought we'd try the Wyoming approach: get to work. We formed a bucket brigade, picked up large rocks from the hillside, and passed them downhill to the bridge. We weren't sure how the rocks would be used but doing something seemed better than doing nothing.

The Tibetans finally got a dump truck and brought some rocks to bale with chicken wire to help in the repair. They also had a Chinese-manufactured earthmover, but it was hardly bigger than a motorized lawnmower and, when fired up, went helplessly around in circles. It didn't take long to see that the rock strategy was futile.

We decided to talk to the truck drivers on the other side of the river. If we ferried our fifteen tons of gear across the remaining twelve inches of the bridge, we would then pay the drivers on the other side to take us to Base Camp. We learned that it was too expensive. Since we couldn't afford any more extortion, Bob elected to wait until the end of the day for the LO to arrive, to see what he recommended. While we were waiting, one driver decided to try to ford the river. He drove his lorry about a hundred yards upstream and plunged in. Although the water went over the top of his fenders and he drifted a bit, with great difficulty he reached the opposite bank. After getting stuck twice in the mud and lurching out, he pulled onto the road. There was much cheering for his accomplishment by the Chinese and the Tibetans, and loudest of all, from the Americans. The river could be forded. But could we talk our drivers into doing it?

While we were discussing how to approach our drivers, two men in a smaller truck started across. They got stuck about halfway. The driver who had successfully done the first crossing drove back into the river, put a rope on the smaller truck, and began towing it toward safety. Suddenly the current caught both trucks and began moving them uncontrollably downriver. Both came to a stop, crosswise to the current. The larger truck was in a precarious position. Water immediately rose and poured through the windows of the cab, in one side and out the other. The three occupants, one an 8-year-old boy, crawled out and reached temporary safety on the cab roof. The two in the smaller truck did the same. But the safety was illusory. At any minute the trucks could turn over from the power of the water broadsiding them. We were sure that the Tibetans could not swim. It became urgent to get the five out of the water before the trucks turned over. Dave Frawley went a hundred yards upstream of the trucks with a rope tied around his waist and tried to swim into the current to reach the smaller truck, but the current was too strong.

Meanwhile the Tibetans began frantically trying to throw a rope to the men and the boy on the big truck. They had to span approximately thirty yards and were not successful. Ignoring the afternoon rain, we watched helplessly while the Tibetans tied their ropes together to come up with one rope long enough to span the entire river, about ninety yards. Carrying one end of the rope, half the Tibetans then crossed the river via the twelve inches of bridge. With Tibetans on both sides leaning away from the river and pulling on the rope, it stayed above the water, and they "walked" it upriver to the cab. A

Stranded midstream, two Tibetans await rescue from the turbulent, monsoon-swollen river outside Xegar. PHOTO BY JIM CLAYTON.

serious game of tug-of-war. The rescue of the boy was completed first. Traveling upside down and moving hand over hand along the rope, he dangled just above the churning river all the way to shore. Eventually all were rescued.

The drama over, we piled into the back of our open lorry to return to the hotel. As we passed a local army outpost, four young Chinese army officers hitched a ride with us to Xegar. The Chinese army compounds of the Tibetan plateau are small and forlorn outposts. It has to be regarded as the worst hardship duty by the Chinese. These men were in uniform and each of them was wearing a huge green greatcoat, lined with yak fur and topped at the shoulders with red epaulets. One, quite incongruously, carried a ghetto blaster. This was a strange sight: the wet and bedraggled American climbers and the four Chinese Greatcoats dancing in the back of an army lorry to what I can only describe as Chinese rock.

AT THE HOTEL. Wonder of wonders, our missing five truckloads of gear have arrived! With luck, we will not be back at the Xegar Hilton tomorrow night.

AUGUST 24, 1988. PHUNG CHU RIVER. Bob Skinner wants to move the gear across immediately. We don't have much time left before erosion undermines the last few inches of bridge. We have almost 29,000 pounds in Power-Ply boxes, made for us by Packaging Corporation of America. Each loaded box weighs between forty and seventy pounds and is just large enough to require two people to lift and move. Maybe we can get everything across and then hire some trucks that are already on the other side to take us to Base Camp. Maybe those drivers are bored by now.

The two abandoned trucks are still sitting out in the middle of the river with water plowing through the windows and over the hoods. About one hundred Tibetans are wandering around, obviously intending to get the trucks out of the river. We're all curious about how they will do it. Meanwhile, the Cowboys are unloading boxes and stacking them on what's left of the bridge. We have to guard all of our gear all of the time. Locals walk back and forth across the bridge eyeing our cameras, recorders, binoculars, and boxes of equipment. Moments ago one tried to casually walk away with a shovel. I was on guard duty and I nabbed him. His smile and shrug of the shoulder as he handed the shovel to me clearly said, "Okay, you got me." The only thing I'm good for today is to guard boxes: my cold has flared up again and I really feel rotten.

4 P.M. We're still unloading the trucks and piling boxes on the portion of the bridge that has not been washed out. We're down to our last truck. The Tibetans who have been watching us all day figured out that they might get a free lunch if they started working, so they've been helping carry boxes and gear off the trucks and onto the bridge. Imagine a 60-year-old Tibetan in native robes walking around with a Burton snowboard under his arm.

As I'm standing here on the bridge—six miles outside of Xegar and fifty miles from the Rongbuk Base Camp, not to mention halfway around the world from home—who do I run into but Dr. Henry King Stanford, my friend from Miami and Georgia. He has been with the Georgia team trekkers who went to the East Face base camp. Their climbing team is still on the mountain. While I've been in Dogtown, Henry has already been to his team's base camp and is now going home. Henry, age 72, and Dr. M. Louise McBee, age 69, twice climbed to the Lama La at 17,500 feet. Not bad for those two youngsters!

LATE EVENING. We're camped on the bridge. We have two tents at one end and four at the other end, so that we can guard our Power-Ply boxes amassed in between. I'm sharing a tent with Rick Dare, Doug Burbank, and Sibylle. Although we're posting an around-the-clock watch tonight, I won't have to do a watch because I'm now officially classified as sick. It's a strange setting, but at least we're in our own sleeping bags and finally self-contained. There is a full-scale party in progress on the bridge to celebrate our escape from Xegar (and Doug Burbank's birthday).

We still don't know whether we will get our own truck drivers to ford the stream tomorrow or have to hire trucks on the other side. Ethan Goldings, a team member from Stanford who speaks fluent Chinese and Tibetan, has talked to the drivers marooned on the far side of the river. They have nothing to do but wait until the bridge gets fixed, which will take at least a week, so for 1,000 yuan or so ($300 to $350 U.S.) per truck, they'll take us to Base Camp if our drivers can't ford the river.

This is the strangest darn situation I've ever been in. This bridge is on the Friendship Highway, the main (and only) road between Lhasa and Kathmandu. There are a number of treks and climbing parties trying to get to different places in Tibet and Nepal. We hear nothing but horror stories. The weather this August is the worst in a hundred years. There are so many roads out, so many bridges out, so many landslides that everybody is delayed, trucks are hung up, buses are hung up, the route to anywhere is horribly stalled. Anybody who is trying to move in Tibet today is walking.

AUGUST 25, 1988. I slept well, although Doug Burbank told me that I kept kicking him all night, and Sibylle said I was snoring. I don't believe either of them.

Breakfast is over, tents have been taken down and repacked, and it appears our drivers may be willing to try to ford the river at about the spot where the two Chinese trucks went in a couple of days ago. Though the water level has receded about twelve inches, the drivers are apprehensive because each is responsible to the government for the truck he's driving. Brian McLean walked all the way across the river to demonstrate that the water doesn't go above his waist and that the current isn't too strong. But the drivers are still afraid to cross because of what happened to the two other trucks. Much time has passed in negotiations. Bob Skinner, 58 years old, has taken off his clothes and started into the water, motioning for the trucks to follow him and showing them the way. The LO calls him back and says that he mustn't do that, he's too old to make the crossing. The Chinese are losing face. The truck drivers are finally shamed into trying.

NOON. The first driver got across fairly easily and our team helped push the truck up the muddy hill on the far side and onto the road. The other four trucks have successfully followed. We're ecstatic. As soon as we reload our fifteen tons of gear, we're on our way to Base Camp. Our problem now is that our bus is long gone and we don't have a sixth truck for us. We are going to have to negotiate once again with the Chinese to get a truck that will carry the team. This saga of travel in Tibet is beyond imagination.

MIDNIGHT. We left what little remains of the bridge over the Phung Chu River at 5 P.M. and are now within a couple of hours of Base Camp. The trucks are stuck in the mud again. We had to leave four team members behind, and those of us banging around inside the back of this truck are beginning to envy them. It has been an incredibly rough journey.

We were unable to negotiate an additional truck, but Bob "the Enforcer" Skinner insisted that we get off that bridge and out of Xegar. So an agreement was reached with the drivers: the Cowboys would ride on top of the loaded lorries to a point down the road where we could unload one truck, leave four people to camp with the unloaded gear, squash all the rest of us into the empty truck, and with five trucks carrying most of our gear and most of the team, head to Base Camp.

Major road washouts and nearly impossible gullies continually impede us. We have been stuck three times by mudslides. At each obstacle, all of us get out, push, pull, and exhort our trucks and drivers to keep moving. These are large military-type lorries whose canvas tops are supported by rounded frames—perfect for rolling. And indeed, one truck came within a hair's breadth of going onto its back. The drivers are scared to death because one of their comrades had gone off the road to the Everest base camps a week earlier and been killed. With the road in such terrible condition, I have to give credit to the Chinese lorry-masters for getting us this far alive.

Because I am still on the sick list, I rode in the cabin with the driver for the first half of the journey. I came close to paralysis from looking ahead at the road. I did everything that body contortions and muscular twists could do, including some major phantom braking, to help the driver negotiate the hairpin turns.

A couple of hours ago, just when I got to feeling guilty about riding in the cabin, the LO in the back of the truck hit his head on one of the many body-lifting bumps. Since he's not feeling well, we have traded places. Now I can't see the road in front, and I'm much more relaxed—but only mentally. There are twenty-two people back here with their personal gear bags, plus three or four boxes that we've retrieved after they bounced out of the trucks in front of us. Being the last person in, I've been balancing on the edge of a box at the tailgate level, with room for only one leg inside the truck. My other leg dangles out the back. Every time we hit a bump, I bounce up into the air and grab the bar supporting the truck's canvas top, so as not to fly out the back end.

This is one hell of a ride.

CHAPTER VI

Goddess Mother

AUGUST 26, 1988. BASE CAMP. 16,700 feet. This morning I woke up to a glorious view of Mount Everest. There is no escaping it, so dominant is this mountain—still many miles away. It is a breathtaking sight. When Luke and Mike came back through Xegar after they'd visited Base Camp, they spoke of the overpowering presence of the mountain. They talked of its power and magnetic beauty. I put their descriptions down to impressionable youth. Today I stand in awe of Chomolungma, the Goddess Mother of the World.

Chomolungma, known as Sagarmatha in Nepal, was first recognized as the highest peak in 1852. It was shown in the Survey of India as Peak XV. In 1865, in honor of Sir George Everest, the Surveyor General of India, the mountain was christened Everest. A second translation of Chomolungma is "the place of the female eagle." I like that.

Today is clear and sunny, in mountaineering terms, a summit day—just beautiful, with a few tufts of snow coming off the top of the mountain, indicating the presence of wind, but clearly nothing like the blasts that can hit the top of Everest. We hope we won't experience the infamous winds. In some respects we feel like we've met our greatest challenge just by getting here.

When our trucks pulled in at 2:30 this morning, the advance party—Courtney Skinner, Dan Pryor, Matt Ellenthal, and Dave Padwa—rushed out to greet us with hot drinks and food, but also with chilling news. There has already been a fatality here. A French team, which had arrived in the Rongbuk Valley base camp area the previous day, lost an experienced search-and-rescue mountaineer, 43 years old, to pulmonary edema. He died during the night and was cremated yesterday.

We were all silent, stunned by the news. I have expected to come face to face with death on this trip. We all do, I think. In January, when we were climbing Gannet Peak in Wyoming, Bob Skinner told me that he was preparing himself for the fact that several Cowboys may die on the North Col. That's not to say that he—and everyone on the team—won't do all that is possible to prevent fatalities, but they are sometimes inevitable in the challenge of climbing mountains. We all know that any death on the mountain could easily be one of us. Within moments of arrival, we were forced to acknowledge our own vulnerability—and mortality.

It didn't take long for the two Cowboy groups to catch up with each other's adventures, and it was clear that Courtney had gotten some much needed rest: his twinkle and famous yodel were back. The advance team, we learned, had been surviving the last nine days at Base Camp with meager food and gear. Among them, they had one small stove and three days of food. Dan had arrived with no sleeping bag (fortunately, Courtney had two). For a reconnaissance hike up the East Rongbuk Glacier, Courtney had only his oxfords. With ingenuity and what they could scrounge from the British, they managed to get along, but there was no doubt, they were happy to see the gear trucks arrive.

"We had no idea what had happened to you guys," Dan said. "And I confess, for the first few days we were here in Base, we didn't think much about you. We thought only that we had reached Mecca."

"Yeah, finally," said Matt. "For months we've all been toiling with this objective—to get to Base Camp. And we had work to do."

"We didn't know anything about what you were going through," said Dan, "till a French expedition passed by. We learned that you had reached Xegar, one day's drive away. Mary Skinner called—"

"That was on day seven," said David.

"—with the good news. It was stupendous! She said, 'The trucks

Base Camp. The communications tent (far right) housed the COMSAT system, our link to home. In addition to two- and three-person sleeping tents, we had the luxury of a cook tent and a dining tent. PHOTO BY BRAD WERNTZ.

have been located. Expect the team tomorrow.' Well, when tomorrow came, we learned what the earthquake had done to the bridge."

The general hubbub of welcoming subsided and we all realized how tired we were. In a most haphazard fashion, we pitched tents and crawled into bed.

The Rongbuk Valley base camp area is shared by the Cowboys; Benoit Chamoux's Equipe D'Esprit expedition, which will attempt the Japanese-Hornbein couloirs; the French expedition that is acclimatizing for a Cho Oyu climb (and has already experienced one fatality); two American expeditions attempting Changtse, Everest's satellite peak; and the Marc Twight–Barry Blanchard Everest Express expedition, attempting a dramatic superalpine (night climbing, no sleeping bag) route to the Northeast Ridge up a snow couloir near the North Col. Our camps are spread out in this wide valley, which is an outwash, or floodplain, created by centuries' worth of sand and gravel carried down from the mountains. The valley is dotted with low rounded hills, or drumlins, formed by ancient glacial sediment. These drumlins provide privacy for the different expedition camps.

The Cowboys have much work to do. The advance team warned us that in the afternoons, any time after 2 o'clock, we can expect rain, hail, or winds. It's 5 o'clock and it's turned windy and overcast, not terribly cold, but not comfortable. I was able to take something of a bath in the Rongbuk River and get into clean clothes, from the skin out, before having to seek refuge in my tent. Earlier, Bob Skinner and Dan Pryor called a team meeting to give everyone direction on setting up Base Camp. The first three days in camp were supposed to be rest days, with intermittent work, but since we're behind schedule by two weeks, there will be no rest. In three days our first yak loads will go up the mountain, carrying food and equipment to Camps I and II. Today we worked on cleaning and setting up Base Camp, sorting and drying out our own personal gear, and locating everything that has come from all parts of the world and finally arrived here in the Rongbuk Valley.

As I moved boxes, I kept thinking about Chuck and the boys. The INMARSAT system is to be used primarily for expedition business and for emergencies, but I hope personal calls will be allowed. We're all eager to get news from the United States. I want to talk to my family, and I am particularly interested in George Bush's nomination and his selection of a running mate.

AUGUST 30, 1988. Base Camp preparations include fixing latrines for our thirty-five team members, setting up the six Chinese personnel with tents and gear, getting everybody arranged in their personal tents, putting up a cook tent and a dining room tent, shoring up the White House with our communications equipment, erecting a medical tent, and making enough improvements to the site to provide reasonable comfort for the next two months.

For the last two days we have worked like busy little ants on the camp and the food distribution system. It is a chore to take all the food boxes apart and separate their contents into breakfast, lunch, and dinner, then reseparate the stacks into Base Camp, Camp I, Camp II, Camp III, and the high-altitude camps. Our camp system contemplates four low-altitude camps: Camp I, Interim Camp, Camp II, and Camp III (the Advanced Base Camp), and four high-altitude camps (IV, V, VI, and VII). The number of tents and sleeping bags and the amount of food and equipment in each camp decrease as altitude is gained. We have space for forty people at Base Camp, for example, but Camp VII will sleep only two. Camp III is an exception, as it is the

Advanced Base Camp (ABC) from which we will launch our attack on the summit. ABC is two miles below the foot of the North Col and sits at just over 21,000 feet. It will accommodate about twenty people to support the high-altitude climbers on the Col and above. It's complicated logistically to get the right amount of food and gear to each camp, then to rotate the climbing teams through, as space and need allow.

Dan Pryor, the Base Camp manager, spends all his time coordinating the rest of us. "How's it going?" I asked him this morning when I was taking a break.

"Not bad at all," he said.

"With all these capable people around you," I said, "it should be a snap."

"Not exactly. But really, I just play an oversight role. Jim Burnett is handling the equipment, John Wayne's taken over the kitchen and sanitation, Matt Ellenthal is on communications. And Ted Handwerk has you and Jim Robinson working on the food, right?"

"All thirteen thousand pounds of it."

"Have you got enough hands?"

"Twelve to fifteen pairs, depending on who else needs help. We've got fifty boxes repacked. We've got about twenty more to go."

"Good show." And off he went to make sure the rest of his operation was running smoothly.

Still, we're behind schedule. One of the things that has hindered our progress is the afternoon weather. In the morning it's absolutely gorgeous and the views of Everest are spectacular. It's clear, bright, and hot. I can wear a T-shirt and shorts in camp, but in early afternoon the winds pick up and we start getting rain or hail. Then there's nothing to do but retreat to our tents until dinner time, around 6 or 7. We go to bed right after dinner because it gets dark and cold.

With all of the physical labor around camp, it's interesting to see who really pitches in and who has to be cajoled into working. I've not been comfortable on that score. Summit team members have been specifically directed not to overextend themselves. Additionally, I haven't felt well, so I haven't done as much as I would like to do. I feel guilty. I'd rather work than sit around and watch, but I sure haven't been the biggest contributor this first week at Base Camp. I've got to get well. I think Bob Skinner feels as bad as I do, but that doesn't stop him. He does the work of about three guys. At 58, he's our oldest member, but he's also one of the strongest. Bob Bohus, my climbing partner, has been working hard, too. We haven't had much time to get to know each other yet, but I can tell by the way he works and how he interfaces with people that I'm going to like him.

I spend a lot of time with Sheri King, my Base Camp tentmate. I enjoy her very much. We've created a comfortable homestead for the next two months, in a two-person tent near the Base hospital. Sheri's biggest concern now is Jim Clayton, who has pulmonary edema. Jim came very close to succumbing to pulmonary edema on our January training climb. He had to be airlifted out in a dramatic, last-minute, window-in-the-weather helicopter rescue. The doctors later said that his lungs were so filled with fluid that he had only three to four hours to live. There are no helicopter rescues in Tibet, so Sheri and the other Cowboy doctors are being extra careful.

Since Jim was our cook, Anne Stroock has stepped in to handle the kitchen. She also has communications and public relations duties—she has been busy. Fortunately for the team, she is a hard worker.

The highlight of today was my call home. Our COMSAT-INMARSAT system operates through the Indian Ocean satellite, connecting us to the States via the earth station in Yamaguchi, Japan. It's a direct-dial call and almost like calling next door. I got no answer in Washington, D.C., where I tried to reach Chuck. I called Miami and talked to Toby. After recovering from the surprise of my call, he relayed that he, Chris, and Chuck had managed to get home from Chengdu through Hong Kong and Manila. He asked me to look for his Brooks Brothers suit, which was palletized on the C-5 and is apparently mixed up with the team gear. I suspect it's somewhere among all the boxes, but what'll I do with it if I find it?

Communication to the United States has already caused a problem. It's a great asset, of course. We check in daily with the Wyoming media and periodically with NPR, CNN, AP, and ABC. We are in regular contact with expedition headquarters in Pinedale, and we have various other specific points of contact relating to our research work. But because of a decision to keep the generator on only two hours a day, one hour in the morning and one hour at night, there is little time for personal calls once the media and research calls have been made. A solid whoop usually goes up from any member of the expedition whose name is called during communication hours. Everybody's excited to talk to the folks back home. I had my first chance yesterday morning. Chuck called and Matt answered the phone and talked with him for five or six minutes but didn't call me because I was in a team meeting. When I heard that, I was very angry and upset and quickly broke down into tears—unusual for me—but I hadn't talked to Chuck for almost three weeks. It was a bad start to the day. Then it turned cold and started to rain and sleet, and I retreated to my tent. I was not good company and not a good team player.

We left the United States just a month ago. The summit group is scheduled to start for the Advanced Base Camp in three or four days. My health is still not top-notch. I'm worried about getting rid of this clinging cold. Right now it's fortunate for me that we keep having delays. We could not get the yaks loaded and out of Base today—they will leave tomorrow. There are not enough yaks for the summit team gear. If my cold hangs on and I have to carry a heavy load, I will have an awfully hard time.

AUGUST 31, 1988. The doctors have Jim Clayton in the portable hyperbaric chamber, and team members are taking turns pumping oxygen into the bag with a foot pump. This lifesaving bag looks like a bloated red frankfurter. It is about eight feet long and three feet wide, with an airtight zipper along the top. It's made of a heavy nylon fabric and has a plastic window above where the occupant's head rests. We have two smaller versions that we will transport higher onto the mountain. Our three physicians, Sheri, Bob Bohus, and Ross Greenlee, will carry out a number of research projects relating to the bag's high-altitude application and potential uses.

Jim looks comfy inside with his books, Walkman, and altimeter. At first I thought it would be claustrophobic, but I tried it and it's not. Designed by Professor Igor Gamow of the University of Colorado, the bag slows the progress of acute mountain sickness by increasing the partial pressure of oxygen (as oxygen is pumped inside), effectively lowering the occupant's altitude. After ten minutes in the bag, symptoms such as headaches and nausea are gone and the heart rate drops as the blood absorbs oxygen. The problem in Jim's case is that as soon as he leaves the bag, his symptoms return. Given other medical indicia, and the close call on Gannet Peak in January, the doctors concluded this morning that he must leave. Today he will depart with a trekking group that has driven into the valley, accompanied by canisters of oxygen, the trekker's physician, and our best wishes.

Late yesterday evening Courtney and I had a lengthy interview with ABC for *Good Morning America*. The show has already done one segment on the Cowboys, using tapes of our training climb on Mount Rainier in May. Last night's voice interviews will be used in conjunction with pictures that are at this moment being transmitted directly from Base Camp to the network in New York. Matt Ellenthal took pictures today of team members with a Canon still-video camera. Using floppy discs and a unit that enables us to play the discs on the TCS-9000, those pictures are digitized and transmitted via our linkup with INMARSAT. They arrive in the ABC studio within seconds.

SEPTEMBER 1, 1988. We have been gone a month. We are quite settled in and comfortable here at Base Camp, with many amenities and some inconveniences. It has turned colder, and getting up from the tent at night to wander out to the ladies' room is not much fun. But we do have the lit and warmed kitchen, dining room, and communications tents, where we can congregate. Anybody can retreat at any time to the privacy of his tent. I've been going to bed early to try to lick my cold.

We had a team meeting this morning at the saddle that rides the drumlin south of Base Camp, just beyond the prayer flags. The saddle gets the early morning sun and affords an expansive view of the Rongbuk Valley to the north and Everest to the south. Courtney leads the meetings with input from everyone. In the end, the decisions are made by Courtney. Today's topics are primarily related to logistics. Our current plan calls for summit team members to start carrying loads of food and equipment to the Interim Camp above Camp I and then on to Camp II and Camp III, our Advanced Base Camp. Each night we will drop back to the next lower camp to sleep. Then we'll go back up to ABC and stay a few days. There is an adage in mountaineering that to properly acclimatize, one must climb high and sleep low. The advance-retreat approach is healthy. Summit team members will carry loads to ABC, rest there, then retreat to Base Camp for four or five days of R&R before making a summit attempt. Because we don't have enough yaks, we have to carry more weight than originally planned. My pack for tomorrow's climb now weighs over forty pounds, and I'll probably have to carry an equal amount each day. So it goes—climbs never unfold by blueprint.

I feel a little envious, though, of teams like the Northwest American Everest Expedition, now on the Nepal side. I'm told that there

Base Camp affords a beautiful view of the Northeast Ridge. We will add the prayer flags we brought from Lhasa to those left by previous expeditions.
PHOTO BY JEB SCHENCK.

are fourteen climbers, including three American women, and forty Sherpas. Courtney's plan is to use young American climbers for transporting the gear on the mountain. He views it as a way to give them an opportunity to climb in the Himalayas. With the small number of Everest expeditions, and the intense competition to get on them, these young Americans will now have a good chance of being invited back.

All climbers who applied for team positions knew of Courtney's plan. They were painfully aware that carrying loads, setting up camps, fixing the route, and breaking trails would sap their strength, thus preventing them, in all likelihood, from stepping into a summit role. But our support climbers are men and women with what Courtney calls an "expeditionary personality," those willing to subordinate their personal ambitions to the good of the team. Climbing the highest mountain in the world requires individuals with a common will who can synergize their efforts, while relentlessly giving the best that each has to offer.

Ted Handwerk talks about it in terms familiar to sports fans. "The critical element," he says, "is teamwork. The critical part of teamwork is self-sacrifice. I have to give my best effort, so that someone else can make it to the summit. To make a play work in football, everyone has to do his job and do it right. It's the same thing climbing a mountain. The linemen in football get little credit—and I won't get the credit that a summit climber does. That's okay. I know I am doing my part."

But make no mistake about it. There is not one climber in the world who could stand in a Rongbuk base camp, with its straight-shot view of the Everest peak, and not covet the chance to stand on top.

Chuck called, which was by far the highlight of my week. Everyone here now knows my feelings about calls from home. When the call came, Mark Pilon came running to look for me. "Sue! Sue! Chuck's on the phone! Chuck's on the phone!" I covered the thirty yards to the White House in about three seconds. I miss Chuck and I know he misses me, too. It may be harder on him because he's in the same routine, coming home after work, where I have greeted him almost every day for three decades. He must have kind of an empty feeling. On the other hand, though I miss him, I'm in the midst of a tremendous adventure, surrounded by interesting people and working on a unique and challenging project. So I worry about him. He told me that he talks to Mary Skinner every day to get status reports. He promised to write to me; the letters will arrive by trekker mail. It is strange to contemplate a mail delivery in this part of the world, but George McCown and our trek support group arrive in Base Camp in a couple of weeks. They will hand-deliver our letters. George, the WCEE chairman, is a great adventurer himself. He's been instrumental in getting the Cowboys this far, and he's bringing other Cowboy supporters to Base Camp en route to the Karma Valley with naturalist Bob Fleming, who for many years has guided trekkers through Nepal, India, and the Himalayas.

I was in high spirits after talking to Chuck and ran around the camp helping with odds and ends of chores. We are constantly filling several large plastic water jugs at a nearby spring to keep the kitchen supplied, cleaning the pantry that we built by stacking Power-Ply boxes on their sides, sorting gear, keeping tarps fitted over boxes we don't want exposed to rain, and fulfilling sponsor commitments with such things as photo sessions and making wands (with sponsor names) to mark our route.

Late in the day Fred walked out of the White House to Julie and Jim's tent. "The summit team is not leaving tomorrow," he said. "Courtney has decided it's more important that Team Four goes ahead. Please tell the other summiters."

Team Four will be setting the route on the North Col. They will need to acclimatize before they can fix the route. We can't climb the Col until it is fixed, so it looks like a couple of more days in Base Camp for me.

Each day, as we spend more time here, I get to know my climbing partner, Bob Bohus, a little better. I like him very much. He's a 36-year-old urologist from Sheridan, Wyoming, and is a real outdoor guy—a jock. He has a great sense of humor and seems to possess all of the caring and sensitivity one hopes to find in a physician. I feel fortunate that he's my partner, but Bob must wonder whether I'm strong enough to make it. He was not on any of our training climbs (except this spring at Rainier, when we did more kibitzing than climbing), so we're both withholding judgment. Knowing how Courtney operates, I'm sure Bob wasn't asked ahead of time whether he would be comfortable climbing with me. It's no small undertaking to commit your life to someone on this mountain, so there must be mutual confidence. Only time on the mountain will tell whether Bob and I are compatible.

SEPTEMBER 2, 1988. Today the schedule was rearranged once again. There is so much snow on the mountain from the late monsoon that we can't move up as quickly as we would like. We have to give the snow at the higher elevations a chance to melt, slide, or blow off. When snow accumulates on the Col, the avalanche danger is high. When snow accumulates elsewhere, climbers are reduced to postholing, sinking up to the thigh in deep snow with each step. And postholing reduces climbers to exhaustion.

Because we need the acclimatization and the physical workout, the six summiters took team gear to Camp I today. My load included a large Nalgene plastic bottle of fuel weighing twenty-two pounds, as well as the medical kit destined for Camp II, which weighed seven or eight pounds. Two bags of company food added another five pounds. Thirty-five pounds is a sensible load for the first carry, but at 18,000 feet it felt like seventy pounds. I struggled with my load and walked at a snail's pace. The trail heading south out of Base Camp is not at all steep. It rises less than a thousand feet over about four and a half miles through a narrow, rock-strewn canyon. At the terminus of the main Rongbuk Glacier, which is ugly—covered with rock, dirt and mudslides—we turn east, following the path of the East Rongbuk Glacier, and start up a steep, 500-foot section to Camp I. Part of the faint trail, high above the valley floor, is obscured by scree and pulverized rock deposited by slides. Camp I is just above the scree slides. On the way up the last steep section, ever-attentive physician Ross Greenlee passed me on the trail.

"Hi there, Sue," he said. I tried to say hello but didn't have enough air in my lungs to get out a word. "Sue, are you all right?"

"Fine," I managed to say. "I'm okay." He could hear me breathing like commercial bellows, I'm sure. I was one of the last to arrive at Camp I. Some of the team made the trip in about three hours; it took me three and a half.

Camp I consists of five tents with sleeping bags, carried up by Team Two, with cooking gear and food stashed in one tent. The area is all dirt and rock with a lot of slide activity. It's unattractive, but it's about the only flat spot since Base Camp. The Himalayas are young mountains. The recent glacial activity and continual upheaval leave the terrain, even in flat spots, haphazard and messy. By contrast, Everest, standing guard in the distance, appears sparkling and clean, its beautiful white mantle of snow continually luring us higher.

After resting at Camp I, we started back to Base Camp. Several of us arrived at the Rongbuk River, which bars access to our Base Camp, at about the same time. The river had risen and no one could find a way to get across without getting wet. Since it was now growing cold, I wanted to stay dry. I stood assessing the different crossing techniques of my teammates to see which one might work for me. Orion Skinner simply walked through in his boots and got wet. David Frawley took about a ten-yard run and leaped—not quite reaching the opposite side. Dr. Bob jumped from rock to rock, and I think he made it without getting wet, but rock hopping was out because my legs aren't as long as his. Fred tried a daring ski-pole technique, charging with both poles in a lance position, carefully timing a two-handed, midstream pole plant while leaping with legs extended like a broad jumper and balancing for some considerable air-time after liftoff. He got a lot of style points but hit short of land. Jim Burnett changed to thongs, walked through, and came back to give Julie a piggyback ride. After depositing Julie, Jim yelled to me, "Sue, do you want a ride?"

"No, thanks," I called.

He yelled back, "Are you sure?" I must have hesitated because he started across the river to get me. I was embarrassed and mumbled to myself, "What kind of a mountain climber are you?" But the ride was welcome. My feet stayed warm and dry.

Jim Burnett, who will turn 23 while we're here, is our youngest designated summit climber and always a gentleman. He is from Kemmerer, Wyoming, close to Pinedale, and has been helping Bob Skinner with equipment and company gear. He's a quiet, strong, and competent young man. He and Julie could be our elite team. We have talked about putting the first woman from the United States on top of Everest and it would be sensational if it were me, at age 51. But the truth is, Julie is faster, stronger, and more experienced. What would really be fun is if we both made it, but the odds are remote.

The first woman to reach the top of Mount Everest was Junko Tabei, on May 16, 1975, via the traditional South Col route. She was accompanied by Sherpa Ang Tshering and supported by fourteen climbers, twenty-three Sherpas, and 500 porters. To date, five women have reached the summit, including Sharon Wood from Canada, the only North American so far.

SEPTEMBER 3, 1988. Sheri, my roomie, has decided that I should go on antibiotics to try to get rid of whatever is afflicting me. I hope it helps because I need to regain my health. At altitudes above 18,000 feet or so, human bodies do not rebuild strength, so I must be strong going up. That will be soon.

Late in the morning our plans hit another snag. The yaks have returned from their first trip up the mountain. They weren't able to reach Camp III (ABC) with their loads because of a morainal crevasse, which was opened either by the earthquake or by glacial movement. It blocks the entire moraine above Camp II. We got a note from Ted Handwerk, via the yak herders, that Team Two is on the scene trying to fix a bridge for the yaks. One more delay.

For me it's a quiet day of rest, reflection, and personal chores. The Rongbuk River runs adjacent to our camp, and on sunny days, washing clothes, shampooing, and bathing are relatively simple—I head downriver with biodegradable soap and a bucket of hot water from the kitchen. I lay my clothes out to dry on the rocks. Toilet facilities consist of two fully enclosed latrine tents, each about four feet square and six feet tall, set up fifty yards outside of camp. They provide privacy, but because they're enclosed, they stink. When we're higher on the mountain, privacy requires more ingenuity, like sneaking off behind a boulder or a snow serac. On a fixed rope even that's not possible. There I just hope the climber on the rope above me has a large bladder and excellent control. At night, when the conditions are so cold and windy that you can't possibly go out of your tent, there are clever systems designed for female climbers, one of which is an anatomically shaped plastic funnel to be used with what men have fondly known for years as a pee bottle. Sibylle, who has spent a lot of time rock climbing and, therefore, hanging off big walls, loves her pee bottle. She talks about it so much that I have become an early convert. The system works nicely when one is caught in inhospitable circumstances. Of course, that doesn't take care of all of one's bodily functions, so some degree of exposure is a sure thing. Fortunately, our high-altitude clothing is designed with special zipper systems, which minimize the area of skin that must brave the elements.

Between taking care of our bodies and clothes, cooking, cleaning, doing interviews, preparing sponsor photos, and performing regular camp chores for thirty-five to forty people, as well as making carries up the mountain, we're busy.

Ted Handwerk organized the food and brought a large variety of bulk carbohydrate foods and canned meats, fruits, and vegetables for our low-altitude camps. He frequently consults a forty-page computer printout detailing the preweighed and prepackaged meals for every person at every camp the entire time we're on the mountain. A building contractor from Boulder, Colorado, he is a long-time Skinner Brothers protégé. He has taught survival, worked as a wilderness and glacier ski guide in Alaska, and done a lot of rock and ice climbing. With Bob Skinner, he also led the Cowboys' training climb in January. Now that Ted has finished his organizational work here at Base, he is leading Team Two.

Our menus, based on Ted's research, are designed to meet the demands of climbing. The food has to be appealing, too, if we are to maintain our strength. He has done well, I think. A typical dinner includes voluminous amounts of hot liquids—soups, broths, teas— and usually some kind of pasta with canned meats and gravy, turkey, or whatever the cooks pull out of the pantry. If Sibylle or Alex is around, we get a tasty dessert. If not, it's canned fruit and packaged candies and cookies. The cooking chores are rotated among team members. Everyone wants Brian to cook—he's really good. Bob Bohus is a worthy cook, too. At least he is with pizza. Our cook tent is large, about fifteen by twenty feet. Bob Skinner, a fanatic on hygiene for the sake of team health, organized a restaurant-quality kitchen, with propane ovens and giant stainless steel pots and pans. At dinner call we wash up, file into the cook tent, fill our aluminum plates and large plastic cups, exit the opposite side, and repair to the adjacent dining tent. This fancy circular North Face dome has a propane-fired chandelier. Using upside-down Power-Ply boxes along the perimeter, we can seat about sixteen people, depending on whether it's six-foot-five Jeb Schenck or five-one Julie Cheney. With some climbers at higher camps, two or three manning the communications system, and our usual one or two not feeling well, we almost always have enough room. It's a time for everyone to relax and mix, and discuss the latest change in plans.

After dinner tonight I went into the White House with David Padwa and David Frawley. We sat around and told jokes. Example: "Did you hear about the expedition cook who, bending down to check the smoking oven, exclaimed, 'Oh, my baking yak!'" Our other jokes

This wild and crazy bunch kept life at Base Camp from being monotonous. Left to right: Dave McNally, Quintin Barney, Doug Burbank, Mack Ellerby, Brad Werntz, Ted Handwerk, Bob Bohus, David Frawley. PHOTO BY JEB SCHENCK.

were similarly sophisticated, though not necessarily printable. The two Davids and I were roommates on our Rainier training climb, where we snuck around like high school kids to avoid cooking meals in the rain at the Cougar Rock campground, and to try to find a nice bottle of Châteauneuf du Pape to accompany the grub.

David Frawley is our self-appointed entertainment chairman. Today I told him he is the first 43-year-old juvenile delinquent that I've ever met. I meant it as a compliment. He has enormous vitality and is simply a lot of fun to be with. He is also one of the hardest-working members of our team. One of the things I like about being around David, with so many frustrations trying our patience, is that he does not feel compelled to be diplomatic, as I often do. "This sucks," he'll say. I stand by in total agreement, but maintaining a reserved and lady-like demeanor.

David Padwa, 56, is our research director. He is an overeducated businessman who figured out how to be a college professor *and* make money. David went to the University of Chicago, Columbia Law School, and the Harvard Graduate School of Public Administration. He has built and sold two major companies and taught at both the University of Georgia and the University of Colorado. Upon returning to the States, David will assume a position as a policy research fellow at the National Center for Atmospheric Research. He is learned and erudite. When any of us has a question about any esoteric subject, we go to David. Only Rick Dare has a shot of challenging David when we play Trivial Pursuit. David has also done a considerable amount of climbing, and though his work assignments are at Base Camp, he hopes to go to ABC sometime during our stay.

Sitting in the White House near the TCS-9000 made me want to call home, but I didn't know which state Chuck was in. I decided the best chance of finding somebody at home early Saturday morning would be Chris. With a thirteen-hour time difference to the East Coast, it would be about 7:30 A.M. in Coral Gables. When he answered the phone, I knew I'd awakened him.

"Mom, where are you?"

"The Everest Base Camp," I said, "sixteen thousand seven hundred feet." He couldn't believe I was calling from Tibet. I gave him our INMARSAT number to call me back because we were estimating a cost of $25 a minute to call the United States from Base Camp, but considerably less to call Base Camp from the States.

"I saw you Friday morning on *Good Morning America*," he said when we were back on the line. "I was in my bathroom shaving and I heard your voice—just like home." So ABC had received the pictures that Matt had sent via the Canon-INMARSAT hookup. "The picture quality," Chris said, "was very good." He also told me about hearing the radio reports that NPR journalist Peter Breslow, accompanying the Cowboys, has been sending out. We chatted for about ten minutes. In signing off, Chris got serious. "Mom, there isn't a day that goes by that I don't think about you being up there," he said. "I hope you're safe and that you have a chance to go to the top." I almost cried, but Padwa's and Frawley's antics captured my attention and deflected a moment of sad introspection.

SEPTEMBER 4, 1988. I was all set to go to Camp I when Fred emerged from the White House with a glum expression.

"What's the matter?" asked Bob Bohus. "Oh, come on. You don't mean—"

"Everything is on hold."

"Again?"

"We've got a radio call from Camp I. Ellerby and McLean. Come in and I'll let them tell you what they've just told me." Mack Ellerby and Brian McLean, two of our strongest climbers, were supposed to make a carry from Camp I to our Interim Camp—a four-hour climb. What could have gone wrong? We entered the White House.

"They said they returned to Camp I 'totally fried,'" Fred explained as he worked to get them back on line. "Brian? Good. Go ahead."

"Unless we get more yaks," Brian said, "there is no way we can climb this mountain. We just can't move all the necessary gear." He sounded angry.

"Look," said Mack. He sounded discouraged. "Here it is September 4, we haven't even made it to Camp II, substantially all of our gear is still in Base Camp, and we don't have enough yaks to move it up the mountain."

For those of us who were standing by at Base Camp, it was a sobering call. How are we going to cope with our loads above 18,000 feet if one carry has fried Mack and Brian? I sat forlornly on a rock outside the mess tent and thought to myself, "All I can do is try."

Worse, we haven't heard from Team Two in several days. We need to know whether everyone is okay and whether the crevasse has been bridged. The beam of our handheld radios is blocked by a mountain ridge. My theory is that Team Two is staying to finish the bridge, and that if they were in trouble, Ted would have sent someone down to get help.

The problem of moving our gear up and our anxiety about Team Two incited a round of leadership bashing, a sport said to run rampant on all expeditions to the Himalayas. I can understand that. Put a group of self-confident overachievers together in intimate proximity for extended periods under harsh conditions, and you have a prescription for friction. The ventilation of feelings is sometimes healthy but not always constructive.

The yak train and Team Three leave tomorrow with Bob Skinner. That will put all our teams up on the mountain, working along our route. The summit team will leave the day after tomorrow, September 6. With all the delays we've had, I'm not going to hold my breath. We plan to move slowly to acclimatize to the 4,500-foot jump in elevation to ABC. When we get there, we have three days of rest—no carries.

After dinner tonight the yakkies, our eight herders, came to our dining tent to listen to tapes on Ted's boom box. We had quite a party, with music our only common language. They're lively and fun and quick to smile. Exposure to the sun has weathered their skin, making it difficult to judge their ages. Their long black hair is braided around their heads and interwoven with red yak yarn, rings, and coins. Many wear turquoise earrings. These Tibetans are named for the day of the week on which they were born, but they also have wonderful nicknames like "Thunderbolt," "Daytime," and my favorite, "Wish-Granting Gem." Some live in villages several days' walk down-valley. Others are nomads who live in tents in the hills. Transporting gear for expeditions is purely a sideline from their major tasks of farming and sheep and goat herding. Since the yaks are the measure of each man's wealth, and the source of heat, food, and clothing, the animals are zealously protected by their owners. When the first American teams came to the Rongbuk Valley after Tibet was reopened to climbers in 1980, these men would ask the climbers, "When you are away for so long, who takes care of *your* yaks?"

The eight men live about 200 yards from our Base Camp in a handmade yak-wool tent complete with smoke hole. They fuel their cook fire with dried yak or goat dung, and bake a flour paste called *tsampa*. They are short, dirty, and pungent from a thousand fires. At

Yakkies Kason (left) and "Wednesday." The lack of a common language didn't prevent the Yakkies and Cowboys from enjoying good, old-fashioned, country-western sing-alongs. PHOTO BY BOB BOHUS.

night they like to visit our camp to hear the music and sing along, especially with our country and western tapes. They can't get quite the right twang, but they are enthusiastic. Music is important to them, and when we turn in, they sit in front of their tent, facing the mountain, and sing their own songs. They say they sing of Chomolungma, the Goddess Mother.

Western technology fascinates them. When we tape their voices and record their pictures on the camp's still-video, they ask us to play the tapes back, over and over and over. At the sound of their own voices and the sight of themselves on the screen, they break into wondrous smiles. One of our medical gadgets is of special interest. Our battery-powered Ohmeda oximeter measures how much oxygen is in the bloodstream via a light probe taped to a finger. We use the oximeters to monitor ourselves, but the yakkies like to have their oxygen levels checked. It seems that despite having spent a lifetime at altitude, they don't have a higher level of oxygen saturation than we do.

Although Ethan Goldings is our Ph.D. Tibetan language specialist, Dan, as Base Camp manager, has more interaction with the yakkies and has done most of the negotiating with them. "You professional students," he says to Ethan, "are too idealistic to barter with professional barterers. And let me tell you, these guys are professionals."

Dan says he was told that Tibetan yak herders were invariably shifty thieves. "The Himalayan climbers I talked to said be sure not to give them anything unless they do something for you first," he says. "I think some of that counsel was based on experience, but the green-eyed monster prejudice may also play a role."

He and Courtney had already agreed on how our expedition would deal with the yakkies: "Treat them with the same respect that you want for yourself," Court told us in one of our early meetings. "Be polite, sincere, and friendly, because they are our equals."

Dan provides them with food, *cha* (tea), flashlight batteries, kerosene, and the cure-all Band-Aid. When they see him working, they silently appear and take his load for their own shoulders. "I have found," he says with a sly smile, "that honorable intentions are not inhibited by language barriers."

In fact, when it comes to the serious negotiations over payloads, Dan thinks that understanding the language is actually a hindrance. "If you know their logic," he told me one evening, "too many of their objections suddenly become understandable. I handle their objections with laughter." The next day, when we loaded up the yaks, he had an opportunity to demonstrate.

The yakkies wanted a twenty-kilo load per side, per yak, supposedly standard. Dan lifted one such load over his head, laughing to show how light it was.

"Mindu, mindu," they said. "No."

Dan stretched out his arms. "Yaks are big," he said. He then threw another fifteen kilos of canned goods into the bag and easily hefted the load to his shoulders.

"Mindu!" they shouted. "No!" But eventually they accepted thirty kilos per side, or sixty kilos per yak (about 132 pounds), raising our total payload by several hundred kilos.

Each yak herder owns at least three yaks. The herders are all of equal status and they draw rocks (instead of straws) to determine the distribution of loads. Some loads are good, some loads are bad, but each load is carefully weighed with a wood and rock balance.

One of the yakkies, Norbu, was fascinated with my Sorel boots (the fleece-lined rubber and leather cold-weather standards made in Canada) and by sign language tried to talk me out of them, gesturing that his feet would be cold going up the mountain. I believe they will be . . . he had on tattered tennis shoes. I don't see how these guys get to 21,000 feet in tennis shoes, but they do. I told him I needed the boots to stay warm, but that I would give them to him when I left for home.

I started to go to bed when Chuck and Toby called from Miami. They reported that the University of Miami had beaten Florida State, 31 to 0. Rick Dare and I have a bet on the national title this year. I'm for Miami; his money is on Notre Dame. We've also placed a friendly wager on the Bush-Dukakis presidential race.

Chuck and Toby expressed concern about the danger here. I explained that the time to worry is when I am higher on the mountain and that it would be pointless for them to expend worry-time now. Comparatively speaking, there simply is not a high level of danger on the route between Base Camp and Camp III. I didn't tell them about the rock avalanches and the death of the Japanese climber, hit by rocks on the route between Camp I and Interim Camp. I can tell from Chuck's voice that he is feeling stress from my long absence. I haven't even left Base Camp and he's wondering when I'm coming home. I don't know the answer.

Chuck said that in the course of the last couple of days, since the most recent *Good Morning America* and NPR shows, he's talked to probably 400 people who have seen us on television or heard the NPR broadcasts, and that a lot of people are following us closely. It's exciting to feel that America knows what we're doing in this remote and inhospitable part of the world. It makes me feel not quite so far from home. I hope we don't let everyone down. Most people have no idea how many things have to go right to summit this mountain. All three of the primary elements—weather, health, and logistics, with their myriad of variables—have to fall into place on one day. On Everest that happens infrequently. You can train all your life, have the best team in the world, and still not make it.

SEPTEMBER 5, 1988. We finally got twenty-five yaks loaded and out of Base Camp. I hope they will get all the way to Camp III.

The luxury of the day was a bath. Bob Skinner has fixed us a bathhouse—a four-foot-square, six-foot-high tent. The top half of one side is made of opaque plastic and faces the sun, so the tent gets warm from the solar heat. Huge galvanized buckets that we bought in Lhasa are placed in the tent. We fill the largest bucket with warm water from the kitchen and climb right in. The women and some of the guys can sit in the bucket as if it were a bathtub. Jeb Schenck and Quint Barney won't fit, so they have to stand and use a scooper to pour water over their heads.

The only people now left in Base Camp are the six summit climbers, our Chinese geologist Professor Kang, Peter Breslow, and a young woman from Germany who has adopted us. Astrid Brenner wandered into the valley a few days ago in a long skirt, long-sleeved cotton shirt, high-top sneakers, and a large, floppy straw hat, carrying a small satchel. I thought maybe she was going to a garden party. Despite being six feet tall, she looks like a pixie. She's 28 years old and going into her second year of traveling around the Orient. She speaks English nicely and is a friendly woman. Astrid is getting room and board from the Cowboys in exchange for helping with cooking, dishes, and other camp chores. I like anyone who cooks and does dishes. She's good company as well. Yesterday, she told me she's going to leave in two days and take a walk to Pakistan. I would find that more intimidating than climbing Everest.

Many nights before I go to sleep I listen to my Walkman. I have never had one before and I got considerable ribbing from the younger crowd early on because I couldn't figure out how it worked. It *is* simple. Now I listen almost every night to unwind. My favorite tape is Vivaldi's "Four Seasons." It has both a mystical quality and drama, just like Everest.

I look forward to starting tomorrow for ABC. I don't look forward to having thirty-five or forty pounds on my back.

CHAPTER VII

Valley of Despair

SEPTEMBER 8, 1988. 7:15 P.M. Eleven of us are at Interim Camp in the big orange tent we purchased from the British. It's mildly chaotic inside. We're all tired but jovial—glad to be heading upward at last. The British tent is large. We can stand up and walk around in it. Along one side is ample space for six sleeping bags, which take up about half the tent space. One quarter of the tent has the cooking area, and the other quarter has communications equipment and a pantry. The dining room is wherever you can find a spot to sit. It reminds me of the home of the Tibetan that we visited in Xigatse. We have no patio with potted flowers, though.

Bob Skinner is in one corner trying to put together an evening meal. He's getting some help, but most of us are stretched out side by side on sleeping bags on a platform of flattened cardboard boxes, necessary on the protruding rocks of the moraine.

"Let's settle the sleeping arrangements," Bob says. "Fred, Orion, Julie, Jim, Sibylle, and David, you all will take the two-man tents. The rest of us will sack out here."

As we await supper, we fiddle with our altimeters, trying to figure out how high we are. The instruments don't agree.

"Okay, so we don't know what height we're at," says Fred.

"We don't know what Bob's cooking, either," David Frawley says.

"We're at nineteen thousand feet," says Bob, without looking up.

"And the outside temperature," returns David, "is just a little bit colder than Bob's hot chocolate."

I like Bob's cooking. Anything he cooks, I eat—it means I don't have to cook.

"Frawley, is your nose still out of joint because Skinner lectured you about that Boston twang?" I ask.

"He just pretends he doesn't understand a word I say."

"The rest of us don't understand you, either," says Orion. "In fact, Sibylle has been rooming with you for two weeks and she still doesn't understand you."

"That's another story," says Frawley.

A chorus of hoots.

Two days ago the summit team left Base Camp carrying full loads to Camp I. A full load is about half of our personal gear (twenty-five to thirty pounds) plus some portion of company gear, such as a tent, sleeping bag, ground pad or food bags. Again the climb up to Camp I was a struggle. My thirty-eight-pound load was off balance because of a large team first-aid case strapped on the outside, and I was beat when we got into Camp I. I shared a tent with Jim Burnett and Julie Cheney. We felt like three vacuum-wrapped sausages. Nobody slept well.

The next day, our chore was to move our loads up to Interim Camp. It took me four hours. Some of the guys did it in under three. It's rugged up-and-down terrain over talus and scree. The overall height gain to Interim isn't so great because of the downhill sections, but it is a demoralizing climb, up and down, up and down, always over unstable rocky moraine.

Camp II is at 19,900 feet, an eight-hour hike from Camp I. The British had decided on the need for the Interim Camp, which we're now enjoying. However, instead of having a logical numbering system, we have Base Camp, Camp I, Interim, Camp II, and then Camp III, or ABC. For sure, I'd rather have this camp here than a logical numbering system.

Above Base Camp, after we turn east, we are in the valley that is the outlet of the East Rongbuk Glacier. *Rongbuk* means "the valley of precipices and steep ravines." An apt name. The entrance to the valley is a terminal moraine—centuries' worth of loose rock, talus, and scree, called glacial till, that has been forced down the valley or fallen from the steep mountainsides. The peaks on either side are in the 22,000- to 24,000-foot range. There is snow on the highest reaches, but mostly they are jagged, stratified, red-veined rock. Daily, rock debris of all sizes crashes down onto the moraine. Often, while climbing through the valley after the sun comes up, one hears the serenade of the rockslides. The terrain is haphazardly irregular: some places it's steep going up, some places it's steep going down, some places it's not steep at all, some places there are large rocks, some places small rocks. Nothing's stable. There's virtually no trail. As we climb higher, we encounter giant frozen snow formations, called seracs. They look like huge white shark's teeth sticking up out of aged, diseased gums. The seracs range from about twenty-five feet tall to over a hundred feet. Spectacular, but eerie. In places, we weave in and out of the teeth, walking on the gums.

My first carry from Camp I to Interim Camp remains so vivid in my mind that I can still feel the forty-plus pounds on my back. Again I'm the slowest, so I'm by myself climbing up this miserable valley. The waist belt on my pack has broken and I can't get the weight properly distributed. The pack straps are cutting into my shoulders. I use any excuse to stop, even though it takes enormous effort to take my pack off, readjust it, put it back on, and try again. I search for a rock that's about waist high to deposit my pack because if I set it on the ground, I have a hard time lifting it back up. If I do put it on the ground, I get it back up by using my sit-and-rollover technique. First, I set my pack upright; second, I sit down with my back against the pack, legs extended, and fasten the straps so that the pack is securely affixed to me; then I lean and roll over into a four-point stance on my hands and knees; with the weight centered over my back, I can slowly struggle up with the help of my ski poles. It's the only time I'm glad I'm alone because I look so ridiculous, particularly since I know that Quint (and some of the others, no doubt) can reach down with one arm, pull the pack off the ground, and swing it up without missing a step. I go through my silly rollover routine several times a day: to take off a jacket, to put on a jacket, to put on more zinc oxide, to get food, to get water, to go to the bathroom, to rest. I am always the last person to make it into camp. Very discouraging. At one point I sat down and started crying because it was so hard. After a few moments of self-indulgence I forced myself to go on. "Crying won't help move a load up the mountain, so suck it up, Sue, and get moving." I talk to myself a lot, and did even before my brain encountered the effects of oxygen deprivation. "Nobody ever said this would be easy, and you're sure as hell not quitting, so move! When you get to Interim, smile . . . Now take a breath, step, exhale, find your pace. Go."

After dropping my first load at Interim, I returned to Camp I to sleep. I had a tent to myself. I needed the rest because we were to carry the remainder of our loads to Interim the next day.

The trail conditions didn't improve overnight, so today's carry was again a struggle. My load was not so heavy and I'd made some progress in fixing my pack, but I was tired from the previous two days' carries. As I lie back in my sleeping bag now, I feel myself back on the trail, struggling under my load. Once again everybody else is far ahead. It is windy and cold. I plug along. I have to stop often. I remind myself to keep a rhythm and to use both pressure breathing and rest-step techniques. The sky looks gloomy. When I am about halfway up to Interim, it starts to snow. It is just too much. My surroundings are bleak, and so am I. I am lonely, cold, exhausted. I sit down and cry. Why am I here? These days are difficult—halfway around the world from home, carrying heavy loads by myself over unrelentingly inhospitable terrain, killing myself slowly. Why? Why am I here and not at home with Chuck and my boys? "Suck it up, Sue. Move." Fantasizing about being at home in Florida with my family helps time to pass: I imagine a crystal blue day on Biscayne Bay, air temperature 79 degrees, water temperature 78 degrees. We have to decide whether to go waterskiing or scuba diving. Maybe we'll do both. Should we barbecue on board our boat, or go to one of Miami's water-accessed restaurants? "Take a breath, step, exhale. Find your pace." Boredom, discomfort, and frustration. Exhaustion, loneliness, and depression. What fun!

I got into Interim about 6 P.M., an hour after everybody else.

Five of us—Bob Bohus, Quintin Barney, Bob Skinner, Brad Werntz, and I—slept in the British tent. I didn't sleep well, probably because the first night at a higher altitude often causes breathing problems. During sleep people take fewer breaths or shallower breaths. At sea level that is not a problem, but at high altitudes a sleeping climber may take several deep breaths, then several shallow breaths. Seconds may pass without any breathing at all. At that point the level of oxygen in the blood is dangerously low. Many people then wake up gasping for air. It feels as if you can't get enough oxygen. I spent a lot of the night gasping and listening to others do the same.

We had an additional problem. A small rodent had invaded. A rat? A mouse? Or some exotic Himalayan plague carrier? Whatever, it was having its way with our food bags. Everybody lay awake trying not to awaken anybody else, but when we weren't gasping for air, we were all listening to the ravenous Rongbuk rodent.

SEPTEMBER 10, 1988. INTERIM. NOON. We're taking a rest day, for which I am very thankful. Yesterday we made a carry to Camp II, which is nothing more than three or four tents sitting on a few rocks in the bottom of this morainal valley. As with all our camps, semiflat rock platforms have been constructed to provide tent space. Nonetheless, unfriendly rocks find ways to protrude into tent floors and invariably attack the most sensitive place on a resting body.

Between Interim and Camp II the seracs become larger and there are many more of them—it's a jumble of shark's teeth sticking up through the rock-strewn moraine. Our loosely defined trail is along a ridge, the crest of a medial moraine. Above the valley floor we weave in and out of the seracs and over the ubiquitous jumble of rocks. It is not steep. We gain about 1,000 feet between Interim and II. We had decided to take three days, rather than two, to move all of our gear to Camp II because in truth, we are all getting tired. I carried a relatively light load and climbed a little over three hours. On terrain where it is not so steep and I don't have a forty-pound pack, I can keep up better. Nonetheless, it was one more day of carrying loads by myself through what looks like moonscape, and wondering why I'm not back home. I think about Chuck and the boys a lot these days. It brings tears to my eyes now when I recall how Chris put his arms around me and gave me a kiss on the steps of our miserable hotel when I left Chengdu, and how Toby ran to the elevator to tell me that his garment bag with his Brooks Brothers suit was on its way to the Everest Base Camp. Why anybody in her right mind would leave her family and do this, I simply don't know.

The carries by the summit team have drained our strength—at least mine. Maybe the conditioning benefits will outweigh the nega-tives. My muscles are tired from four days of carries, but I feel accli-matized to 19,000 feet. I had no trouble at all breathing last night.

When the summit team gets to ABC, all the Cowboys except for our Base Camp crew will be back together. We'll be able to make some decisions about whether the summit team goes down to Base Camp for R&R, or up the Col to capitalize on the good weather. Historically, climbers have rotated to lower elevations to rejuvenate before attempting a summit. But if the Col route has been fixed and the weather holds, it could be to our advantage to move fast. It depends on the Col route, the weather, and how everybody is feeling.

After dumping our loads at Camp II last night, we came back down through the moonscape to Interim. Just the summit team and Brad Werntz are here. Brad hasn't been feeling well, so he's resting with us. We now have daily radio monitoring at specific times, morning and evening, among all of our camps. Sometimes it's hard to make contact, because the terrain interferes with the radio beam. Base Camp has been in contact with the outside world. Last night they told us that the team received a surprise phone call from Wyoming Governor Mike Sullivan, chairman of the expedition's honorary board of governors, wishing the team well.

In other news, we learned that another trekker has come down with a severe edema problem; Sheri King is taking care of her in our hyperbaric chamber at Base Camp. So far it appears that our M.D.s have saved at least two lives. Everybody here tonight seems to be in good health and good spirits. I'm in better spirits now, too.

Coming down from II last night, I had a chance to talk to Fred. After these initial carries, everybody recognizes that we need a shift on the summit team. Jim and Julie appear to be working well together and are compatible climbers. Fred and Orion have climbed together for twelve years, so they are well matched. But Dr. Bob and I simply are not. Bob is a strong, fast climber. It's detrimental to him to be teamed with a slow climber. At the higher elevations where a climber must keep moving to stay warm, it could be life threatening. He can't afford to stand and become chilled while waiting—WOW! I'm sitting here talking and the day's biggest rockslide comes careening down the gully just north of me. The rocks bounce off each other and ricochet wildly in all directions. Some of them are as big as Volkswagens. These rockslides create the lateral moraines that run up both sides of this glacial valley. Because of them I don't wear my Walkman when climbing in this valley. I want some sound to reach me before a rock does. I haven't forgotten about the Japanese climber who died this spring on this section of our route.

Fred told me that Courtney and Bob are reevaluating our summit

I can always manage a smile for the camera, even climbing through the seracs with a heavy pack and aching muscles. PHOTO BY JEB SCHENCK.

teams. We don't sit down and discuss these things—they more or less evolve. Courtney and Bob have years of living and teaching survival in arctic conditions and they know my capabilities, so I have confidence in their judgment. I'm also convinced that if it is at all possible, they will give me a chance to go for the top. One plan under consideration is switching from two-man summit teams to four-man teams. That may be safer. With four people, if one is in trouble, there are three people to help. One climber can assist the distressed person, leaving two climbers to try for the summit. It's not as fast, of course, but I know that speed is not the means by which I am going to attain the summit. For me to be successful, it will have to be a careful, deliberate, step-by-step approach, with protective camps in place. My move to the top must be closely timed to my climbing rate for the distance and for the oxygen supply.

Four-person teams have negatives, too. I would be the slowest, and either I would have to climb alone or other climbers would have to adjust their pace to mine. Or someone else would take my summit spot. Another troublesome negative to me, assuming I'm still on a summit team, is that if we use four-person teams, it's likely that we'll stage our summit attempts from a 26,000-foot camp rather than 28,000-foot camp. We would not put in Camp VII as originally planned. I'm not sure that I can cover 3,000 feet at that elevation fast enough to make the top and get down alive. To my knowledge, no climber has ever summited Everest from the Northeast Ridge and been able to get back to a 26,000-foot camp the same day. I must remember to ask Quint about that. He's read everything that exists in print on Everest and is the team historian. We will have to wait and see what conditions develop. Certainly I want all decisions to be made in the best interest of the team. I also want a chance to go to the top.

Meanwhile, the summit team is resting here at Interim. It's a beautiful, blue sky day, with a few cumulus clouds. I am on a bluff that looks down the valley of the East Rongbuk Glacier. There are some spectacular knife-edged seracs directly in front of me. Up the valley toward ABC there are bigger seracs and a postcard view of the Northeast Ridge. A few clouds are flowing in toward the peak, indicating some wind. It's quiet here, except for the occasional snap, crackle, and pop of the earth's changing surface.

Mountain climbers are weather-worriers. We must find out when the monsoon season ends and when the polar jet stream will descend. It is then that we'll get the strong northwestern winds that make this side of Everest so dangerous. The winds can be hellacious. Already it's getting colder. Last night the temperature dropped well below freezing. My water bottle was frozen this morning, so it'll go into my sleeping bag from now on.

Last night Fred, Orion, Julie, and Jim stayed in the company tents, while Dr. Bob, Brad, and I slept in the British tent. The little devil was back, with his rodent chums. I heard them around 2 A.M., happily munching away. When I turned on my headlamp, I saw one. I had been envisioning a giant wharf rat with fiery eyes, yellow teeth the size of razor blades, and long stringy hair like yaks. When I saw it was just a meek field mouse, that was quite enough for me. After telling Bob Bohus the good news, I went right back to sleep. But Bohus got up and spent the rest of the night big-game hunting, throwing rocks inside the tent at any little rodent that raised its head. He got at least one (he says). He was quite happy about that this morning. I was happy, too, because once I had gotten Bohus working on the project, I slept soundly until 8 A.M.

Psychologically and physically, I am in better shape today, except for this lonely feeling that I've acquired since coming here. Few members of my team can relate to this curious 51-year-old woman scrambling around a glacial moraine in Tibet. Most can't relate to my life-style back in the States, either, so with few exceptions, our conversations are relatively superficial. I withdraw into my own thoughts, and I am not great company.

I hope that Chuck and my boys are getting my mental messages and know how much I miss them and how much I love them.

EVENING. Some Team Two escapees have arrived at Interim. Doug Burbank and Mark Pilon have descended from ABC. The rest of Team Two—Ted Handwerk, Dave McNally, Steve Gardiner, and Alexandra Hildebrandt—are still above us.

Doug Burbank is a tenured geology professor at the University of Southern California in Los Angeles. He has a grant to study the geology in this area of the Himalayas. Doug is working with a Chinese geologist, Professor Kang Jian-Cheng of Lanzhou University in Lanzhou, Gansu Province. Professor Kang joined the team in Beijing and is now a full-fledged Cowboy, but since he is not a strong climber like Doug, he is doing his research in the Rongbuk Valley near Base Camp.

Mark Pilon, also from Colorado, was a late addition to the team. He is a technology expert and seems to be able to make anything work, at any elevation, from generators to computers.

The Team Two overachievers call themselves the TRACTORS, for Teaching, Rocks, Art, Climbing, Telecommunications, Official Research Support. The TRACTORS' original charge was to establish the low-altitude camps. But since the yak train couldn't get across the crevasse to ABC, they first had to build a bridge that satisfied the yak herders. They have put in ten grueling days on the mountain and are now cycling down to Base for a well-earned rest.

MOUNT EVEREST

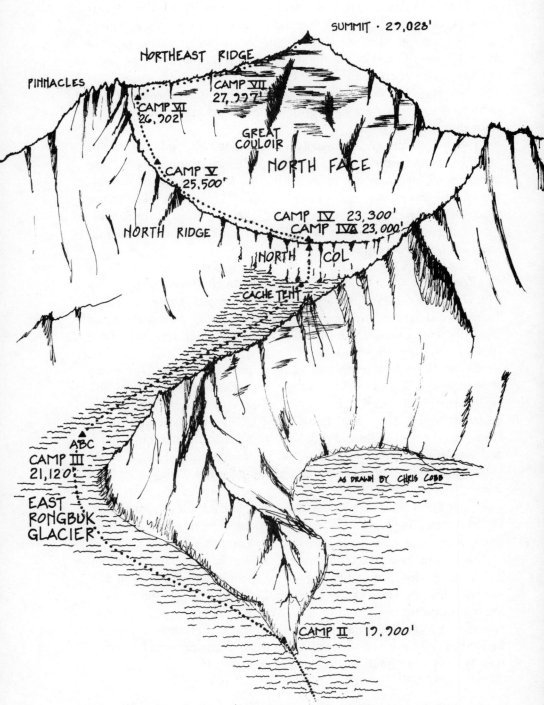

SUMMIT · 29,028'

NORTHEAST RIDGE

PINNACLES

CAMP VII
27,227'

CAMP VI
26,702'

GREAT
COULOIR

NORTH FACE

CAMP V
25,500'

CAMP IV 23,300'
CAMP IVA 23,000'

NORTH RIDGE

NORTH COL

CACHE TENT

AS DRAWN BY CHRIS COBB

ABC
CAMP III
21,120'

EAST
RONGBUK
GLACIER

CAMP II 19,700'

LOOKING UP THE EAST RONGBUK GLACIER
TOWARDS THE NORTH COL & THE NORTH FACE.

CHAPTER VIII

Attitude Adjustment

SEPTEMBER 11, 1988. CAMP II. 8 P.M. What a spectacular landscape. Our camp is on the rocky moraine covering the glacier, penetrated irregularly by giant white ice seracs. Just above us to the southeast is the glacier that will lead us to the North Col. To the southwest is the snout of the Changtse (Beifeng) glacier. Where the two glaciers meet, their inner lateral moraines merge to form the medial moraine, a rock ridge that runs up the center of the now joined ice fields. Here our camp sits. There are large seracs skipping down the valley to the north and a 3,000-foot cliff to the northeast. To the northwest, rising directly above our camp, is a 1,500-foot vertical rock wall, which periodically hurls rocks in our direction. Fortunately, a natural moat between the bottom of the rock face and our little tents captures most escaping rocks, so it is unlikely that any can reach us. I hear the slides at night, however, and with a little imagination, I can visualize them ricocheting across the moat and reaching my sleeping body. We also hear the ice consolidating in the seracs, making loud cracking noises—like gunshots.

The weather is excellent. The route from Interim to Camp II has splendid views of our route on the north and northeast ridges of Everest. I'm excited about getting there.

Dave McNally and Steve Gardiner came through this afternoon on the way down to Base Camp. They said the route to ABC is a steep 1,000-plus feet, but the camp itself is established and comfortable. Our plan is to make carries during the next couple of days and move up to ABC. Dave and Steve reported that the snow is coming off the mountain, giving us better climbing conditions.

Dave McNally is from Jackson, Wyoming, and is the expedition artist. His challenge is to capture the spirit of the natives and the essence of the cultures we've seen and to record the strain, the camaraderie and the magnificence of a full-scale siege climb in the Himalayas. Back home Dave works in oil on canvas, painting realistic portraits and Western subjects. He will be taking back to the United States compositions from our expedition and from our travels in China and Tibet. Dave and Steve Gardiner trained together in Jackson. Coming over on the C-5 Steve told me about our handsome 34-year-old artist: "Dave is an incredible find for Cowboys on Everest. He is a strong, solid climber filled with determination and drive. He is also patient and understanding, with a good sense of humor." Steve was right. Dave's both a strong climber and a gracious young man. At this point, I'm not sure which I value more.

Steve Gardiner, also 34, teaches English and journalism in Jackson, Wyoming, loves climbing, and has published numerous books and articles on the subject. He won the Wyoming Outdoor Council-expedition scholarship, given to the Wyoming high school teacher who best exemplified the traditional goals of mountaineering, and can best convey the experiences in China to students throughout the country. From Everest, Steve will prepare and transmit to his high school students lessons on geography, geology, the history of China and Everest, communism, Chinese family life, and Chinese education, art and literature.

Three other Cowboys were finalists in that same statewide contest: Jeb Schenck, Rick Dare, and Carl Coy. Courtney thought all the teachers were so terrific he brought as many as he could.

Team Four, led by Brian, is doing a reconnaissance of the North Col today. They will start putting in the fixed route tomorrow. If all goes well, by the time we have moved to ABC, the fixed route will be in on the Col, carries made to Camp IV, and Camp V scouted out.

Only the summit team is now at Camp II, with Brad Werntz, Dave Frawley, and Sibylle, who has sustained a mild shoulder injury. My roomies are Brad and Bob Bohus. Brad is an engaging young man. At 22 he is the youngest member of our expedition, a few months younger than Jim Burnett. I first met Brad on the Aconcagua climb. He was 19 then, but more mature than a lot of 30-year-olds I know. He's strong and like most young guys, likes to have a good time. I was most impressed, however, with his literary background and his interest in poetry. I sensed a spiritual quality in his approach to climbing and a philosophical approach to life. In South America that year, he was a thoughtful, willing worker. He hasn't changed.

The scheme I came up with in today's lonely hike up the mountain is a four-person rope team consisting of myself, Bob Skinner, Julie, and Jim. If the four of us could reach the summit, we would set five records: first United States woman, oldest United States woman, youngest United States woman, oldest United States man, and youngest United States man. Oxygen-deprived daydreaming. We still have many obstacles before anyone gets a shot at the summit.

I have a headache tonight, which is unusual for me. It is probably a dehydration headache from not drinking enough liquids. We need to drink five or six liters a day, which is not easy to do. I try to drink one in the morning at breakfast and one at dinner, with the remainder during the day while climbing. It's just darn hard. I don't know if I can make a carry tomorrow. I have to consider, though, that summiters must demonstrate that they are mentally and physically in condition to climb—or lose the slot to a fitter candidate. I want to show that I can do the job. I know I can. I am always last coming in, but I usually get there in pretty good spirits and am ready to go the next day. I hope I can keep it up. Tonight is not a good night.

When I really get to feeling sorry for myself, I think back to something I read during our forced stay in Xegar. In *Faces of Everest*, Major HPS Ahluwalia described how the 1965 Indian Expedition moved its gear up the mountain. Almost half of the 800 porters were women. The expedition, in fact, would have preferred more women because they drank less and made less fuss about carrying sixty-pound loads. And when a male porter got too drunk to manage, his wife would carry his load, too. One day, the major wrote, a woman porter gave birth to a child. "For a day or two after delivering the child she did not carry a load, but then she resumed her carries. This is not very unusual. She probably delivered the baby at a height of about 9,000." Now that helps keep things in perspective.

SEPTEMBER 13, 1988. This morning we woke up to two or three inches of snow, which was a surprise because yesterday was an absolutely clear blue day. Today there are some clouds. I wouldn't be surprised if we got more snow later.

I am now about a third of the way from Camp II to ABC, taking a little break, sitting in the sunshine and drinking my Gatorade. I use a lot of Gatorade powder in my water bottles. It has some electrolytes, which may be beneficial, and it covers the iodine taste. Most of us are continuing to iodine the water to be sure that we don't get any gastrointestinal problems. The rest assume their bodies have adjusted to foreign invaders.

The route up from Camp II is more rock moraine—scree and talus covering the glacier. We're climbing the medial moraine. The underlying glacier has cut a valley, or glacial trough, between twenty and forty yards wide out of the mountain side. The trough is lined on each side by a combination of snow banks and serac walls, eighty to ninety feet high. Climbing through this section is like walking through a white-tiled tunnel with no roof. The route to ABC covers about four miles and is not terribly steep. Nonetheless, it's a tough haul because we're getting up to the 21,000-foot level and, of course, we are still carrying loads. Today I have some of my personal gear and a tent that needs to be moved higher. It's about thirty-five pounds—over a quarter of my body weight.

Yesterday I also carried a load to ABC. I made it, but I was worried because I hadn't felt good when I arrived at Camp II. I tried to analyze what could be slowing me down and I think I haven't been eating enough. I have had the equivalent of a bowl of cereal in the morning, one or two candy bars at lunch, and at dinner half a bowl of noodles and half a retort (a foil bag of meat and gravy heated in boiling water). That isn't enough to keep up my energy at this altitude with these loads. I have to eat more or I won't make it.

Early yesterday, when everybody else took off to carry their loads, I lounged around with Dave Frawley and Sibylle. After four peanut butter and jelly sandwiches for lunch, I felt better and started for ABC. About halfway up the route, I could see two figures descending. As they drew closer, I recognized Courtney and Matt Ellenthal (now affectionately known as Yak). I was surprised to see them heading down. It was apparent that Court was not well. He was moving slowly. As soon as he saw me, he sat down on a rock and waited for me to get up to his rest spot. Courtney is a seriously polite person, in the tradition of the Old West. He inquired about my health and about other teammates before I could learn what was going on with him. It seems he's been coughing badly for several days, not telling anyone, and trying to ignore signs of pulmonary edema. Finally, Ross, our Camp III doctor, insisted that he go to Base Camp and commit himself to the hyperbaric chamber.

We sat together on a rock for about thirty minutes. We talked about how traveling alone for so many days can bend the mind. I enjoyed visiting with him because we have been out of sync on the trip. He and Bob seem to have confidence in me. We've been in some difficult spots together, like Aconcagua. At about 23,000 feet, Aconcagua is the highest mountain in the Western Hemisphere. The Normal Route is not technically difficult and hides the dangers of Aconcagua's altitude and unpredictable weather. It is a mountain that lures people to their deaths with its gentle approach. Many more climbers attempt Aconcagua and more climbers have died on Aconcagua than on Everest. Four men died while we were there on our training climb in February 1986: two Japanese, a Frenchman, and a Spaniard. I also heard about the Argentine climber lying frozen near the peak. No one had been strong enough to carry the body down, so he was lying there, as he died, trying to remove his parka. At the moment he froze to death, he had felt warm.

On our climb, the team had carried gear and stashed it above the Berlin Huts, at about 19,800 feet, then returned to camp at about 18,000 feet. We were in position to go for the summit. The following day a powerful storm struck. We climbed in blizzard conditions for over an hour. I was cold and shivering, but kept going—head down, one foot in front of the other, following the climber in front of me. When the storm became so fierce that we could no longer make upward progress, Courtney and Bob called for a bivouac. As my teammates frantically fought the gusting wind and driving snow to get tents set up, I watched from a few yards away, without concern. My shivering had stopped and I felt warm, even though the temperature was 15 degrees below zero and falling fast. I sat down in the snow and took off my parka. "Jesus Christ!" Courtney yelled. "Get Sue into a tent!" I was half carried and half dragged to the closest tent. Fred Riedman plied me with hot Jell-O and other warm drinks, and overnight the warmth returned to my body. They had saved my life.

Exercising to exhaustion and high-altitude hypoxia (oxygen deprivation) predispose the body to hypothermia. Hypothermia (from the Greek *hypo* "less than," and *therme*, "heat") is a lower-than-normal core temperature. The core tissues are generally considered to be the vital organs, particularly the heart, lungs, liver, and brain. The body's survival mechanisms, in a cold environment, shunt blood-carrying oxygen away from appendages and to the vital organs. Thus, the increased risk of frostbite.

Keeping warm by keeping active can help maintain a normal temperature in the neighborhood of 98.6 degrees F. Even vigorous activity, however, generates only a small amount of heat compared with what can be lost in severe cold. An individual who relies on muscular activity to generate heat must eat copious quantities of food. Metabolization of food provides heat and energy. Consumption of the energy substrate in the muscle, the muscle glycogen, is the end point of the ability to continue muscular activity. After the energy substrate is consumed, the core temperature takes a sudden plunge. The decrease in core temperature then depresses one's mental capability to properly cope with the serious threat.

To help increase heat production, the body resorts to uncontrolled, irregular contractions of voluntary muscles, or shivering. Violent shivering is the body's last serious defense against sliding into potentially lethal hypothermia. A hypothermic individual usually stops shivering when the core temperature drops to 90 to 92 degrees F.

Wind significantly increases the danger of hypothermia, since it removes large quantities of heat. Heat loss increases not in proportion to wind velocity but as the square of wind velocity. A healthy, warmly dressed person can withstand a temperature of 15 degrees F., but the same temperature is life threatening in a 20- to 25-mile-per-hour wind, which produces a windchill factor of minus 17 to minus 22 degrees. On Everest, when ambient temperatures reach below minus 30 degrees F., a 15-mile-per-hour breeze will create the equivalent of minus 70 degrees; a 40-mile-per-hour wind will mean an effective minus 101 degrees F.

As Court and Yak continued their descent, I trudged upward. I am climbing alone again today. There is nobody pushing me, nobody to offer aid or comfort, no moral support. It's all up to me. I have been getting so depressed during the day with these loads. It's been eight days now. Sometimes I just don't want to take another step. Yesterday, when my load began to feel heavy, I fantasized that when I arrive at ABC, Courtney and Bob had decided that I couldn't have a shot at the summit and I'd have to stay at Base Camp. I picked up my pack, headed back to Base, hitched a ride to Kathmandu, and went home. That sounded good.

Being in shape is only part of this battle. The higher you go, the more mental a climb becomes. Yet, the higher you go, the more your mental capacity diminishes. I remember Jim Wickwire, one of America's famous climbers, saying that altitude is the worst hazard a climber faces, not the objective dangers of rockfall, icefall, avalanche, crevasses, storms, or winds. Clearly the risks to a climber are greater on a Himalayan climb, because the altitude factor is magnified. Many climbers believe that the majority of accidents on big mountains are errors relating to the unnoticed diminution in intellectual ability. Oxygen deprivation constrains the ability to make decisions. Even with total brain power, there are certainly few things in the world that require more focused attention, more controlled physical effort, or more emotional stability than climbing Mount Everest. "I guess that's why you're here, Sue," I told myself. "Now see if you can keep your head screwed on straight and get moving."

I got up to ABC and saw my next challenge: the North Col. It is indeed formidable. Visualize a dead-end canyon blocked by a 2,000-foot vertical wall of snow and ice. Look closely and you will see the giant seracs, as well as steep avalanche chutes swept clean of new snow by recent avalanches, and below, the slough of years of avalanches. It is the most dangerous area through which we will travel, the place where our director of mountaineering fears the loss of several lives. The snow changes frequently on the Col, avalanches are an omnipresent danger, crevasses lace the face, and seracs fall unexpectedly. From 1922, when seven of George Leigh Mallory's porters were swept away, to this spring, when three more climbers were crushed in an avalanche here, the North Col has always exacted a grim toll.

Just after I arrived at ABC, Bob Skinner, Brian McLean, and others on Team Four came down from their reconnaissance. They say they have found a reasonably safe route snaking through some high seracs toward the right side of the Col, then angling left to the top. They seem satisfied that it's about as good as we can do.

"The snow appears relatively stable," Brian said. "We'll start work tomorrow to put in the fixed line to the top."

In steep and dangerous areas such as the North Col, where ava-lanches abound and there is a high probability that a fall would be fatal, the route is "fixed" with ropes which remain in place for the duration of the expedition. The route is secured in sections, each generally the length of one rope, perhaps 130 to 300 feet. Each end of the rope is attached to an appropriate anchor, such as a dead man (an aluminum plate), an ice screw, or a metal picket, three to four feet long, hammered into the snow. The fixed ropes follow the chosen route upward. For the duration of the climb, each climber clips into the fixed ropes to ascend and descend.

Advanced Base Camp is very nearly at the base of the Col—the gate to the mountain and the toughest technical challenge we'll face. From ABC we can see our route on the North and Northeast ridges and, of course, the peak itself. It is hard to believe that we still have almost 7,000 feet to go. But we can move more quickly now.

The sight of the peak renewed my energy and enthusiasm. It was late in the day, 6 P.M., when I started my descent to Camp II. Dave Frawley told me that he made it down in fifty minutes, so I figured I could do it in ninety, max. I was wrong. I was still well above Camp II when darkness closed in. I stopped to put on my headlamp so that I could make my way through the rocky terrain. Several times I had to stop to flash my light around to find the route. I descended carefully, so as not to fall or twist an ankle. More than once I slipped in loose scree, but I managed to remain upright. Then the battery of my light went dead. I sat for a few minutes to let my eyes adjust to the dark-ness. Fortunately, Bob Skinner had insisted that I take a radio, so I was in voice contact with both ABC and Camp II. I was also able to pick up Camp I and Base Camp. I learned that Courtney's condition had turned more serious and that Fred, Orion, Dr. Bob, and Dave Frawley had joined Yak in escorting Courtney down. There was concern that they might have to carry him to Base Camp. After monitoring radio calls and relaying status reports from Base Camp to ABC (since the curvature of the mountain makes the radio contact between ABC and Base Camp sometimes difficult) I continued my descent in the dark. When I reached the last steep section, I called Camp II and requested that somebody come up with a light. Brad came and we descended together to a nice warm tent.

On the route, halfway between Camp II and ABC, is Frawley's Cairn, a three-foot-high stack of rocks that David built up to mark a

Yaks carried some of our load up the East Rongbuk Glacier; we carried the rest. The Cowboys employed no Sherpas. PHOTO BY JEB SCHENCK.

break in the snow wall where we can see the peak of Everest. It is a wonderful spot. I rest there, gaze at the peak, and contemplate life on the mountain. How can I describe how tough this is? Imagine being 6,000 feet higher than on any mountain you have ever seen in the continental United States. Imagine that the only air to supply your lungs must be sucked in through a single straw. Then imagine taking seven or eight five-pound bags of flour and strapping them onto your back. Now start climbing an endless flight of stairs, the steps of which are either marbles or unstable, shifting rocks. Do that four or five hours a day by yourself. Then go back down and do it again. And again. And again. For eight days.

My body seems to have adjusted reasonably well to this self-imposed torment. I have had only a couple of physically "down" days. I go slowly to pace myself and I think that helps. It's my psyche that's a problem. I have to remind myself that the most successful climber is not necessarily the fastest, or the physically strongest, or the greatest technician, but the one who doesn't burn out prematurely, who remains focused, and who is in the right place at the right time. Studies of summiters show that they excel mainly in will and determination and that they have the ability to endure pain and press on. My forte.

Nonetheless, psychologically, it's tough not to be among the finest and the strongest. In athletics I have always been one of the best, out in front. Here I am the tail end. It bothers me, but the fact is that my body is not the equivalent of younger specimens; I must pace myself, I must keep things in perspective, and I must maintain some degree of humor. After all, as one of the guys said when joking with Bob Skinner, Dave Padwa, and me, "The three of you are exemplary members of the Golden Years Club."

Between Camp II and Camp III is the chasm that stopped the first yak train. Twelve to sixteen feet deep and three to five feet wide, it crosses the entire thirty-five yards of moraine that separates the valley walls at that point. Such crevasses appear when a glacier works its way downhill over any protrusion in the underlying terrain—a rock step, for example. Since the ice flow cannot bend, it cracks under the pressure, opening a V-shaped chasm. Morainal crevasses are not so dangerous to climbers as snow crevasses. On a snow field, or firn, the crevasses become covered with snow and are often invisible. Moraine crevasses are easy to see and can usually be circumnavigated or jumped. This one, however, was too big for the yaks to cross.

The TRACTORS have constructed an engineering marvel. Or at least, a marvel in ingenuity. Under the direction of contractor Ted Handwerk, they threw rocks into the crevasse and built a three-foot-wide fill right to the lip of the crevasse. With fragments of bamboo and rope discarded by a previous expedition, and some strategically placed boulders, they framed in the sides. The top rocks are flat pieces of shale, making a three-foot-wide, perfectly passable bridge. The yaks, though, didn't recognize good construction when they saw it and refused to cross. Wish-Granting Gem finally took a yak that had a ring through its nose and pulled it across. All the others followed.

About two and a half miles up the narrow moraine from Camp II, the glacier curves almost due south. Exposed to view is the entire north side of Everest, including the North Col. Yesterday when I rounded this corner and saw the peak, I thought to myself, "I can do it. I know I can do it." No thoughts of turning back now. Today, a few clouds block the view of the approach to the summit and give some suggestion of what it might be like to have limited visibility on the upper reaches. But the winds are the most critical element—winds in excess of 100 miles per hour have defeated many teams on this route—and they will arrive in early October.

At the head of all glacial troughs is a cirque, an armchair-shaped hollow that accumulates snow. The back and sides of the armchair are usually steep walls. On the East Rongbuk Glacier, the back of the armchair is the North Col. The cirque accumulates decades of snow on its seat, creating a firn field. Depending on the underlying terrain, a firn field may have a few or numerous crevasses. Where the gradient of the cirque becomes steep, the ice flow is accelerated, and fissures appear where pressure exceeds the strength of the ice. Where the gradient is very steep, ice falls are created. Our Advanced Base Camp sits below the crevassed firn field, about two miles from the foot of the North Col. Hiking up to ABC, I can see some areas that have avalanched and some areas on the Col that will avalanche. I hope we're not in them.

4:30 P.M. I have been on the trail now four hours. I'm above 20,500 feet, resting again and coughing badly. A discarded oxygen canister marks the spot from which a climber can first see ABC, another 300 yards away. I'm tired and look forward to getting there and having a hot drink before I head back down to Camp II. Wispy cirrus clouds are dancing around the peak of Everest; thicker clouds are looming in the west and will undoubtedly bring snow. Brad just passed me. He's in ABC now and is probably anxious to get back to II. I really should descend with him, as we'll be traveling after dark again.

I pick myself up and struggle on towards ABC. This camp has a large, green, army-type mess tent that serves as a kitchen facility, as well as a twelve-foot-square tent for communications and dining. A dome tent that can sleep about six is several yards away. It is our medical facility. Scattered around on the talus are a number of smaller two- and three-man tents for sleeping. It's a comfortable station, considering that we're now at 21,120 feet.

8:00 P.M. I had a bowl of soup and a can of tuna and am now back at Frawley's Cairn on the route down to Camp II. Brad went on ahead and I had to tell myself one more time to keep my own pace. The competitor in me always wants to turn up the speed, but I'm not in competition with my teammates—only the mountain and myself. I've achieved my big goal for the evening, to pass through the crevasse zone before dark. I probably have another hour to go to Camp II. While at ABC, I learned that Team Four, now known as the Col Boys, have about a third of the route fixed. With the help of some Team Two and Team Three members it looks as though it will take about three more days, if the weather holds, to finish the route. Tomorrow I will make one more carry to ABC. Then, the tenth day out of Base Camp, I get to rest.

SEPTEMBER 14, 1988. 2:30 P.M. I knew today would be a killer. I waited to carry the heaviest load—fifty pounds—till the last day, in anticipation of being able to rest the day afterward. It's remarkable what the human body will do. I'm fully acclimatized at this elevation, but I know that from here on deterioration is greater than acclimatization. Still, my strength and stamina are good. I have also been sleeping well, which is a good sign at altitude. When the guys steam past me on the trail, I get discouraged, but then I tell myself that *they* should be thinking, "I hope I'm in as good a shape as Sue when I'm her age." It gives me a minor kick. Before I left home I got what medical analysis is available for this kind of thing, and the prognosis for my success at altitude was relatively good. I did some muscular strength tests at the Sports Medicine Center in Washington, D.C., and I did treadmill and other tests at the University of Maryland Physical Fitness Center in College Park. Then I based my training routine on the results of those tests. My VO_2 max (the ability of the body to deliver and consume oxygen during maximum exercise) is extremely high, according to the doctor who monitored that exam. He said it was the equivalent of a 22-year-old college football player. That must be an exaggeration, but my body's capability to utilize oxygen is why I have acclimatized with few altitude symptoms.

No one, however, said that I had the muscular strength of a 22-year-old, so during my training program for several months prior to the expedition, after doing aerobic exercises like running and cycling, I worked with weights at a health club. I concentrated on upper body strength because, like most women, I've always been weak in that area. Years of running, skiing, and playing tennis have given me reasonably strong legs. In any event, I think the training, my general level of health, and our long, slow trek to Base have all gone into successful acclimatization.

It has been six weeks since we left home—three and a half weeks traveling across the United States, Japan, China, and Tibet before arriving at our Base Camp, and two and a half weeks setting up our supply lines and our route over the fifteen miles between Base Camp and the North Col. Six weeks is a lot of preparation time. We're looking forward to some real climbing.

The sky is cloudless, unbelievably beautiful. These are true summit days—there's not a breath of wind discernible on the peak. We will be so blessed if we have weather like this for our summit attempts.

I've been resting in the sun at Frawley's Cairn for thirty minutes now. Brad, David, and Dr. Bob have all gone by. It's going to take me another two hours to reach ABC. I'd better hit the road.

SEPTEMBER 15, 1988. 2 P.M. I am lying in my bag at ABC, eating some of my own words. Yesterday I was carrying my monster load, patting myself on the back, marveling at how much strength and stamina I have, even remarking that my teammates should wish at 50 to be as strong as I. Pride goeth before a fall. Shortly thereafter, as I was picking my way through the rocks, I simply ran out of gas. I seemed to be breathing okay but I had no strength. I could take only about five steps before I'd have to stop. My pack suddenly gained twenty pounds. My legs would move only after intense pleading from me. My progress was pitiful. I was exhausted and depressed. After 6 o'clock some of my teammates began to wonder where I was, and Brad started down to find me. When I saw Brad heading toward me, I grew angry at everything and everybody. However depleted I was, I wasn't about to let anyone help me at the last minute, not after I'd worked so hard, made all my carries, and almost reached ABC. Brad read my mood immediately and simply said, "I thought I'd see if you were okay." He didn't say any more, just swung into step beside me. Brad is so thoughtful, his mere presence dissolved some of my anger and tension. Moments later David Frawley appeared. Neither of us said anything. I just swung my pack off and he carried it the last 200 yards into camp.

Ross Greenlee insisted on checking me out. I sank onto Ross's bag in the medical tent and took my pulse. It was only 84—really low, given the level and extent of my exertion. The doctors have suggested that we take our pulses regularly. It is one indication of how we are faring at altitude and whether we are getting enough liquids. For the last several days my pulse has ranged between 60 and 66 on awakening, and up to 120 when I am climbing. I know it's been much higher during exercise at sea level. Maybe I am not taking it when I am working my hardest. Why did my body come to a stop? Maybe it is lack of food. I must eat more.

Today is finally a rest day and I am doing exactly that, lying in my bag, reading a book, eating and drinking liquids. I am really indulging myself, too. I feel decadent eating Nestlé's Crunches and granola bars. With a good book—Sibylle recommended Isabel Allende's *The House of the Spirits*—I may never move.

Even with this welcome rest from carrying loads, I know that I am in a fragile emotional state. It is unusual for me. The exhaustion and the isolation, being away from my family, and being unable to make any real contact with my teammates—all are taking their toll. I guess I need some moral support.

In a magazine article last spring, Bob Skinner was quoted as saying, "Sue is tough and ambitious and has a better chance to get to the summit than some younger women." (Of course, in another article he also called me "just a middle-aged housewife.") I was flattered (about the former), because of all the people I've ever met, Bob is the toughest. Well, I used to think I was tough. I'm not. I used to think I was emotionally independent. I'm not. I used to think I was always in control. I'm not. Small wonder no one lives for extended periods above 17,000 feet. It turns people into mush.

CHAPTER IX

Fixing the Col

SEPTEMBER 16, 1988. ABC. I stayed in my bag most of the day. Late in the afternoon I wandered down to the galley tent and encountered two of our lead climbers, Brian McLean and Mack Ellerby, who'd just come off the North Col.

"You went a long way," Brian said. "Was that a 250-foot rope?"

"Just about," said Mack.

"From that ramp, do you think you can continue up and left, or did it look like you go up and right, over the top there?"

"I don't know. I wasn't quite as far as those two bodies."

I listened. Mack is a 36-year-old fence contractor from Denver. He's been climbing for about twenty-five years in North and South America and in the Alps. He has several first ascents in Alaska and is one heck of a climber, as well as a nice guy. I joined the conversation after viewing the route with our high-powered scope.

"Mack, those bodies—what do you think? It doesn't look like they were swept there by an avalanche."

"No, they weren't. They just became part of the mountain. You die up there, someday you'll come down here. They could have had hypothermia and died, or fallen, or an ice block could have crushed them. There're a lot of little things like that."

Little things? I'm thinking those are not so trivial.

"The one on the left looks weird. Maybe it's just a piece of garment, but it looks pretty distinct. It's red."

"Arms or legs sticking out of the snow?" I asked.

"It could be, or else just abandoned gear."

"You can tell it's from years and years ago," said Mack. "It's coming straight out from the center of the ice cliff. So it happened a long time ago. Just next to them is really a nice ramp. Once you get up that steep part, past that point, it looks pretty mellow."

"It's a little cracked up in there," said Brian, "but we can move one way or another to find the easiest path. Before you get to the bodies, there seems to be a ramp that goes up and right. That might go . . . Oh, and now there's another object. This one's blue and red, just left of the earlier ones." He motioned for me to take a look.

"I see what you're talking about. Something's in the ice."

We zoomed all the way in. No bodies. We were looking at clothing remnants from an old expedition. Not that there are no bodies up there. Everyone knows the story of Hannelore Schmatz, who reached the summit of Everest from the south side in 1979 with climber Ray Genet and two Sherpas. Mrs. Schmatz, as she is known among climbers, tired on the descent, and on a bitterly cold night, she and Genet bivouacked above the South Col. By morning Genet was dead. One of the Sherpas climbed back up to help Mrs. Schmatz down, but she collapsed almost immediately and died. She guards that route now, lying fully clothed and half-encased in ice.

Carl Coy joined us.

"Can you see the route, Carl?" I asked.

"I can see the first third. It looks like we may have to go far to the right to get around the crevasse."

"What do you think the total vertical is between here and the top?"

"About two thousand feet," Brian said.

"And what's the steepest part?"

"The center section is part of the crux," Mack answered. "Maybe there's another above. I don't know yet."

Brian was now studying the route again. "Mack, even farther to the right you could probably top out, too."

"Yeah, but then you're on top of that snow cornice. If you can avoid that . . ."

"By keeping to the left, maybe?"

"That's what hit me. There is a ramp that leads up, but it's kind of sloping and it looks like the serac hangs over it."

Seracs are ice blocks that can grow as tall as a seven-story office building. They're formed when snow melts and refreezes, and builds into massive, solid blocks of ice. The danger lies in not knowing when one will come crashing down on your climbing route. Seracs are even less predictable than avalanches.

"I know there have been routes over to the right," Mack said. "There have been ropes there. But without ladders, we are still going to have to shoot back, way left, to get over the main part of the icefall."

"I think we have done a reasonably good job of minimizing our exposure to both serac and avalanche," Brian said. He must have been reading my mind. "I'm still worried about the big basin at the very top. Mack, any idea how much spillover we'll get when that whole slab releases up there?"

"It's hard to say. I was breaking snow, but it was real soft, like snowfall. It wasn't avalanche debris."

"Take a look over here, Sue." Brian pointed out a large buildup of snow he called a crown. "On the right side is one way up. Mack went up the slot on the left side. It's steep ice. I'm just wondering if that crown will slide while people are on it. I would advise staying off it."

"You can't get to the top from where I was," Mack said. "There's a mother of a crevasse. We'll have to make a ladder to put over it. It's tricky climbing—real sheer. That will all have to be fixed if we top there. It'll be a lot of work, and a lot of exposure." I like Mack's calm, businesslike approach to his job.

Brian, 34, has spent parts of the last nine years as a National Outdoor Leadership School instructor. He has a master's in materials science and engineering from the University of California at Davis, and has an engineer's analytical mind. Everything about Brian's voice and manner spells teacher. Well-trained himself, he is willing to train others. I had a chance to see some of his teaching skills on one of our training climbs. On Rainier we practiced crevasse rescue and self-arrest under Brian's tutelage. He made an impression on me when we were doing one of the self-arrest moves. He demonstrated the proper technique, then said: "Learn to do it right the first time—you won't get a second chance."

Brian always said that he wanted to do everything he could to help make the team successful. I admire that attitude. He has worked hard and unselfishly. At one point, before we left the States, Brian was teamed with me as a designated summiter. That changed, however, in one of the thirteen reorganizations of team structure. It may have been when Todd Skinner, Bob's son, was hurt. The team needed Brian's leadership and physical work on the Col. But for a freak accident, we would have had two other experienced climbers standing here with us right now. Todd Skinner and Paul Piana were on the team, but earlier this year, after completing an almost impossible free climb of the Salathe Wall in Yosemite, both suffered serious injuries from being hit by a dislodged boulder. Todd and Paul are outstanding climbers. Todd has over thirty-five first ascents to his credit and is considered one of the world's best rock climbers.

"What do you guys think about the weather here?" I asked. "It's been so good."

"Exceptional," Mack said. "We haven't had a real bad storm for a month. That should really help us on the Col. The only reason it's so nasty is because it's the lee side of the mountain. All that ice is formed by the wind transporting snow over the top."

"But still, better the North Col than the Khumbu Icefall?" There were agreeing nods.

The Khumbu Icefall is an area of jumbled ice blocks on the South Col route, on the Nepal side of Everest. It is one of the most dangerous spots on the mountain because it moves unpredictably and has crushed many climbers. As on the North Col, a climber seeks to minimize the number of times that such a dangerous area is traveled. I couldn't believe it when Dick Bass told me he'd been through the Khumbu Icefall eight times on his last trip.

Dick Bass and Frank Wells are two extraordinarily successful businessmen who first met in 1981 and decided to climb the highest mountain on each of the seven continents. When they began, neither was an experienced high-altitude climber. In fact, Frank had virtually no climbing experience. In 1983 they conquered six peaks. On April 30, 1985, Dick reached the seventh summit, Mount Everest. The book *Seven Summits* tells their story.

Dick was 55 years old when he reached the top of the peak I'm looking at right now. Both Frank and Dick are personal friends, and their example had a strong impact on my own decision to climb Everest. These aren't middle-aged guys suffering midlife crises. They are men who have always challenged themselves in life. And they have always been willing to take a properly calculated risk for a meaningful reward, in both business and sports.

While Mack and Brian have been finding our route, several other Cowboys have been carrying loads and helping to set the fixed line. Carl Coy, Jim Robinson, Jeb Schenck, and Quint Barney are playing major roles. Jeb has the additional burden of being the high-altitude still photographer for the team, so he's always climbing weighted down with his equipment. Bob Bohus and Brad Werntz are also helping to fix the route. Brad and Mack were surprised by an avalanche yesterday. Fortunately, it was a small one and though it knocked Brad over, he was not injured. Mack was able to jump out of its path, and both returned to camp all smiles.

Another of our strongest climbers is Ethan Goldings. I admit being partial to Ethan because he goes to my alma mater, Stanford University, where he's working on a Ph.D. (He got his B.A. at a less well known institution called Harvard.) Ethan, a terrific climber and skier, speaks both Chinese and Tibetan. I've been impressed with his sensitivity to his colleagues, whether they're Cowboys, Tibetans, or Chinese, and whether he's on the mountain or in an urban setting.

Today's bad news is that Bob Skinner had to leave ABC. Ross Greenlee is accompanying him to Base Camp. He was in the ABC hyperbaric bag last night because of accumulation of fluid in his lungs—clearly the early stages of pulmonary edema. It was obvious this morning that he had to descend. As director of mountaineering, Bob's job is to oversee all tactical moves on the climb. He has been supervising the route finding, as well as carrying sixty- and seventy-pound loads. He may well be suffering the effects of overexertion and extended time at altitude. Now we are without both Skinner brothers.

I'm not concerned about leadership getting our route in, with Fred, Brian and Mack here, but I feel bad that Bob and Courtney are gone. This is their trip and we're now at a crucial spot. Many expeditions that have come to this point haven't gotten past the North Col. It is the critical technical point of the route. With Bob and Courtney gone, I feel that some of my underlying strength has been taken away. They may be the only two that have confidence in me. I can understand that it's difficult for the younger members of the team to relate to or care about my desire to climb this mountain. They have seen, demonstrated daily, my cautious, slow-paced approach. They have no reason to believe that I have the capability of reaching the summit. The Skinner brothers, however, have climbed with me in other parts of the world and they know, as I do, that with the right conditions, I can reach the top.

Now that I'm rested, when I look up at the mountain, I know I can do it . . . if I can keep myself from getting upset and focusing on negatives like missing my family and my lack of integration on the team. I have to fight so hard to maintain an even keel here, tonight I'd rather just quit and go home.

SEPTEMBER 17, 1988. NOON. After breakfast this morning I lay down in my tent to rest and decide whether to carry a load up to our cache tent. We have placed a dome tent about eight feet in diameter near the top of the firn field, just a couple hundred feet below where our fixed rope starts up the face of the Col. This tent, about an hour and half's hike above ABC, is there both for safety purposes (any tired, cold climber coming off the Col can stop there, get warm, and get a hot drink before descending to ABC) and also to serve as a stash spot for all the equipment we must haul up the face. Loads will be carried from ABC to the cache tent and deposited there until it's time to start moving them up the fixed line. I fell asleep thinking about the hundreds of pounds of equipment that have to go to the cache tent, and then up the Col.

Moments ago I was awakened. The sound of bells drifted up the valley and seeped into my tent. I gradually revived and recognized the symphony in the background. The yak train had arrived. With it were two notes for me, hand-carried by Norbu. The first note was from "Yak" Ellenthal, with five messages jotted down from a telephone conversation with Chuck, who has been calling Base regularly:

1. Chris—extensive knee operation—in hospital three days. Successful transplant of ligaments.

2. Everyone well and praying for you.

3. Went to Detroit for Michigan–Miami game, Miami won.

4. Had dinner with Luke Omohundro in Georgetown.

5. Lots of love.

So, of course, now I'm anxious about Chris's knee.

My other note was from Sheri, reporting on Base Camp activities. She was informing me that, with other responsibilities, she couldn't take over communications, too. Too bad. She has a wonderfully seductive voice, which even over our handheld radios evidences a physician's soothing bedside manner. The guys love it when she handles the evening radio call for Base.

Ethan is going to try to talk the yakkies into taking our gear higher to save five or six days of hauling by team members. Sometimes the yak herders, however, do not have much incentive. Even money can't entice them to do extra work—they have no place to spend it. But they do like to trade, and we do have goodies from the faraway Western world that the yak herders covet. We might begin trading anything from our Sorel boots to tents to save several days of load carrying. Ethan is working on it right now as I lie in the sack, trying to recapture the energy that I lost in the nine days of carrying loads to ABC.

Yesterday Brian led a refresher course on safety, on ascending and descending fixed ropes, on rappelling, and on due care in general. I don't think anyone knows that I've never been on a fixed rope in my life—I sure didn't tell Courtney or Bob. I listened closely to Brian as he reviewed each rope, each safety line, each carabiner, and how each is affixed to a harness. Although falling is not necessarily the most dangerous aspect of the North Col route, it can be deadly because of the crevasses. The unstable snow and the potential for movement of snow and ice are the biggest concerns on the Col. Seracs can break off, casting giant chunks of ice as big as tractor-trailers onto the face, crushing any human body in the vicinity. Avalanches, of course, are common. Entire slabs descend the face. Each climb through the Col is a roll of the dice. We are conscious of the danger, but no one is frightened—it is part of climbing. I'm not unaware that some of my friends back home think it's crazy to be here. But I rationalize that in the United States every year, we have numerous avalanche deaths in ski and winter recreation areas, thousands of boating accidents, and other recreation-related disasters. This isn't all that much different. It all relates to defining your own limits of acceptable risk.

The yakkies unloaded and left. They would not take our gear higher. I'd better gain sufficient strength to do my share of the carries. Maybe our guys on the Col will get the route finished today, but unfortunately, it has been snowing. Snow is one thing we don't want to see. If we have to hold here in ABC, it could be several days before the new snow consolidates and the avalanche danger abates. A weather report last night from Base indicated that some of the late monsoon weather on the Nepal side of the mountain will filter over to us. But my altimeter dropped this morning, which suggests that the high-pressure system is still above us. Oh, if only we'd gotten here on schedule! Anyway, a snowy day is a good day to stay in bed.

My two-person tent is on a rocky ridge about thirty yards from the mess tent and overlooking the latrine area, which is nothing fancy — just large boulders to crouch behind. I don't have a tentmate yet, but I think David Padwa is headed this way. My stuff is spread all over the floor and I've had a luxurious day of resting and sorting gear: sun lotion, film, batteries, tapes, medical supplies, vitamins, sewing kit, extra socks, gloves, glasses, all sorts of miscellaneous items that I or a tentmate may need.

It is strange to be lying on the flank of Mount Everest, halfway around the world from my family and everything that I know of as real life. It's easy to ask why, but it's hard to answer. Although there may be common threads, the answer from each member of our expedition would be different. Extreme climbers want to live intensely. They spend more time on the edge, living at a higher level of vitality than most any other of life's sojourners. For them, Everest is a symbol of excellence, of the barely attainable. It is the mightiest challenge: a brutal struggle with rock, ice, altitude, and self. The satisfaction, as I have experienced it on lesser climbs, comes from enduring the struggle, from doing more than you thought you could do, from rising — however briefly — above your everyday world, and from coming, momentarily, closer to the stars.

Alpinists couldn't pursue the challenge without the exceptional support of their families. Everyone on the team I've talked to has the same concerns about being away for so long and expresses the same appreciation for those who have given them the opportunity to be here. There will be strain on our families, and perhaps a few cracks, but they all know, I think, that great achievements mean effort and risk, not lounging in front of the television set.

Mountain-climbing goals are at once tangible, measured in feet above sea level, and subjective, beyond measurement. This expedition originally captured my interest not because of its intent to put the first United States woman on top (initially, I didn't even know none had made it) but because of the metaphor. Here was a chance to go beyond the comfort zone, to aim high — literally.

So here I am, waiting to go the last few thousand feet on Mount Everest. It has been ten times tougher than I imagined, physically, mentally, and emotionally. I was not properly prepared for the mental

Julie Cheney, our strongest woman climber, makes her way up the fixed line on the Col. PHOTO BY JEB SCHENCK.

side. But I wonder if it isn't even harder for some of the others. Fred Riedman got married a few weeks before we left the United States; Quintin Barney has a ten-month-old daughter who has started to walk since he left home; Ross Greenlee's wife is pregnant. Others have similar stories. Like all the Cowboys, I am making my adjustments. And we still have, as of today, a very good shot at this mountain.

SEPTEMBER 19, 1988. There is a dramatic difference in living at 21,000 feet. My teammates who have been working here have noticeably lost weight. Their faces are lined and burned, their lips cracked. I hear their coughs in the night. The effort to cook and boil sufficient water for our needs is much greater than at Base. Mere survival requires extra effort. Black alpine choughs, known to fly as high as 26,000 feet, circle this camp, like vultures waiting for our dead. Every day as we carry loads to the North Col and contemplate the dangers that lie ahead, we hear the rumbling of avalanches on the Col.

I did a carry today to our cache tent. I arrived there at 9 A.M. The lovely, sunny day turned to snow by 1 P.M. I watched Jeb and Julie go up the ropes to see what the last two days of snow had done to the fixed line. They were able to go only a few hundred feet. With two to four feet of unconsolidated snow, the postholing was exhausting. Julie

111

is sick tonight, nauseated and vomiting. This worries me because Julie is stronger than I am. How will I do?

Tomorrow the guys are going up early to get to the last section that hasn't yet been fixed, about a hundred yards below the top of the Col. Today, at that point, they encountered the formidable crevasse Mack had seen. It's about twenty-five feet wide and at least 150 feet deep. If the snow stability on the route is okay, they'll put a ladder across the crevasse. We don't have any bolted aluminum ladders like the ones used on the Khumbu Icefall. The Cowboys had to make one. I watched Carl Coy do the job. He used some of our fixed-line rope and three-foot metal pickets, tying the rope into holes drilled into each end of the pickets. The finished product can be rolled up to carry up the Col. It resembles the rope ladders ships carry to drop over the side for rescues. If the Col Boys get the ladder in today, the entire route will have been fixed. We will be taking almost a ton of equipment from the cache tent to Camp IV at the top of the Col. I'll be going up the Col in a day or two. Fred will go with me on my first ascent, to make sure my skills are up to the task before I am turned loose. I expect it to be a terribly difficult day. I have some apprehension about exposure to avalanches, as well as crossing the ladder. But I know that if the rest of the troops can do it, I can do it, too.

When I arrived here at ABC, I was drained mentally, physically, and emotionally from the nine days of carries. Anne Stroock, who is working with Steve Marts on the video documentary, wanted to do an interview the morning after I arrived. She came to my tent with her video camera. Her first question was: "How do you think it's going so far?" I started to cry. I was so down, so depressed, feeling that the team had zero confidence in me, did not appreciate what I'd already done and was not offering any kind of support. Anne was perplexed. "Look, Sue," she said, "if you'd like to talk later, that's fine." I couldn't speak—just nodded my head. "Is there anything I can help you with?" she asked. I was embarrassed at being unable to keep my normal composure, but since Anne seemed sympathetic, I bubbled something about doing carries for days on end by myself, with nobody seeming to care one way or another. She was straightforward. "You've been pretty reclusive yourself," she said. "It takes effort on both sides. This is serious business and everyone has their own concerns." I ought to shape up, she was telling me, get down to the mess tent and take part in things.

So I did, and things have been better the last couple of days. The whole exercise is so exhausting in every respect for everybody, we all have to go the extra distance to make the team work. Anne helped me focus on that and I plan to have a higher, more cheerful, and more productive profile.

Everyone is very aware of what each of his or her teammates is doing—or not doing—for the team. I've been worried about that because I simply am not as strong as most of the others. They are all much younger than I am. Now that the Skinner brothers have gone down, there is a couple of decades' difference between me and the others here in camp. They recognize that I am not as strong, but they also feel, I think, that I haven't put out as much as I could. Perhaps they are right. I have been trying to pace myself to get as much out of a 51-year-old body as possible. But with the stress that everyone is under, that is resented.

I got one thing off my chest this morning. Carl Coy has been working hard on the Col and he is getting pretty tired himself, but I heard a comment, attributed to Carl, about my not doing my share, that I wasn't going to let go by. Sitting in the mess tent with three or four others, I complimented Carl on the ladder and said to him: "Listen, I know some of you don't think I've been doing my share and I'd like to discuss that a little." Carl was surprised. I continued, "It's unrealistic to expect me to carry loads that are as heavy as you guys can carry or to fix the route on the Col. And I don't have the talent you have, Carl, to make a bridge. But we all knew what our roles were when we started this venture, and the package included different people with different capabilities, each of whom brings a special talent to the table." Without expressly stating it, I wanted Carl and some of the others to give a little thought to which team members had been doing the work in organizing this trip, and who had been out raising the money to get everyone all the way across to China to Everest. I wasn't ever looking for a free ride, but I did want a little understanding and respect. The air seemed to clear a little.

The friction inherent in any pressure-cooker environment is, in my view, often exacerbated by a democratic approach. Since what is planned and what actually transpires on big mountain climbs are rarely the same, thoughtful decisions must be made by leaders on short notice. In my view, team members, having already made such a commitment by signing on, ought to be prepared to follow. Now, both the Skinner brothers are still down in Base Camp recovering from their respective edemas. Our deputy leader, Fred, and the climbing team leaders, Jeb and Brian, have had to take on the enormous responsibility of high-altitude decisions: who does what jobs, who is fit to carry loads, what days are rest days, whether the Col route is stable, and a myriad of other things. Each of the climbers, particularly those who have worked hard setting the Col, interpose strong views. Worry about the weather makes us edgy. We're all conscious of time slipping by. We've made up some lost time, after having been two weeks late arriving, but already our weather service at Penn State hints that the polar jet stream may soon shift in our direction. Last night we met at dinner to discuss our situation.

Everybody agreed that we have so much work to do that we must all pitch in. Summit team members must carry loads up the Col like everyone else. I suggested that we should think in terms of full team support for Julie. "Let her go lighter," I said. "She obviously is our fastest woman climber and has the best chance of getting to the top." My suggestion to rally around Julie was well received, I think, but inspired no further discussion. I can't tell if the guys are discouraged about anyone's chance for the top, or if they have retreated into their own thoughts. We're in an unusual position: the two expedition leaders are not in camp, and people who have known each other for a very short time are trying to pull off one of the toughest jobs that mankind has devised.

SEPTEMBER 19, 1988.

POSTED: SUN   SEP 18, 1988   10:51 PM EDT   MSG: EGII-3743-2591
FROM: EVEREST BASE
TO: PENN. STATE

GOOD MORNING! IT IS 0915 ON MONDAY 19 SEPTEMBER 1988. THE DAY HAS DAWNED CRISP AND 20% ALTO CUMULUS CLOUDY. THERE IS A MELTING LIGHT LAYER OF SNOW FROM LAST NIGHT. WE HAVE NOT SEEN MOUNT EVEREST FOR THE LAST TWO DAYS, AND IT APPEARS TO BE MISSING AGAIN THIS MORNING. ABOVE WHERE THE EVEREST PEAK SHOULD BE (WHERE THERE IS NOTHING BUT A CLOUD BANK) IS A LENTICULAR TYPE CLOUD. WE HAVE NOT HAD RADIO CONTACT WITH OUR UPPER CAMP TO FIND OUT WHAT THE WEATHER WAS THERE YESTERDAY.

THE TEMP HERE IS 34°F. THE LOW WAS 26° AND THE HIGH 56° OVER THE LAST 24 HOURS.

THE WINDS ARE CURRENTLY CALM, ALTHOUGH THEY GREW TO 10 MPH LAST NIGHT LATE. THE BAROMETER READING IS 30.85. THE ALTIMETER READS 16880!! HAVE A HAPPY . . .   SHERI

The weather at Base seems balmy, from Sheri's report to Penn State. I haven't heard their forecast for us today. Everyone in this part of Tibet now knows we have daily weather reports from Penn State. Even the yak herders go to Dan at Base and by pointing to the electronic mail depository, inquire about the day's forecast.

I feel good tonight. I did a carry to the cache tent and will do at least one, maybe two carries, tomorrow, while the guys are finishing the route at the top of the Col. The thing that still bothers me the most is that I have no opportunity to talk to Chuck or my family. I miss them terribly. I miss my friends, too. There are things I miss relating to the comforts of home, but they're trivial. Mostly I think about Chuck. He's been my teammate for almost thirty years now, and I can't wait to see him again. I hope everything is going well for him and for Chris and Toby and that they are not worrying too much.

I've been thinking a lot about the numerous changes from the original format of this climb. The most difficult for me so far has been carrying loads. Sometimes I lie in bed at night and think how nice it would be to have a Sherpa. He would bring me tea in the morning and do my dinner dishes at night. I would just pop my things on his back and walk while he carried the weight. When we got higher, he would carry extra oxygen for me. But that's not the way it is on this expedition. Everyone carries loads.

Another change is our highest camp. Courtney planned to have a high camp, Camp VII, in the neighborhood of 28,000 feet. That appealed to me, because given my speed and the altitude, I was never sure I could make the 3,000-foot ascent from 26,000, where most expeditions put in their last camp, fast enough to be a contender. Camp VII made summiting seem very feasible to me. Now it appears that we won't have a Camp VII. A less significant problem is being without trained cooks. Cooking hasn't been a burden on me, because nobody wanted to be poisoned. However, the irregularity of the situation and the different types of meals don't encourage me to eat much. I should be consuming 5,000 calories a day to maintain my weight. I can't do it.

Psychologically, the loss of Courtney and Bob also affects me. Being closer in age, they understand my struggles more than some of my younger teammates do. I hope one or both of them will be up soon. It remains unclear what changes will be made on the summit team, and whether we will go with two people or four people. It's clear that Dr. Bob does not want to be on a rope with me. That's okay. I understand it. He must think of his safety. He doesn't know me well enough to know that given fair weather, I will make it. And he doesn't know Courtney and Bob well enough to know that they will give me the chance.

Tomorrow is another 6 A.M. day. I need some sleep. If this machine that I am talking to has the power to send a message halfway around the world, please tell my husband I love him and I miss him.

SEPTEMBER 20, 1988. 3 P.M. It's very cold . . . maybe 5 degrees F. Team Three, with Jeb, Sibylle, and David Frawley, left about 7 this morning to carry loads to the cache tent. I left a little later. It was a beautiful, crisp morning and a splendid walk up the glacier. The valley we travel is about a mile wide. As I go toward the North Col, the northeast face of Everest, capped by the Pinnacles, watches my progress. Our British friends, whose tents we purchased and are now using at Interim and ABC, made the first-ever ascent of the Pinnacles just before we arrived. The face below the Pinnacles is steep avalanche territory, with a few couloirs. To my right, 3,000 or 4,000 vertical feet of fantastic jagged rock rise above the valley. A slice of the famous yellow band runs horizontally through the rock just below the peak line. The rock is loose, always crumbling. Day and night we hear not only the thundering sound of avalanches but also the continual rockfall from the west side of the valley. ABC is in the center of this glacial cirque, below the firn field in a place where it would be virtually impossible for an avalanche to reach us, but not necessarily impossible for the rocks to bound our way. As seasoned a veteran as Mack Ellerby announced a substantial rockfall two days ago in a most memorable fashion: he came dashing from our latrine area, yelling, "Rocks! Rocks!" thereby calling to everyone's attention the rockslide, his presence, and the absence of his pants.

The walk up to the cache tent is easy. I feel well acclimatized at 21,000 feet. On the route there are some crevasses, but they are small. The cache tent is 200 feet from the bottom of the Col, which pitches up impressively from the glacier at a nearly perpendicular angle. That is the spot where we clip in to the ropes. I had lunch by the tent and watched Team Three working their way up the ropes to reach the spot that needs to be fixed with the ladder.

Lunch consisted of some broken Ry-Krisp crackers and a squeeze tube of chive cheese I found in the cache tent. After I'd managed to adorn some pieces of the crackers with cheese—like putting tooth-paste on a toothbrush—I arranged them on my carefully spread table-cloth (my parka) and poured myself some tea. I had a flashback to the years right after college, when I'd served my apprenticeship (as we all did at that time) with various ladies' volunteer organizations. Before I had built up the confidence to say I really hated those ladies' teas, I attended quite a few. Well, here I was at the North Col having a dainty lunch of tea and finger sandwiches, crusts already removed.

It now appears the summit team will go down to Base in a few days for R&R. We need to make some space available at ABC for Team Two, fresh off R&R, to start carrying loads. We must set up Camp IV before we can make our summit bid. We have about sixty-five loads of thirty-five pounds each to get to the top of the Col. With seven climbers carrying every day, getting all the loads to IV will take over a week. Tomorrow morning the summiters will leave early, make a haul to the cache tent and check out the fixed ropes. If Team Three has fixed the crevasse, we may go all the way to the top. Then we'll go down to Base.

On our radio call today we heard about some bad news from the Nepal side. There was an avalanche on the West Ridge that has killed one or two Sherpas of the Spanish team. Also, it appears that a French team on the South Col tried for the summit yesterday and was stopped at 26,000 feet because of heavy snow.

In addition to that French group, the Spanish team and the American team on the south side of the mountain, there are a Korean team attempting the South Pillar and a Czech–New Zealand team on the Southwest Face. We've heard that there are more than a hundred climbers at the Nepalese base camp. It sounds like Yosemite on a summer weekend.

We are all anxiously awaiting the arrival of George McCown's trek, presumably in two or three days. Given our delays, we know better than to hold our breath. Betty Bohus, Bob's wife, is coming with George, and each of us expects to receive mail from home. I am looking forward to getting word from Chuck.

CHAPTER X

Conflicts

SEPTEMBER 22, 1988. Yesterday I had my firsthand introduction to the North Col. Let me describe the encounter. Leaving ABC by 6 A.M. requires getting up by 4:30 or 5. The temperature is zero. You must put on several layers of clothing, something like this: expedition-weight underwear next to your body, followed by a synchilla jacket and pants, a lightweight windbreaker, and then a suit (or pants and jacket) of either down or a downlike synthetic. Everything is layered and must be easily removable, because as you climb, you quickly become overheated. You load up your pack and hike about an hour and a half to the cache tent, using ski poles as walking sticks. While hiking up, you have to take off one or two layers because you get hot, but you must have them immediately available to put back on in case it gets cold. At the cache tent you add about six or seven pounds of weight around your waist: a waist harness, carabiners, a figure-eight descender, and other hardware. You put on insulated supergaiters that go over your climbing boots and zip up to the knee. You may also put on overboots. Next you affix your crampons and trade ski poles for an ice axe. Then you add about three ten-pound bags of weight to your back, more if you can handle it.

The 2,000-foot ascent to the top of the Col is essentially vertical.

The imposing North Col dwarfs our cache tent, where we have stashed gear and supplies for our continued ascent. PHOTO BY TED HANDWERK.

Three quarters of it is about the inclination of a steep staircase. But remember the altitude, what you are wearing, what you are carrying, how you are breathing through your one straw, and then imagine climbing a 2,000-foot staircase with no defined steps. There are some footholds, but you're basically kicking in your own steps. You are attached to the fixed rope by a handheld ascender, or jumar, that grips the rope with metal teeth and slides up, but (unless it ices) will not slide down without your express permission.

You step up and place one foot, then move the jumar up the rope with one hand. With the other hand you jam the spike of your ice axe into the snow as necessary for stability, and step up and kick in with the other foot. Before long your steep staircase, now all gleaming ice, turns totally vertical, like a ladder from the recesses of a ship's hold. But there are no rungs. As you step higher, you must kick in with the two crampon points on the front of each boot, balance on the two one-inch teeth now planted a quarter of an inch in the ice, move the jumar, move the ice axe, and move your body weight and pack weight up the ice wall. Where one rope ends and a new rope starts, and at each anchor point along the way, you must affix yourself to the mountain as best you can with the four crampon points and with your ice axe, remove the carabiner attached to your safety strap (which runs from the fixed rope to your waist harness), place the carabiner onto the upper rope above the anchor, then remove your jumar from the lower rope and attach it to the upper rope, all the while balancing the load on your back and trying not to lose the glove you took off because you couldn't get the carabiner unlocked with it on. Meanwhile, your glacier glasses have fogged up because you're breathing so hard.

You continue doing the same thing, every rope length upward, while trying never, under any circumstances, to look down.

Yesterday it took me about three hours to go approximately 900 feet. Rick Dare took advantage of the situation, when I was huffing my way up the wall and he was zipping down. As we passed, he grinned at me and yelled, "Vote Dukakis!" I was too breathless to respond.

I dropped my load at a cache that we had established halfway up and began the process of descending. There are different techniques for descending, depending upon the slope of the mountain and the type of snow or ice. On the steep sections you must face the mountain and attach the figure-eight (a metal braking device, which slows the rope by friction) to your harness, and rappel down. In rappelling, you

step back and down, blindly into space, and kick the two front crampon points of one foot into the ice somewhere below, alternating one
blind downward step after the next. You still have to contend with
changing your hardware at each anchor point.

Understand that while you are doing all this, both ascending and
descending, you have below you deep crevasses and above you giant
ice seracs, none of which look very stable. To your right are the rock-
falls, and all around are avalanches waiting to happen. It is, to say the
least, inhospitable terrain.

When I made it down to the cache tent, Jim Robinson was waiting
with a welcome hot drink. Jim is another guy who's really worked
hard, both in setting the Col and in many other ways. He, Dan Pryor,
and Yak are our three Middlebury grads.

Meanwhile, up higher on the Col, Mack, Brad, and Carl had
reached the crevasse that blocked our path. After affixing our home-
made ladder, they ascended to the top of the Col, where Camp IV will
be established, and returned to ABC with big grins. Our route is fixed.
We're on our way to the top!

I got into ABC last night about 8 o'clock, and woke up promptly
this morning at 11. Nothing like fifteen hours of sleep for weary
bones. My first climb on the Col was a thrill, at least the first half.
The remainder of it, I'm told, is more dramatic—more crevasses and
seracs, and tougher because of the gain in altitude. It really is fun,
much better than moraine climbing.

7 P.M. The latest news is that the camp above 27,000 feet probably will
be eliminated. That could also eliminate any realistic chance for me to
get to the summit. I'm not a happy camper. I was counting on that
high springboard. Meanwhile, the day has brought a crisis in both
leadership and morale. While Bob and Courtney have been at Base,
Brian and Mack have led the effort to get the Col fixed. Everyone here
knows how hard they've worked, and we've agreed on an all-out push
to get our gear to the top of the Col. Now Penn State predicts that a
major storm may hit us soon, in all likelihood the day after tomorrow.
Brian has called for all hands to carry loads tomorrow. Then comes the
message from Courtney and Bob: Team Four is to descend in the
morning for R&R.

"ABC to Base, ABC to Base. Do you read me? Come in, Dan. Do
you read me?" We're in the mess tent and Fred is trying to establish
communication with Courtney and Bob, who are camped at Interim

on their way back up the mountain. We cannot talk directly to Interim, but we're able to get a clear signal to Dan Pryor at Base, and Dan has a clear line to Interim.

Fred: "This is Fred at ABC. I hardly picked up anything Courtney said—there is too much static. What's the story? Over."

Dan: "This is Base. Bob's at Interim. How's everyone? Over."

Fred: "Three are still up on what's called Hooter's Ledge on the Col, bringing Peter Breslow down. Everybody's A-okay."

Dan: "Ten-four. Do you copy that, Courtney Skinner?"

Courtney, from whom we hear only static, arranges with Dan to relay a message to us. He wants a 10 A.M. radio conference tomorrow.

Doug Burbank, with us at ABC, relays to Courtney that he will take radio duty because everybody else will be on the Col. Hearing that, Courtney asks us to stand by for five minutes while he and Bob have a discussion. There are about fifteen of us in the tent, and we all roar when someone in the back, recalling the crisis in Lhasa, yells out: "This is it—they're sending us all home!"

Fred continues his conversation with Dan: "Okay. Anne Stroock's got the quotes you wanted to send to hometown newspapers, but none are printable. Stand by."

While we're waiting for Courtney and Bob to call back, Anne Stroock relays one quote from each climber. It's true that most are not printable. Urologist Dr. Bob's is marginal. Asked about conditions at ABC and the health of our group, Bob responds: "The pecker-checker says this ain't no weenie roast." Dan groans.

We discuss the current disagreement, whether some of the strong climbers who have been working on the Col should go down for R&R, to be rested to climb later, or whether they should stay one more day to help carry loads before the storm comes. The climbing team needs the help on loads. The Skinners want the support climbers to rest.

The call comes, and again our comments are relayed to Courtney and Bob via Dan at Base.

Brian: "All we want is one day to get enough equipment up so that we can have a Camp IV. Today was the first day that a lot of people got very high on the Col. Tomorrow is Friday and we can get another ten to twelve loads up before Saturday's storm. If we don't get the loads up and then have to dig out the entire route after the snow, or worse yet, wait several days to let it set and avoid the avalanche danger, we could lose a whole week."

Orion: "Tell Courtney we'll do anything he says, but the situation up here is difficult and we would like him to trust the leadership that he has up here. We will send the climbers that he wants down on Saturday. Over."

We hear only static as Dan relays our messages to Courtney and Bob and picks up their reply.

Dan: "Courtney says he does trust the leadership up there and he says you are doing a bang-up job, but he is taking more of an overall view as opposed to focusing solely on Camp IV. He wants six people down so we will be in a position to summit."

Ethan: "Dan, can you read me? Listen, I know that Courtney and Bob are thinking of the whole picture, and we may not be seeing it, but let me tell you what we're seeing and then maybe they can make a judgment from that. When the team that goes down comes back up after R&R, we will still be putting in camps. It is so hard up here, I don't think Courtney and Bob realize it. It has taken us so long, it is so difficult. Their summit schedule is too soon. When Team Four comes back up, we still won't have the mountain ready for a summit bid. Over."

We listen to the static as we wait for the decision. Finally we hear Dan's voice.

Dan: "Courtney still wants four to six people down tomorrow."

Brian: "We read you, Dan. Tell Courtney we will do anything he wants, but we feel it is critical to climbing the mountain that Team Four stays tomorrow and goes down on Saturday. If that storm moves in, we are going to lose four to five days on the Col, and that will put us another week behind."

The Col Boys, with virtually unanimous assent inside the ABC tent, argue vehemently that one day doesn't matter for R&R but matters desperately for moving the loads up the mountain. Courtney and Bob hold firm. The conclusion, about 9 P.M., is that Team Four must descend. Brian and several others are angry. They have been in charge at ABC when many important decisions have had to be made. Now they are being second-guessed by those not in their shoes. On the other hand, the Skinners, as the expedition leaders, have constructed an overall plan for rotating teams that they feel gives the Cowboys the best chance. Tension is high tonight.

I escaped to my tent. My roommate tonight is Ted Handwerk. We have climbed together on Rainier and in the Wind River Mountains in

Wyoming. He's an experienced winter mountaineer. After we snuggled into our bags, I told him how tough I thought the Col was. He listened quietly to my impassioned report. When I finally wound down, he said, "Yup, that's Everest."

SEPTEMBER 23, 1988. All of us at ABC got up early and headed up to the cache tent, where we picked up loads to go to Camp IV. Everybody started up the Col except Brian, Mack, Jim, and Carl, who patiently waited at the cache tent for the call Courtney had set for 10 A.M. The Col Boys wanted to seek permission, once more, to continue up the Col with their loads. When no radio communication could be established, they had no choice but to follow Courtney's orders. Reluctantly they headed down.

It's unfortunate to have such conflicts. There appeared to be merit in both positions. The issue was awkward for me because as a general rule, I believe that one person should make the important, and final, decisions. Someone has to be the C.E.O. Yet I respect Brian's and Mack's views and the leadership they've provided. I also want to move up as fast as possible. Finally, I suppose, I was swayed by Dr. Bob's comments: "Medically and traditionally, climbers cycle down. Safety, not the summit, is the top priority. I don't want to die for the mountain. I don't want to go out of here with a pile of rocks in the Rongbuk Valley as a memorial." Hard to disagree with that.

Under our original schedule today was one of our first summit days. Instead, I lugged a load of gear up the North Col. Fred and I had to wait until the last of the climbers ahead of us had moved up the ropes and spread out. We started up in the early afternoon. Fred took the lead and said that he would wait for me at Lunch Ledge, an interesting spot to even contemplate lunch, let alone sit down for a meal. Though there is an inviting snow platform about six feet square, giant seracs cling to the side of the mountain and hang right overhead. A few steps down is a yawning crevasse. From Lunch Ledge up, the route was steep and more technical. No amount of acclimatization can eliminate completely the desperate gasping for air during strenuous exercise at 22,000 feet. Breathing deeply and resting periodically, I moved upward at an acceptable pace and came to a section of deep, soft snow. It was slow-going: take a step, slip back in the soft stuff, hang on, climb higher, slip back and repeat.

Mack had scouted and put in one particularly difficult section we called Mack's Lead. It is a section of vertical blue ice just above a

Steve Marts, Anne Stroock, and Ethan Goldings enjoy a break at Lunch Ledge. This small, level spot in the snow partway up the Col provided a welcome rest from the strenuous climb. PHOTO BY TED HANDWERK.

crevasse, created when the ledge we are ascending had broken away from the face. Mack's Lead would require ice-climbing technique: front-pointing with the crampons, using one ice axe with the fixed rope (or two axes without the rope). I was apprehensive. Not only had I never been on a fixed line before, I had no ice-climbing experience. Zero.

When Fred and I reached Hooter's Ledge, just below Mack's Lead, four of our climbers were descending. They were each at a different level in rappelling and Fred and I had to wait about half an hour for them to get off the ropes. Finally, about 5 o'clock we started up Mack's Lead. This was to be my first ice climbing: heading up Mount Everest at 22,500 feet. Fred encouraged me by taking off ahead of me and calling back casually, "Let's make this one fast, Sue." Obviously, he expected me to make it with no trouble. And I did. It was, indeed, steep and icy, but between doing something that resembled ice climbing and something that must have resembled a vertical duck-foot walk, I made it through quickly. I had to hang on at one precarious perch halfway up, so that four more Cowboy climbers could come down. Kicking in hard with my crampons and flattening my body against the ice wall, I made room for them to descend. It had begun to snow and Matt "Yak" Ellenthal had developed symptoms of hypothermia. He was wearing his Lycra tights, not the best gear in cold, snowy conditions. It was imperative that he get down quickly. Dave McNally was helping Yak down along the fixed line with Anne Stroock and Steve "The World's Greatest Climbing Photographer" Marts coming slowly behind to help if necessary. Descending the rope directly above me, all of them were kicking snow down onto my head and neck. When they reached me, they had to unhook their safety lines and reattach them below me, a potentially dangerous maneuver, particularly since it was almost dark, it was snowing, and everyone had cold, inept fingers. Yak was stiff and nonresponsive when I spoke to him. Clearly cold. Meanwhile, poor Fred waited higher up. I started out again and was making good progress when David Frawley came ripping by, carrying probably his fifth load in five days. He hollered some words of encouragement and raced on up to the cache area that we'd established just below the crevasse bridge. It was getting late when I reached the corner of the next crevasse, where passage required tiptoeing along a narrow ledge above the chasm. Frawley, having already deposited his load, was headed back down to help me. He is such an upbeat guy, always helping. I thought about David teaching Peter Breslow how to use his avalanche beeper. "This device will help us find you if you get buried under four feet of snow," David explained.

"Great," said Peter, "but what if I get buried under twelve feet of snow?"

"We'll call your family," came the quick reply.

David took my pack the last hundred yards up to the cache spot. I climbed up along the edge of the crevasse. The weather had cleared and there was a spectacular view down valley. It was nothing less than intoxicating. Below, even in the twilight, I could see all the way down the East Rongbuk Glacier, past ABC to the point where the glacier turns west into the rocky moraine that heads toward Camp II. There above me was the Everest peak, bathed in alpenglow. The North Ridge, the route we will be heading up, looked broad, smooth as a highway, and wonderfully inviting. I said out loud: "I can do that."

Fred, David, and I didn't leave until after 6 o'clock. There are a couple of sections that have to be rappelled because of their steepness, but we got down quickly. I loved it. On some sections I thought I was flying. Putting a carabiner on the fixed line and my trust in it, I could lean out, hang on with one hand, and take giant leaping downward steps. Other times, I'd wrap the rope around my arm and behind my back to brake my descent. I had no fear. It was dark, so I couldn't see anything anyway. I just hung on to that fixed line and visualized a gazelle bounding downhill. Somewhere below Lunch Ledge I fell, but I was attached to the line with my safety strap. I held my crampons away from the snow and slid down to the next anchor. It was like the body surfing I sometimes do while skiing. No problem.

We stopped at the cache tent briefly and headed on back to ABC, getting in around 9:30. I was tired, and because of falling on the way down I looked like a frozen little bunny. I considered it a successful day. In fact, I was exhilarated. It was tough, but I know I can do it, however many times are necessary. I just have to remind myself that the North Col is one of the most dangerous areas on the mountain. Thrilling to climb, yes, but too much like Russian roulette. If all goes well, I only have two more round trips through it. We've now gotten a lot of the stuff moved up from the bottom of the Col to the top. The fellows are working on establishing Camp IV.

While I was climbing the Col that day, my family was roughing it, too. Chris, Toby, and Chuck were dining on strawberries, champagne, and smoked salmon at a brunch at Florida's Boca Raton Hotel & Club. When I got home, they rubbed it in—showing me a photograph of themselves with President Reagan. Well, I always said I liked contrasts.

We heard after returning from the Col that the Seattle team, with three women climbers, is going to be attempting the summit in the next few days. It's quite possible that all this "first United States woman" stuff will become moot.

SEPTEMBER 24, 1988. The summit climbers have been advised to descend to Base Camp. So this morning, with a tired body, I prepared to descend. Julie, Jim, Orion, and Bob all set off early. Fred and I didn't leave until sometime after 1 o'clock. We stopped at Camp II to visit with Courtney, who was on his way to ABC with Sheri King, and we discussed the conflict that had stirred up all camps. Courtney said that he and Bob have been very concerned about giving our climbers sufficient rest and having fresh teams on the mountain as we get higher—both for safety and for getting the job done. He feels that we at Camp III didn't fully appreciate that need.

A study in contrasts. While the Cowboys were struggling up the North Col on the fixed ropes, Chris, Toby, and Chuck Cobb were with then-President Ronald Reagan in Florida. PHOTOS BY SUE COBB AND LUCIEN CAPEHART.

Courtney wanted to know how I was feeling and who I wanted to climb with, since Dr. Bob and I were not a well-matched pair. Feeling confident, and thinking there were even some members on my team who were gaining confidence in me, I suggested one or two names. We discussed the pros and cons. I told Courtney that I felt very relaxed about it, that it would work out one way or another. It would be nice for the team and an honor if we were to get an American woman to the top, but Julie should definitely be first choice. I suggested that we push her as hard as we can, with some of our best, fast climbers. Whether she makes it or not, I still want a shot. I want my climbing partner to be comfortable climbing with me, and to understand the pace, and most of all, I want to make sure that we're a safe team. I don't want to put my life in unnecessary danger, nor do I want to endanger anybody else. We'll just have to see how things go and how everybody's health is. In all likelihood the issue will resolve itself.

After an hour's conversation with Courtney and Sheri, Fred and I began meandering down the valley. The glacial moraine looks much different than when we went up almost three weeks ago. There are so many changes, it's a bit scary. Not for a moment do I forget that this is

128

where a Japanese team member was killed by rockfall in May. The premonsoon climb was called the Asian Friendship Expedition and included 252 Chinese, Nepalese, and Japanese. The mammoth undertaking cost $7,000,000 and produced the first live television broadcasts from the summit.

It was turning dark when we reached Camp I. In my wildest dreams I wouldn't have thought we could negotiate the route below Camp I at night, but we never even needed a headlamp. The moon came up, almost full, and lit up the night like a klieg light. This is the night I dreamed of starting up to the summit. Instead, I was on a moonlit walk down to Base.

When we arrived at Base Camp, we found George McCown and the trekkers in camp. By the time Fred and I appeared, they had gone to bed, spread out in Cowboy tents all over Base.

I'm tired. I still suspect that the largest part of my fatigue is from poor diet. I can't seem to do much about it, particularly on the days that we're climbing. I climbed the Col on a cup of hot chocolate for breakfast, and a granola bar and a candy bar at the cache tent. Lunch was another candy bar. There was no dinner left when we returned late to ABC. Today my fuel for the descent to Base was a bowl of instant oatmeal and another finger sandwich—a cracker with peanut butter and jelly. Halfway down the fifteen-mile hike to Base, I had another candy bar and water. That is not enough food to sustain anyone working at these heights. I don't know how to discipline myself in that area. It could be a serious problem later.

CHAPTER XI

R&R

SEPTEMBER 25, 1988. BASE CAMP. 9 A.M. I was awakened with the news that George McCown's wife, Karen, was ill, suffering from acute mountain sickness. She and her daughter, Amy, were leaving the trekking group to descend to a lower elevation. I ran out and gave Karen a big hug. She looked terrible, with signs of both pulmonary and cerebral edema. Karen and Amy took off in a jeep with a Chinese driver. The trekking group was downcast. I look forward to visiting with them, but I am too tired today. My goals are to call home, take a bath, and rest. Tomorrow I'll socialize.

Base Camp seems startlingly luxurious, now that I've been up on the mountain. When we were first here, we were building the camp and seeing it progress slowly, as you see a child grow. Dan Pryor has practically turned the place into a luxury spa (at least by comparison with the places I've been the last three weeks). I feel like I'm at the Boca Raton Hotel & Club. We have hot water to bathe. We are waited on, fed, and pampered.

Fred and I have been taking a lot of kidding because of our evening descent of the Col and our stroll into Base Camp much after dark. We're now known as the Night Stalkers. Someone has even suggested that by climbing at night, we can sleep by day and thereby avoid camp chores.

SEPTEMBER 26, 1988. I called home last night and talked to Chuck and Toby. We discussed the family news, world news, presidential campaign news, and Christian's knee operation. I'd like to talk to Chris. Maybe I can sneak in a call while I am here in Base Camp. I'll have to remember to tell Rick Dare that Bush is leading the polls by four points.

Chuck wants me to go to Budapest with him. His plan is for me to leave Base with George and his trekking group on October 13 or 14. By that time we should have made our summit attempts and be back in Base Camp. From Kathmandu I would fly to New Delhi, or Hong Kong, then meet Chuck in Europe. All expedition members are to stay and help clear the mountain. If Chuck's plan works, I'll be leaving early—and feeling pretty guilty.

Chuck and Toby said they had been frightened by pieces of information that an avalanche on Everest had killed two people. They tried to call Base but couldn't get through. It wasn't until they reached the Nepal desk at our State Department that they learned that it was the Spanish team on the Nepal side that had a fatality. They also mentioned a *USA Today* report that the Seattle team is ready for their summit attempts and will have at least one American woman on their first team. I've thought more about this contrived race to the top. It's not a terribly big factor. The challenge here is so great that if anyone can make it, under any circumstances, I congratulate him or her.

Chuck sent me some more articles on our expedition. This is unlike the trip to Aconcagua. There, we had no media coverage. Not one single person on the trip knew me, where I lived, what I did, or anything else about me. I could go down and climb that mountain and have a lot of fun doing it. It was even more fun for me to come back after four weeks and have my friends in the office notice the tan and ask where I'd been. "Oh," I said, "I went down to South America to climb the highest mountain in the Western Hemisphere."

Or, after Memorial Day weekend: "What did you do this weekend?"

"I climbed Mount Rainier." That's what I like. No need to talk about it—just go do it.

10 P.M. I spoke to George about the possibility of leaving with his group. They must depart by October 12 to make their connections out of Kathmandu. That's over two weeks away and just might give me enough time to get up, make a summit attempt, and get down. I hope

131

so. I really have been homesick. I hope my friends at home haven't forgotten me. I stayed up for a long time tonight writing postcards home, thinking about what's going on in Miami and Washington, what's happening at my law firm, how the University of Miami Hurricanes are doing, how the Dolphins are doing, what's going on with Miami's Super Bowl. I regret having had to resign the chairmanship of Miami's Super Bowl Host Committee because of my long absence to climb Everest. For eight years I led the negotiations with the NFL and team owners to persuade them to bring the Super Bowl to Miami. Finally we got the 1989 game and I'm gone during the critical pregame phase.

There's at least one team member who shares my concerns about what's happening in the financial world while we're gone: Alexandra Hildebrandt, who has worked on Wall Street for the past five years. She's a very attractive woman, with long blond hair and an expressive face. In fact, she started out as a model and actress.

"I didn't get any intellectual satisfaction out of modeling," she told me one day in Base Camp. "The acting was a little broader, more stimulating, but the intellectual basis was still lacking. I went back to school at night and studied business. I got involved with the stock market and loved it.

"The world of venture capital and investment banking in New York is thrilling," she continued. "I get to deal with the whole spectrum of people in business, from the top investment bankers to the entrepreneurs working night and day to make a dream come true. I can participate with those people and help them realize their goals, and work with all the consultants and attorneys in between."

That is exactly what I had found to be one of the pleasures of doing bond financings—working with a variety of bright and stimulating people to put good projects together. "How old are you, anyway, Alex?" I asked.

"Thirty-five."

"Our careers have some parallels," I told her. "I started out in competitive athletics, but along the way I realized that I couldn't rely on my body for the rest of my life, that I had to train my mind and move in the direction of intellectual satisfaction. You went from modeling to finance; I switched from sports to law. One difference between us, though: you could still pick up some modeling jobs." Alex flashed a quick smile. I wanted to continue talking with her, but I had to do my Base Camp chore for the day. I'd drawn a real plum: cleaning up the latrines.

My ribs are killing me. I know that climbers up here can break their ribs coughing. I don't think I've done that, but I've torn something. When I'm lying down, I can't sit up unless I bring both knees to my chest, put my arms around them, and sort of rock forward, without using my stomach muscles. I'm painfully sore, but I don't want anybody to know about it. I'm talking to my body about being back in good shape by the time I leave here Friday.

If the fatalities on the Spanish climbing team, caused by the avalanche on the Nepal side, are confirmed, they will bring to four the number of climbers who have died since we arrived. First was the Frenchman who died of pulmonary edema the day we arrived at Base. A member of another French team, who chose not to descend with his teammates to a lower camp after encountering bad weather at about 25,000 feet, has now been missing for over a week. There's no chance that he's alive. I am apprehensive as I look ahead. It's like one more run through the mine field, and if you make it, you're home free. But you can't be scared and be successful. I've got to keep focused on the goal.

MIDNIGHT. I can't go to sleep. All the way up the mountain I have been sleeping like a baby. Tonight I have been tossing around. Everything comes down to these last two weeks. We have worked so hard for so long. For me it started with that first meeting in Jackson Hole in August 1987, when the board of governors got together and gave general approval to the plan and a million-dollar budget, and we started raising funds to get thirty-five people through China and up Everest. Now most of the research projects are nearly complete, the high school students, enriched by travel, are in college. We still have the four Wyoming teachers with us and a few thousand feet left to climb. So many ideas that Courtney proposed have borne fruit, but in the eyes of most people, success on an Everest expedition is to reach the summit. To have that kind of success, everything boils down to the next two weeks. We also face the greatest amount of danger in the next two weeks. I lie here and pray that all thirty-five of us walk out of this valley.

3 A.M. My ribs ache horribly, I still can't sleep, and I have the return of an old nemesis on my lips—vicious, bubbly sun blisters. I have been tossing and turning, and in the middle of the night I can't escape the questions asked by my friends: What is the meaning of all this? Why do it?

George Mallory made a statement that is famous among climbers. It sneaks in and out of my mind. "If you cannot understand that there is something in man which responds to the challenge of this mountain and goes to meet it, that the struggle is the struggle of life itself upward and forever upward, then you won't see why we go . . ."

I asked Julie for her thoughts the other day. She loves the challenge of climbing.

"It's so demanding, mentally and physically," Julie said. "When you are up there, you can't just rush down to a doctor or a hospital or evacuate yourself quickly. You have to go in prepared to deal with the consequences. The risks are high. And that poses the challenge for me, as a mountaineer."

Certainly the high risk is something we've all thought about. In an emergency, teams on this side of Everest (in contrast to the Nepal side) have no chance whatsoever of rescue by helicopter, even from Base Camp.

"Have you found Everest easier or harder than you expected?" I asked.

"It's just about what I expected. The North Col is very hard, but I have done things equally hard."

Whew, I thought. The whole exercise is more difficult than I expected—mostly because of the length of time, the remoteness, and the totality of the effort, emotional, mental and physical. But Julie and I agree that climbing this mountain is analogous to other things in life: if you have an opportunity, take it. Set your goal high, and then go for it. This we are doing in the literal sense: Everest is as high as you can go. We hope that in the summit—or its attempt—we will achieve something beyond the physical feat.

"I don't know what I am going to run into as we go higher," Julie continued. "I might be totally overwhelmed. I mean, on the North Col, you can see the top, you can see what you need to do. But higher up, I have no idea. The terrain is unfamiliar, the lack of oxygen, the exhaustion . . . Are you nervous, Sue?"

"No. Apprehensive, but not nervous. The Col was tougher for me than it was for you—I hadn't done any ice climbing—and it was tiring. I've always been told you need legs of steel for ice climbing. But I wasn't the least bit scared. I don't know what right I have to be so cocky, but I was comfortable. My concern is the weather. If it holds, I'm just sure we can do it. We, the team, I mean. How high *I* personally will get, I don't know—there are so many variables."

"Over the past two days," Julie said, "I've felt really anxious about the climb. About what's up ahead. It's finally hit me that nobody on our team has been up there before, and we are going to be putting in the first footprints."

"But that's exciting, too, don't you think?"

"Definitely. Or I wouldn't be going up there. But I'm anxious."

My feeling is that as a group, we're in good shape, and that will be one of the keys to our survival. In competitive athletics you try to time your physical peak and mental peak to coincide with your biggest challenge: the finals, the playoffs, whatever. On that score, I have confidence. We just have to use good judgment, both personally and collectively, in the areas where we are inexperienced. We know it's not like climbing in South America or the States, where there is much less worry about the effects of oxygen deprivation. At least there, your brain works better. And it can be 50-below back home and yet not nearly so cold as it will be on Everest because of the lack of oxygen.

"I hope we use good judgment," I told Julie. "Much as I want us to be successful, I'd rather we both went home alive."

"We can always come back."

Spoken like a 31-year-old.

SEPTEMBER 27, 1988. I finally went to sleep after taking a codeine pill to stop the pain in my ribs. I was awakened about 9 by a phone call from Chuck. He's acutely interested in the precise details of who is going where and when, which I can't supply right now, because our situation remains so fluid. Chuck has gotten to know the team by phone. He calls Base Camp all the time, whether I'm here or not. Today he asks me, "Where are Brian and Mack? Is Yak back at Base? Are Anne and Steve still at Camp IV? How's Courtney's health?" And so on.

I took a walk today to pay homage to Marty Hoey and to others who have died trying to climb the north side of Everest. Marty has been on my mind. She wanted to be the first American woman to climb Everest and went with my friends Dick Bass and Frank Wells on the 1982 North Face Expedition. She was climbing on a fixed rope on the Great Couloir with Jim Wickwire, one of America's great climbers. At 26,000 feet, they stopped to rest. Marty apparently leaned back on the fixed rope. She fell backward, tried to grab the rope, and missed. Simultaneously, her harness came open. Marty plummeted thousands of feet to her death. Her jumar remained attached to the rope and her harness belt hung dangling. It happened so fast that Wickwire, above her, was unable to help. It appeared that Marty had failed to loop the belt back through the buckle of her harness, allowing the belt to work its way free of the buckle. There was no way to retrieve her body. She is now a part of Everest—forever.

The tradition here is to build a memorial cairn to honor the lost teammate. On a small drumlin not far from Base Camp stand numerous small stone altars with names scratched in rock. I stood before these cairns, framed by the peak that lured these men and women to their deaths, and said my prayers for Marty. I thanked her for the inspiration, and I thanked her for the warning.

SEPTEMBER 28, 1988. My strength is coming back. I feel great. Tonight we had another telephone interview with *Good Morning America*, and then I helped Dan transmit some pictures of the Cowboys taken on the Col, so that the ABC network can run them with the phone interviews. I also had a challenging interview with a newspaper reporter in the United States who denigrated my effort here because I'm not a world-class climber. I do not assert that I am. I'm not even anything close to it. For this kind of trip my experience is limited. But it doesn't bother me when I am attacked for lack of Himalayan experience. Facts are facts. The reporter asked me what I thought our chances were, both mine and Julie's, to get to the summit.

"If the weather holds," I told her, "Julie's chances are excellent. My chances are good." I hope I am right. I hope the weather holds, because Julie and I are going to just suck it up and go do it.

Fred said tonight that our summit days are possibly eight or ten days away. The tents are in place at Camp IV and our advance climbers will be going up to Camp V tomorrow. We're ready for the final push. I feel good.

SEPTEMBER 29, 1988. Another beautiful day. Another summit day. Another day of messing around in Base Camp, reading, finishing postcards, taking pictures of each other, sorting gear, not doing anything strenuous. If we are not climbing, our orders are to either eat or sleep. That's what I've done the last few days and I'm bored. I can't wait to go back up.

We had radio contact with Camp V today. The camp's not in yet,

After the austerity of the higher camps, Base seemed like a luxury spa to Dave Frawley and me. PHOTO BY MATT ELLENTHAL.

but Ted Handwerk and Doug Burbank were both at the 25,500-foot site on reconnaissance. Tomorrow we leave.

We have another trekker in the Base Camp hospital. I don't know how people in the Rongbuk Valley have survived without our three Cowboy doctors and all of our equipment. They have been taking care of everybody who comes through. There is a young German girl here now who has pneumonia or something worse. She is very sick. Since Ross Greenlee is on his way to ABC to trade places with Sheri King, and Sheri isn't back, Bob Bohus is the only doctor to care for this girl, which means Bob can't go up with us tomorrow.

SEPTEMBER 30, 1988. 9 A.M. If the weather holds another ten days, we are going to be ecstatic.

Over breakfast I talked to Sibylle. I haven't really gotten to know Sibylle very well. I have noticed two things, though. One is that unlike me, she eats all the time—and no matter how much she eats and how little I do, she is still skinnier than I. The other is that she always travels light. As far as I can tell, she has only one set of clothes for the entire trip. She told me she loves to sew and she makes her own things, including climbing gear. I was curious about Sibylle. Like everyone on the team, she has an interesting résumé: Reed College in Portland, Oregon, grad school at the University of California in Irvine, a Ph.D. in biology, all interspersed with climbing, skiing, and bike racing. She was born in Germany, where her father was a famous climber.

Last year, Sibylle said, she climbed in Central Asia with a Seattle group. The climbs were 3,000- to 5,000-foot vertical granite walls at altitudes of 17,000 to 18,000 feet, with ice climbing on the approaches.

"Is big-wall climbing your forte?" I asked.

"There are a lot of American women who are excellent wall climbers, way better than me, who lead at high levels of difficulty, like 5.11 and 5.12, every day. But very few women do any serious ice climbing, and not many bother to do big walls these days. Walls were fashionable in the 1970s. Now it's short, hard climbs, anything over 5.12.

"I was lucky that a woman who had intended to go to Central Asia decided not to, and that the group wanted another woman and invited me. Some of the guys were much more experienced than I, much better climbers, very experienced in the Himalayas. One had just done a new route on Gasherbaum, which is often called the hardest mountain in the world. That's when I got the idea of coming here: I was with those guys and I turned out to be one of the strongest people. I was the only one who could keep up with the leaders."

"How do you like Himalayan climbing?" I asked her.

"I'm definitely coming back. I want to get on two expeditions next year. I have no idea whose, but I am going to get on one in the spring and just stay over the summer and get on one in the fall. I like living here. I like the mountains here."

"They are beautiful, and there's no doubt that your strength shows up in this kind of environment. How old are you?"

"Thirty-seven."

"You're not all that far behind me, for crying out loud!" Really, I thought she was 33.

Before the morning was over, Chuck called again. He is aware of the dangers of the upcoming days. His last words to me before our departure for ABC were "Come home, sweetheart, please come home." I thought about Marty Hoey and I understood him to be saying "Please don't stay there forever." I fought back tears and prepared to leave Base Camp.

INTERIM CAMP. 8:00 P.M. The summit group, with Peter Breslow in tow, left for Interim this afternoon. Dr. Bob has to remain at Base to take care of the sick German girl (who apparently has a pulmonary embolism) until Ross Greenlee or Sheri King can get down to Base.

I was pleased to find that the steep hill leading into Camp I didn't seem very steep. The hill hasn't changed, but I have. Three weeks ago it took me more than three hours to go from Base to Camp I, today it took an hour and a half. Obviously, we are all acclimatized and in better physical condition. We made record time to Camp I, had a snack, and set out for Interim. Three of our group were already there: Bob's wife, Betty Bohus; Astrid, our German camp jack; and Dan Pryor, who has left his chores at Base Camp to help at ABC in the final days.

Last time I talked to Astrid, three weeks ago, she had decided to head for Pakistan. A few days later we heard by radio that she was back at Base Camp. She has rejoined our team. She obviously is doing her round-the-world trip on a shoestring. I think I would choose the security of being with thirty-five American Cowboys over the freedom of walking alone through Tibet and Pakistan. Astrid is not a climber, by any stretch of the imagination, but she is spunky and willing to work in camp. She will help Dan at ABC during the summit attempt.

Betty Bohus had joined George McCown's trekking group in the States and arrived in Base Camp the same day we got down for R&R. Courtney proposed that Betty, who is a nurse, stay on as a camp jack for us, too. When the rest of the trekkers took off for the Karma Valley, Betty stayed. Now she is working her way up to ABC with Dan and Astrid. Betty is strong and capable, a welcome addition.

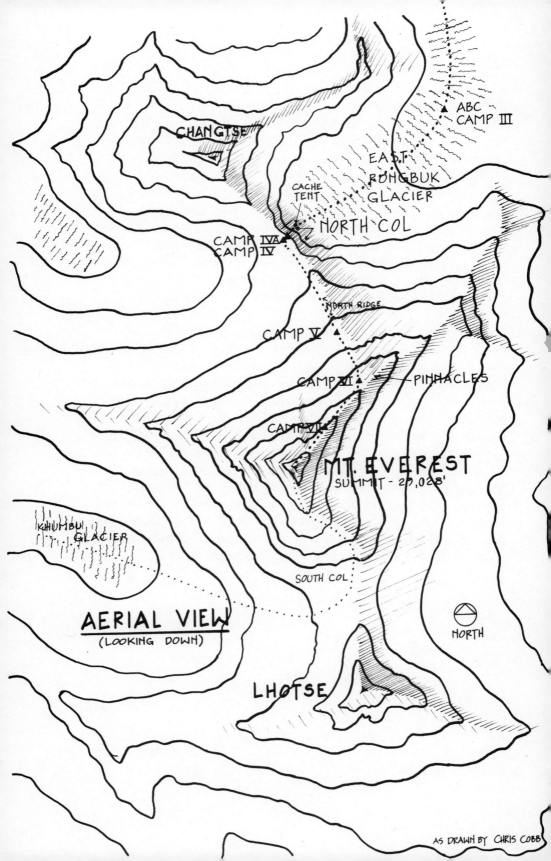

CHAPTER XII

Peaking

OCTOBER 1, 1988. After a night at Interim, the summit group set off for ABC around 10:30 A.M. It was by far the best day I've had. I climbed with the entire summit team, just bounding along the route.

"Hey, Sue!" Fred called. "What did you have for breakfast, anyway? You're moving like a jackrabbit."

I was euphoric, I was so happy to be feeling well. We did the trip between Interim and Camp II in excellent time. As we arrived, Fred motioned for us to come listen to the radio report from Base.

"Could you repeat that, Dan?"

"Right. The first woman from the United States has summited."

"Who was it?"

"Was it the Northwest group?"

"South Col?"

"Take it easy," Fred said. "Let the guy finish. Go ahead, Dan."

"Stacy Allison, from Portland. She summited with a Sherpa, Pasang Gyalzen. Over."

I looked around for Julie, but she was still coming up.

"Are you disappointed, Sue?" asked Peter Breslow, ever the journalist. I hesitated a moment to sort out my feelings. It was always distinctly possible that someone would get there ahead of me, and that I might not make it at all, so I've never had all my eggs in that basket. That was for the media to dwell on.

"Had I been the first U.S. woman," I told Peter, "it would have been a fairy tale." Not that the idea hadn't appealed to me: I like fairy tales. "Imagine, a woman in her fifties, and an unseasoned climber to boot, making the summit. Now that I know just how difficult it is, I can only say, 'Congratulations! We are proud of you!' She is an accomplished climber, and she has earned the reward."

"What about the difficulty of the route?" Peter asked. "Wasn't her route easier?"

"From what I'm told, our route is not technically harder, but it is definitely longer and less familiar to climbing teams. We will be spending more debilitating time above twenty thousand feet, and more time in the Death Zone. And it's colder in the shadow of the mountain. We won't feel the morning sun until 9 A.M. And the difference between direct sunlight and shade is as much as 25 to 30 degrees. At 30-below to start with, that can make a dramatic difference. You know, many American teams have negotiated the South Col route, but no American team has ever made it on our route. In fact, Peter Erschler is the only American who has summited from the north side. I suppose that says something."

Breslow went off to get Julie's reaction to the news. When I said that Julie should have the first opportunity, I meant it. She is a mountain guide, and success here would have a greater impact on her life. To her credit, Julie refused to make a big deal out of it when we talked later. We agreed, though, that neither of us would mind if we were to be the second and third United States women at the top . . . or the sixth and seventh. We just want to get there. Of course, records can still be set, if that's the game. I could be the oldest American woman to summit. And even if I don't make it up, every step I take above the Col will probably set a United States women's age-group record. Age, in fact, may be more important than gender. As David Frawley said to me last night, not entirely facetiously, "In these our golden years, we have undertaken a difficult challenge. I hope we set an example for others. Someone who may not want to climb Everest might yet attempt something similarly difficult. 'If Cobb and Frawley can go climb Everest,' he or she would be saying, 'I can do what I set out to do.'"

The Northwest American team, led by Seattle attorney Jim Frush, used forty Sherpas to carry gear, establish camps, and fix the difficult portions of

the route with ropes and ladders. Using oxygen, they climbed the now tradi-
tional South Col route made famous by Sir Edmund Hillary and Tenzing
Norgay on the first ascent of Everest in 1953. Stacy, a 30-year-old Portland,
Oregon, house framer and building contractor, is an experienced Himalayan
climber, having summited Ama Dablam and reached 26,000 feet on the North
Face of Everest only last season. Her final assault was launched from the
team's Camp IV at 26,070 feet, in nearly perfect weather. Two more climbers
on the Northwest team, Peggy Luce and Geoff Tabin, would summit three
days later. Diana Dailey, the third woman on the team, was weathered out. In
all, twelve climbers on the south side of Everest reached the peak on September
26, while I was sitting in the Cowboy Base Camp.

The Camp II area was abuzz with climbers. There were two
Changtse expeditions, one of which, an American team, had failed
on their summit bid and were preparing to depart. The snow on
Changtse is so deep and soft that the climbers had to posthole, and
couldn't make it. We also passed the Canadian Everest Express team,
on its way toward our Camp III, to climb one of the couloirs on the
Northeast Face leading to the Pinnacles. They're going to have a tough
climb. They had hoped to do a less dangerous route in the same area
but lacked the proper documentation; the easier route was permitted
to the Japanese team for preparation for a winter ascent. The Japanese
have now arrived, so the Canadians get a leftover couloir.

Several good luck messages have been relayed to us. Word is out
in the States that this is our summit week. Yak and David Padwa,
manning our TCS-9000, are going to get lots of calls. If only those
callers knew how much the summit depends on the weather.

The stretch up the glacial moraine from Camp II to Camp III looks
different. Most of the seracs have been deformed by continual melting. Several have disappeared. Again we did the section in record
time. I felt terrific when we arrived at ABC. I am secretly quite pleased
with myself. Perhaps I've succeeded in properly pacing myself, being
in top shape for the most important climbing now to be done.

As I was hiking up from Camp II, I thought about the last time
that I had done the same section. It had been September 15, the ninth
day of our load carrying to ABC. I hadn't been strong enough to climb
with the rest of the climbers and I had struggled along by myself,
exhausted and depressed. I wanted to quit. Now, weeks later, tough-
ened by the Everest crucible, both my mind and my body are in
excellent shape. I finally feel that I'm doing my share and that I am

really a part of this team. And I think my teammates feel the same way.

When we arrived at ABC, Bob Skinner was sitting in front of the mess tent with binoculars, watching the North Col and the ridge. We could see Handwerk, McNally, and Burbank putting up a tent at Camp V at 25,500 feet on the only flat spot on the North Ridge. Our route follows the North Ridge up and joins the Northeast Ridge above the Pinnacles. There it veers right, through the First and Second Steps, to the summit. By the time the Cowboys go to dinner tonight, Camp V will be installed.

Bob had really hot-footed it up to ABC after the arguments on carries versus R&R. It's clear to me that Bob had been very worried about safety on the Col and about the health of climbers who have stayed at high altitude. He feels personally responsible for the life of every person on the team. He had been anxious during the days he'd been forced to stay at Base Camp. Bob wants to be on the scene and take the responsibility he knows is his. Now he appears to be some-what relieved, in that the Col looks stable, and with Camp V set, we are in position for a realistic assault on the summit. He admitted to me that when we'd been two weeks late arriving at Base, he thought we could have bagged it right then. But now that we've made up time and the weather is holding, I sense an undercurrent of optimism in that stoic demeanor.

I can't tell whether he hates the job or relishes it, but Bob is always the one who has to come down hard on any climber who is not relentlessly and unfailingly giving his or her utmost for the team. In a weak moment he admitted that if he were to do it again, he'd rather not have the same assignment. "By the requirements of the job and by my own personal nature, I find myself always gnashing my teeth, always focusing on people's weaknesses, to find a way to make each person a stronger, more committed team player. I just can't be satisfied with less than the best effort, and of course, I know a lot of our decisions are unpopular." Calling himself a "raging beast," he really does hammer on us to get the team pulling together. Although he knows that each person has to regulate his own development, he also knows that each person has to reach down inside and come up with more than he thinks is possible.

Bob wants the summit team to stay in ABC tomorrow. I don't mind. My legs, being the combined age of 102, could use the rest before we start the ice-climbing routine again. The concern that the Skinners continue to express is that over 20,000 feet our bodies will disintegrate rapidly. We will get weaker each day. I'm worried about the cold, too. Our guys are saying that it is bone-chilling on the Col. Dave McNally had to come down because he didn't have his over-boots. He had on supergaiters, the insulated gaiters that go over our insulated climbing boots, but that wasn't enough.

I'm thinking carefully about my warm clothing. I will wear a Wild Things high-altitude suit, which I won't take off until I'm back down to ABC. The suit fits over a Makalu high-altitude parka. Underneath I'll wear either one set of expedition-weight underwear and a pile suit or two sets of expedition-weight underwear. I'll have gaiters, over-boots, gloves, overmitts, balaclavas, hats, face masks, goggles. No area of skin will be left exposed. Skin freezes in sixty seconds at minus 20 degrees F. At the same temperature, if a thirty-mile-per-hour wind comes up, exposed flesh can freeze in thirty seconds. We will need our special Dana packs, designed to carry the oxygen units. Food, sleeping bags, and oxygen cylinders will have been placed at the higher camps by our advance teams. I will carry my survival gear en route, including my down bag, which I will probably need to survive in each camp. I am ready to go. I'm excited and I flat out can't wait to get up there for our summit attempts.

8 P.M. The route through the Col looks safe. The snow on the North Ridge looks solid—no postholing. The biggest concern is the wind. Ted Handwerk said the wind at Camp V yesterday was sixty miles per hour. That's about all you can take and still stand up. If it gets higher, it could create insurmountable problems. We are also experiencing some attrition. Mark Pilon went to Base because of severe headaches. Anne Stroock has had to descend because of what seems to be a slight case of pulmonary edema. Quintin and Ethan are not well. They are both strong climbers and their loss will hurt us. Bob Skinner still doesn't look like he's gotten back to normal.

I hope Anne gets back up here. She quit her job at a Wyoming television station and moved to Pinedale to work on the expedition. Originally she signed on as a cook. When Steve Marts joined us to do the video, Anne became his right hand. Steve has probably shot more high-altitude documentary films than any other Himalayan climber. He has cast his experienced eye upward from this exact spot before. Steve and Anne got to ABC early and Anne's been up here close to a month. She has done several carries up the Col, and she and Steve have the video set up at Camp IV so that Steve can stay in his tent and keep a camera trained on the summit teams all the way up the North Ridge, the Northeast Ridge, to the summit.

Anne is always upbeat, works hard at whatever she's doing, and adds zest and humor to every situation. She's also bright (a Williams College grad) and has both feet planted firmly on the ground. Not being an experienced mountaineer, she happily admits that she has surpassed even her highest expectations in climbing to Camp IV. She goes into one of her infectious laughs when she describes the thrill of getting to the top of the Col for the first time and then realizing she couldn't see a thing—she'd reached her 23,500-foot milestone in a total whiteout. "I didn't care, I was soaring five hundred feet above the clouds anyway!" My guess is she'll whip the edema and get back here before we leave the mountain.

Ted Handwerk, my former roomie, has left ABC to work up at Camps IV and V and help push on to Camp VI. My new roommate is Carl Coy. It amuses me how we all move in and out of tents and sleep with a different person, male or female, each night. Elsewhere such behavior might be frowned upon; here it's business as usual. It's a good way to get to know people.

It is probably twenty degrees colder here at ABC than it was a week ago. That's what happens in October. The arrival of the Japanese team that's come to set up for their winter ascent reminds us that winter is not far off.

Living on the edge of Mount Everest made me think of the many red ant colonies on the ranch where I grew up. As a child I would watch the ants building the mounds of dirt at the entrances to their underground labyrinths. I even had an ant farm so that I could study the subterranean tunnels. But my brother and I had no qualms about stepping on ants. Sometimes Pete and I poured fuel into the ant holes and burned all the ants out, simulating major catastrophes to humankind. Life is insignificant to the greater force that perpetuates the disaster, whether it's fire, earthquake, or avalanche. Here, to see a person on the top of the North Ridge, against the backdrop of Mount Everest brings clearly into focus the awesome exposure a climber faces. Either the forces cooperate or we get killed.

Tension in camp is mounting. Tempers are short. With the need to conserve energy now paramount, each climber seems less willing to step up to perform a camp chore. Everyone is getting worn as we who are left start the most dangerous part of our trip. We won't know who will go on what summit team, on what day, until we get above Camp IV. There remains the possibility that those who have been designated for the summit will be told that they are not going, that someone else is stronger. There remains the possibility that one team will have good weather and the next team will have a bad day. There remains the possibility that we'll be weathered out entirely.

Carl came off the Col today, exhausted and still numb from the cold. When he came into our tent, he flopped down on his bag and stated succinctly: "It's a bitch up there."

After giving him a chance to catch his breath, I asked him for more information.

"The daytime temperature is down to ten below," he said, "and the winds have picked up, even below the ridge. Carrying loads is inhuman. It's almost impossible to stay warm."

While he's talking, I'm thinking: I am cold *here.* I am going to need everything that I can possibly put on my body to stay warm. In my bag right now, which is rated to minus 40 degrees, I have on a Capilene undershirt, expedition-weight underwear, a down vest, pile pants, and two pairs of wool socks. Both my Makalu and my down jackets are thrown atop my bag. I also have a hot water bottle in the bottom of the bag to warm my feet. I know that one of my biggest challenges will be keeping my fingers and toes warm. I've had mild frostbite two or three times before. My feet get cold if I drive north of Fort Lauderdale.

It's discouraging to see some of our strongest climbers, like Carl, showing the withering effects of having been at altitude for so long. Carl rotated through Base Camp for R&R, as I did, and he's been back only a day or so, gone only once up to the Col, and he's exhausted.

Brian McLean looks tired, too. Even Mack seems to be going slower. Clearly, we don't have a plethora of climbers with great reserves of strength. Since there is no recovery here at 21,000 feet, if someone is shot, he's shot. *Fini.* Jeb's team is coming up from below, which will give us a little strength, but we may not have enough climbers to get everything as high as we would like for the summit attempts.

Every night at dinner, the conversation commences with an accounting of each climber's health. Each recites a litany of ailments, which is met with understanding and sympathetic nods. Self-help remedies are exchanged, and attention then shifts to the climb. Tonight Brian reported, "We've got a good facility at Camp IV now. Four tents are in, plus the large cooking tent. We can sleep twelve and more if we need to."

"We got two tents up to Camp V," Carl said. "I didn't think it would take that long to get up the ridge to our site."

"How long was it?" I asked.

"It's a tough two thousand feet," Mack answered, "probably four or five hours. The wind is a problem."

Damn, I'm thinking. If it is four or five hours for these guys, it's six or seven for me. I'm pleased with the progress, though. With Camp V in at 25,500 feet, we have only 3,500 feet to go.

OCTOBER 2, 1988. ABC. Another rest day. Brian's team will try to put in Camp VI tomorrow. The summiters will stay here tomorrow and go up the next day.

Ted just came down from Camp V and stopped by to get some things that he left in my tent. He's on his way down to Base, coughing blood. With a punctured lung, he's all through. He looks rotten. He's pale and moves pathetically slowly. His spirit, however, is as strong as ever.

"Sue," he said, "we've hauled every single bit of gear on our backs, we've secured a safe route through the North Col, and we've gotten the next two camps set in on the North Ridge. We've come 13,000 miles and we have about a half-mile to go. I'm really proud of the Cowboys. Particularly, I'm proud of my team. What a great job they did! I'd climb with them anywhere." I nodded assent and sat up in my bag. "But I'm worried about the timing now," he continued, "and how weak everyone's getting. We've still got a good shot, but it's got to be soon, before it gets any colder, and before the winds pick up more. You know, if we'd had Sherpas, we'd have been to the top. I'm sure of it. We had the climbing strength and we had the weather. I sure wish I didn't have to go down." With that he ducked out of the tent.

According to Ted, Camp IV is comfortable and Camp V is habitable, but windy. Take every bit of warm clothing, he advised. The winds, over sixty miles per hour, are now the challenge. If they continue, it is not likely that we can do it. By arriving late and not using Sherpas' help, we have literally cast our fate to the winds.

I feel bad for Ted. He has worked for years on this expedition and now he has to descend a few days short of the finale. I stuck my head out of the tent flap. "Thanks, Ted," I said, "Thank you very much for everything you did to get us to this point." But he was already gone, starting the long, lonely walk through the moonscape to Base.

Ted is right. The length of time we've all spent over 18,000 feet is taking its toll. The cold weather setting in will exacerbate our decline. This mountain pokes and prods until it ferrets out any weaknesses in any human body. Yak was ill last night. He's going down today. Quint Barney left. Ethan is not feeling well and may have to go down. Jimmy Robinson looks like a ghost with blue lips—the telltale sign of oxygen deprivation. Everest is sapping our strength. As we head into the final days here, we are saying a lot of prayers for the weather, and for all of us to hold out and return in good health.

It was a bitterly cold, windy day at ABC. Mark Twight and Barry Blanchard of Everest Express started up their couloir today and had to turn back because of the cold and the winds. I'm told that Mark is one of America's best climbers, so it's not terribly encouraging to me that they had to turn back.

This was the day that the Georgia team's attempt on the East Face was finally thwarted by the winds and a massive avalanche that wiped out their high camp at 24,000 feet. Joe Dinnan, the Georgia expedition leader, recounted later the "total terror" of fighting avalanche after avalanche, as the fair weather of September slipped into the arctic cold of October.

Fresh troops have arrived—Dan, Astrid, and Betty Bohus. Betty was in great spirits, but she is nauseated and vomiting tonight. She hasn't had as much acclimatization time as the rest of us. We also had a visit today from the other American team that attempted Changtse but was turned back by deep snow. There are no successes on this side of the mountain yet.

We got word on the radio today that Ross Greenlee has left Base Camp for Kathmandu with the West German girl, who is seriously ill. He will not be back. With Sheri King at Base, that leaves only Bob Bohus, on the medical side, on the upper reaches of the mountain.

Our weather report is for continuing high winds. Bad news. We are going to have to push hard and fast. The present plan is that tomorrow Brian's team, which has been our strongest, will start for Camp VI. If they make it, two of the guys will drop back to V, and if the remaining four are in good enough shape, they will make an immediate summit attempt. If only four people get to VI, two will drop back to V, and the two strongest will have the shot at the summit. The first summit team will be followed, presumably, by another team, which would include, if they're all healthy, four of the original six summiters. Since I am not one of the strongest six, I would not make that round. If we still have time, maybe I would get a chance. Or if somebody has a problem and I stay healthy, I may get moved up. The odds are getting slimmer. I feel the best that I have felt since leaving the United States. I would love a chance. But I want a team success more than anything. Keep it in perspective, Sue. Getting as high as safety allows will be a thrill. We've said from the beginning that our goal is to get everyone home—no fatalities and no serious injuries. We don't want to stretch ourselves out above the Col in high winds and double-digit below-zero temperatures to the extent that someone gets killed. Bagging the summit isn't worth it.

Carl and I have retired to our tent. Mixed with the tension and excitement in camp is considerable introspection. There's not one person on this mountain who is not looking forward to getting back to his or her loved ones. While we were preparing for bed Carl started to talk about his family. "My son Ryan is 4 years old today. I wish I could be with him. Someday maybe he'll understand. I also miss my wedding anniversary by being on this trip. Fortunately, my wife does understand." Carl's last words were not, however, said with total conviction.

"Can anyone who does not climb mountains really understand?" I asked.

"I don't know," came the quiet response. "I really don't know."

OCTOBER 3, 1988. Team Four, including Carl, has gone up. They won't be off the mountain until the job is done. If all goes well, they will get Camp VI set for our potential summiters, who could still include me. Bob Bohus is having second thoughts about going up, even though he might have the best shot for the top, with Mack. I don't know how Mack's feeling, but I just stopped to talk to Bob. He was sitting on a rock outside the mess tent. Yesterday he had said he didn't feel well and today he looks pretty blue. "How're you feeling, Doc?" I asked as I sat down next to him.

"Not too well. I'm not sure I should try to go up again."

"I'm sorry to hear that. Any edema signs?"

"No, I'm just feeling pretty shot. You know, after I left my down pants and Gore-Tex suit and camera at Interim, I began to wonder if I wasn't showing signs of mental decline. I know I need those things up high, but I just forgot all about them."

It was worth worrying about. Oxygen deprivation to the brain causes atypical behavior. Probably more deaths are attributable to errors in judgment and outright climbing mistakes from a muddled mind than from the objective dangers of avalanches, crevasses, falls, and other traumas. I thought about Marty Hoey's failure to double-back her harness belt. As a physician, Bob has studied the effects of oxygen deprivation.

I wondered, too, whether the presence of his wife in camp might cause Bob to rethink the risks involved in a summit attempt. After all, he knows that for every climber who makes it to the top of Everest, one dies trying. Would the thought of Betty watching and listening at ABC be enough to dissolve the resolution of this strong, gentle man?

Whatever the reason, Bob definitely does not look up to climbing today. Perhaps it would be best for the team if he chose not to go, because he is our sole physician. Knowing Bob, I'm sure he's considering that, too. "Don't go if you're not feeling up to it, Bob," I said. I was remembering Lou Whitaker's words: "There are only two kinds of climbers: old climbers and bold climbers. There are no old, bold climbers."

8 P.M. This afternoon I took my hardware and personal gear to the cache tent so that tomorrow, when I take a couple of the British cylinders of oxygen, I won't have such a heavy load—at least for the first two miles. Then it's up the Col again. The hardware weighs a lot. My crampons, waist belt, carabiners, figure-eight, ascender, the safety webbing, and miscellaneous items easily add up to ten to twelve pounds. It was not an easy hike. The day before I went down to Base for R&R, that hike took me less than an hour and a half; today, over two and a half hours. Carrying a forty-pound pack really makes a difference. I also fell once. I slipped on the ice in a relatively flat spot. I wonder if I'm losing strength. It's a haunting little thought.

I ran into Doug Burbank at the cache tent. He just finished his last carry on the Col. He has worked hard for the team and is going to spend the next few days finishing his geological research. I can tell by the smile on his face and the bounce in his step that he's glad to be going down. He's dodged the bullet.

We leave tomorrow for Camp IV. Going up the Col will be difficult with my bulky pack. Camp IV is fit to sleep twelve, so when we do get there, it should be reasonably comfortable. Jim Robinson suggested to Julie that she take one of the 36-inch aluminum pickets so that if the wind gets too bad, she can pound the picket in, clip herself to it, and not get blown off the mountain. That's a little scary. If the wind gets that bad, I think I am going to crawl back to the next lower camp and book a charter to Miami.

I've sealed all the tapes of my Everest diary into a weatherproof bag for transport to Base. If anything happens to me, I want them to get to Chuck. The Col has set firmly. The snow is not nearly so soft as it was before, which is tough for me because it's icier, but with more stable conditions there is less chance of avalanche. So, I expect to get through the avalanche and serac territory without mishap. The next step will be to exercise good judgment as I go higher. I am mentally prepared now not to make it to the top. I hate to say that, because that can take away some of the drive, but I am going to go as high as I can. We have been living at these weight-melting altitudes for seven weeks now and are experiencing attrition and weakness. I am apprehensive about the cold above the Col. Returning teammates have warned us that it's bitter. A couple of the guys had to come down to avoid frostbite on feet and fingers. Brian says he wakes up at least twice every night to rub his feet. Naturally such incidents inspire macabre climber jokes, like, "He who dies with the most toes, wins."

Bob Skinner carried another load up the Col today. The guy's almost 60 years old! He carries a full load, and more, and climbs 2,000 vertical feet just like the 25-year-olds, even though he hasn't been feeling well. He and Jeb, David Frawley, Rick, Alexandra, and Sibylle have returned to ABC with the latest plan. Brian, Mack, Jim Robinson, Ethan, and Carl will attempt to put in Camp VI tomorrow. My group, with Brad Werntz and Courtney, leaves tomorrow and overnights at Camp IV. If there are two strong members from Team Four available after putting in VI, they get a shot at the summit. It seems doubtful to me that they will have the strength. The day after tomorrow four summit climbers—probably Fred, Orion, Julie, and Jim Burnett—will move to Camp V. The following day they will move to VI. Their summit day is October 7. I will go one day behind them. My ability to try for the summit will depend on how well I can endure the cold and the wind when I get above the Col. Since I have lost my original summit partner, Courtney and I will climb together, and whoever is strong enough gets a chance to go for the summit.

My tent is like the inside of a freezer tonight. I have taken my warmest clothes to the cache tent, so I am going to have trouble staying warm. Having another body in this tent keeps it a lot warmer, but Carl is on the Col.

Four of our team members have had pulmonary edema, one a hole in the lung. We are all tired. No illusions now. Just the final days of hard work and due care. Our systems have been stressed close to their limits. We will be living on the edge of human survival.

The mountain is so immense and the distances so great that human frailty and accidents can't be dealt with easily. The recovery of bodies is not even attempted. We will have the greatest exposure when nobody is above us. Support from below is psychologically comforting, but if something happens, there is little chance anyone from a lower camp can climb up quickly enough to help. However, a climber who is above can descend rapidly, providing some hope of rescue. Support climbers will be above the summiters until the final night at Camp VI. Until that last day, then, if we go according to plan, I should be relatively safe.

I keep hearing the last words Chuck said to me on the phone: "Come home, sweetheart, please come home."

CHAPTER XIII

Winter Descends

OCTOBER 4, 1988. BIVOUAC AT 21,300 FEET. The wind is howling outside. It's 4 P.M. and five summit team members are huddled in the cache tent seeking protection from the hundred-mile-per-hour winds. We left ABC this morning, intending to go up the Col. Gusts pushed me out of our track into the soft snow, and I had to struggle to stay upright. By the time I got to the cache tent, I was cold and feeling rotten.

Fred started up the fixed line. He soon returned. "I couldn't keep upright on the rope," he said. "I'm over two hundred pounds with my pack, and the wind just blew me over."

But we are under orders to get to the top of the Col tonight. Courtney insisted on starting up, so Brad Werntz took off ahead of him and placed a tent about halfway up, in case Court doesn't get all the way. Courtney didn't begin the ascent until 4 P.M., and he's not a fast climber. It's likely that he'll need that tent.

The rest of us don't want to take a chance on having to overnight among the crevasses and seracs on the Col in hurricane-force winds. I'm worried about Courtney, but he's a big boy. David Frawley and Rick Dare decided to go up and left the cache tent midafternoon. They'll help try to hold down the tents at Camp IV.

The news from Penn State this morning is not good. There will be high winds today and tomorrow, with a possibility of a break later in the week. We won't know until we are higher whether the mountain is climbable. Courtney's strategy is to get us in position so that if there's a weather window, we will have a chance to make a push for the top. The Col Boys tried to take loads to Camp V today, but the winds were too high. They stashed their loads and have dropped back down to IV. There are eleven people there now, so tent space is at a premium.

It has been a bad day for me. I felt bum when I got up this morning. I was hoping that in the excitement of going up, and in the fresh air, I would feel better. I had an insignificant load to carry to the cache tent. Even with that, every step was an effort. I had a hard time breathing. The winds were troublesome. When I got to the cache tent I knew that I would not be able to climb the Col today. To say that I was disappointed in myself would be a gross understatement. I decided to lay over at the cache tent, get up early, and climb the Col tomorrow in the morning. After Fred was blown off the fixed rope, the other four summit team members decided to hold, too.

6 P.M. The situation is not good tonight. We have Courtney bivouacking at about 22,500 feet and one climber yet to be accounted for. Alexandra began a descent from Camp IV and hasn't yet reached Courtney. She doesn't have a radio and it's unclear whether she has a headlamp or proper clothing. We're concerned. It's almost dark, the winds are still gusting sixty to eighty miles per hour, and the ambient temperature has probably dropped to minus 10.

I am worried about my health, too. I seem to be okay lying here inside my sleeping bag, but getting up takes everything out of me. Jim Burnett has been fixing hot drinks and I've had a cup of soup and some tea. I must feel better tomorrow. I must get up the Col and go on to Camp V.

What if I get hypothermic again? I had the feeling today that it wasn't far away. Climbing the Col should keep me warm, but if I can't move fast enough, I could be in trouble. I am also having problems with my ribs, which have hurt so much since I went down to Base Camp. When I fell on the ice yesterday, I exacerbated the problem by jamming a ski pole into my side. Any movement is excruciatingly painful. That I can deal with, but hypothermia will take me out of the picture.

Everyone's tired. There was so much lethargy inside this tent this

As weather conditions and my health deteriorate, I continue to wonder whether I'll make the summit. PHOTO BY JEB SCHENCK.

afternoon that we couldn't even get through one round of Password. Orion suggested that we play cards, but when he got his cards out, nobody got as far as shuffling them.

Good news! Alexandra has reached Courtney's tent on the Col. Court called us on the radio moments ago and said that he will follow her down—a wise decision. She does not have a light. Courtney has given her a red emergency blinker so that if she gets into trouble, she can flash us at the cache tent. Now we're all peeking out of the tent watching for a red light. Alex is apparently in good shape and both of them will stop in here for some hot tea on the way to ABC.

9 P.M. More bad news: a radio message has just come in from the top of the Col that David and Rick have not arrived. That's astounding—they left about 2. The weather has taken a turn for the worse, and conditions are deteriorating rapidly. The winds are hellacious, and it has started to snow. With dropping temperatures and wind-blown snow, we're hoping David and Rick get to Camp IV soon. We will monitor our radio until we hear that they have arrived safely. Soon Mack will start descending to look for them and will radio us if he needs help. Courtney and Alex have passed through and are headed to ABC.

9:35 P.M. David and Rick made it into Camp IV, so everybody's accounted for. We're ready to sack out. The cache tent can sleep five comfortably, except now we share space with several packs as well as all the climbing gear and equipment that's been stashed here. With a little maneuvering we can stretch out. I am against the entry flap on the windward side of the tent. I've piled a couple of packs between the tent wall and me. The wind is ferocious, shaking the tent violently.

OCTOBER 5, 1988. ABC. What a horrendous night. The wind howled unrelentingly, tearing at our tent, probing for weaknesses. The fly on my side and a portion of the ceiling ripped apart. Snow was blowing in at both entryways and through the ceiling. This particular tent is not designed for 21,000 feet, but it's so spacious that we wanted to use it for stash purposes and for an emergency bivouac, which was our need last night. Several times, the power of the wind bent the tent poles horizontally and both the frame and the fabric were pushed flat against us. The tent wall would lie across me, covering my face. When the gusts abated, the poles would pop back up and the tent would resume its original shape. Blowing ice crystals were hitting my face through the tent membrane. I got up and moved my feet around to where my head had been, because it felt like I was being smothered when the tent covered my face. Not that any of my buddies would have noticed—all four of them were burrowed way down inside their bags trying to stay warm. With the spindrift covering them, they looked like moguls on a ski run.

The winds never let up. Amazingly, the tent stayed in place despite major rips and two broken poles, one of which had gone through the ceiling. Inside, we looked as if we had slept outside in the snow. Everything—climbers, gear, cooking equipment, packs— was covered with two to three inches of snow. It took a while to shake ourselves out.

I was desperately hoping that we would be able to get up in the morning and go right up to Camp IV, but the visibility is poor, with high winds, blowing snow, and avalanches on the Col. Camp IV reported in at the 9 A.M. radio call among us, the North Col, and ABC. They had a miserable night, too, with winds gusting over one hundred miles per hour.

Ethan told of trying to go from Camp IV to Camp V yesterday.

"Twenty feet out of camp we were getting blown around so that we had to plant our ice axes, hunker over them, and hang on for dear life. It got worse and worse. We could hardly stay on our feet. The terrible thing was we couldn't rest at all. It took every muscle we had and all the strength we had just to hold on. It was incredibly exhausting." Lou Whitaker called the winds on this route in 1984 "more powerful and more constant" than anything he'd ever seen. Marts's video that year was entitled *Winds of Everest*.

"Don't kid yourself about a two-day window," Ethan continued. "It's going to be real hard to punch this thing through. It's going to take both a weather window and strong climbers. It's going to be a bitch from V to VI. There's not going to be any retreat from VI to IV. Our climbers are going to be *way* out—really out on a limb."

Since no one can move on the Col today, we five will return to ABC. Tomorrow, weather permitting, we'll go back up. I am sorry that we have to lose ground, but I don't feel well. In fact, I feel rotten. I hurt. The possibility of reaching the summit is diminishing daily. My strength is less every day and the weather is worse every day. That combination pretty much precludes back-to-back 1,800-foot ridge walks for me, even if I get to Camp V.

My body doesn't have enough fuel or heat-generating capacity to keep me warm. This morning at the cache tent, when I woke up, my toes felt frozen. I rubbed them for over an hour, but they did not warm up until three hours later, after I had hiked all the way down to ABC. Inside my bag I'm still cold. The inability to generate heat is a serious problem here because one can so quickly become hypothermic. If there is no source of external heat, hypothermia is inevitably fatal. As weak as I am now, if there is any real wind, I can't justify trying the last 3,500 feet above Camp V. I couldn't protect myself, I couldn't protect a partner, I couldn't help a partner, and in all likelihood, a partner couldn't help me. I am going to rest today and tonight, eat as much as I can, drink as much as I can, and see how I feel. I am awfully discouraged.

Steve Gardiner and Dave McNally descended earlier today from Camp IV. Steve's used up. He looks ghastly, surely pre-edema, and Dave's not far behind him. They are going to Base tomorrow. Ethan is going down too. Those guys spent a lot of time up on the North Ridge and they all look like refugees from a concentration camp. The summit climbers are standing by now at ABC. I don't think Bob Bohus is prepared to go back up. Fred and Orion are hanging tough. Orion grew up in the Skinner environment, where everybody's tough. He had pulmonary edema on Aconcagua, but he seems to be doing all right here. Fred's been through many Wyoming winters with the Skinners and he's climbed McKinley, a good, long-haul test. He's strong, but has to be concerned about edema, too, since he had cerebral edema on Aconcagua. Jim Burnett and Julie are quietly going about their preparation. They seem to be in fairly good shape, but it's hard to tell about someone else's condition. I'd say Mack has the best chance to make it. He's at Camp IV now. He's been working hard for the team and he's an extremely strong climber, competent and self-confident. Brian or one of the Col Boys may be strong enough, but they all may have spent too much time at altitude. I sure hope they make it, though, because they deserve to. If any of the rest of us get a chance, that'll be gravy.

Coming down to ABC from the cache tent, I had a recurring fantasy that I gave Dan Pryor a message to call Chuck at home and tell him that I was off the mountain, that I was safe, and that my Everest climb was over. An appealing thought, but it made me break down in tears because I don't want this to be over until I do better than I have so far. I am not through trying.

Besides, I feel better tonight. We had a sensational dinner. We have adopted John, one of the support members of the Canadian Everest Express team, who is a fine cook. There were about eighteen of us at dinner, including a couple of guys from Everest Express, the halt and the lame from the Cowboy team, as well as the summit group. A few days ago David Frawley went down below the Rongbuk Monastery, bought a lamb, slaughtered it, and carried some meat up to ABC. John fixed roast lamb, rehydrated peas, mashed potatoes, and canned fruit. It was the best meal I've eaten in weeks.

8 P.M. I am in bed with several layers of clothes on and everything else I own thrown on top of my bag to keep out the cold and wind. There is three inches of new snow on the ground. We are worried about the condition of the Col. Our only chance now of getting someone to the summit is a weather window. We have to get someone in position and ready to go if the window opens. We can't stay all winter. We have been advised by Penn State that squalls will continually come through, but between squalls there may be brief respites. *Brief* is a bad word. We need at least three to four good days.

All the delays of getting to Base Camp put us far behind schedule, and now, in early October, the snow and wind are slowing our progress. At Advanced Base Camp we're resting before making a renewed effort to establish higher camps.
PHOTO BY JEB SCHENCK.

The Cowboys have done so many things I won't think of the expedition as a failure if we can't summit. Even today, when the weather was horrible, Doug Burbank was out climbing the area around ABC to collect geology samples to continue his research. Steve Gardiner, so drained he hardly has the energy to speak, sits in his tent drafting lesson plans to educate his students about China, Tibet, the Himalayas. That makes me feel better. I am proud of the team for getting the camp in at 25,500 feet. We still may get higher. It's not over, but knowing we will be leaving soon, I am beginning to reflect on this journey. The best part is just trying . . . trying to do something so incredibly physically demanding and logistically complicated. There's considerable satisfaction in getting this far, climbing as high as we have, and testing ourselves at every step.

The worst part—by a large measure—is being away from my family this long and knowing that I am causing them such worry. I had no idea how homesick I would be. At the same time I felt isolated from the team. The Sisyphean solo walks up the moraine exacerbated my loneliness, and precluded any opportunity to get to know my teammates, to become friends with anybody. That was hard. It almost broke my spirit. I was also concerned about the publicity that was focused on me, as opposed to the team, and about failure. Now when I think about how difficult climbing this mountain is, not just for me, but for everybody, I know that each step is a victory and that not making it to 29,028 feet is not a failure. Anyone who wants to be a critic should spend a few days here.

It has also been a pleasure to watch the Skinner brothers bring this operation into being, to have it unfold before our eyes, with all the disappointments and hardships, and to see the successes. With this expedition they have touched a lot of lives. As with most Himalayan expeditions, there has been considerable criticism of the leadership. Some perhaps valid, some not. The route itself has made team communication a problem. We are spread out over many miles, with little opportunity for all of us to come together and pull in the same direction at the same time, and little opportunity for discussion and explanation of sometimes unpopular leadership decisions. Group consultation and unanimity on all issues are not possible on the Northeast Ridge route.

Will I do it again? No. I've had this experience. It's too big a sacrifice for my family, and that is too big a sacrifice for me. Lying here tonight I can't think of a single rational reason why a middle-aged housewife would want to do this twice. I have been honored to be on this team; I was pleased by the selection as a summit climber, by the faith put in me. I have been overwhelmed by the outpouring of good wishes and prayers from those who knew I was challenging the highest mountain in the world. Overwhelmed. The experience has been a nine-plus out of a possible ten. But no, not again.

OCTOBER 6, 1988. 2 P.M. We can't move again today. The weather is clear and brittle, with high winds. We may have been able to get to Camp IV today, but there is no sleeping space unless the climbers now at Camp IV can move up to Camp V. They have radioed down that the wind conditions on the ridge are beyond human tolerance.

In the several meetings we had this morning, we changed our plans to suit the mountain. The climbers now at Camp IV—Brian, Carl, Mack, Jimmy, Steve, Jeb, Rick, David, and Dr. Bob—have become the summit team. We at ABC are the support climbers. If they can't move within the next day or two, they will have to come down. We will then go up and would again be the summit team.

If we try to climb tomorrow, we may have problems on our route. Bob Skinner went to look at the Col today and thinks there are some spots that could let go. The guys will first have to down-climb from Camp IV to kick loose potential avalanches and dig out the ropes.

This morning after breakfast I told Courtney that if we're off the mountain, I plan to leave with George McCown to get to Kathmandu by October 15. That did not please him. Even though I am not instrumental in getting the team packed up and out of Base Camp, he feels we should stay together. I agree, but I probably won't do it. If I can't meet George, I will try to arrange a jeep to get to Kathmandu (while patting myself on the back for having gotten a Nepalese visa while I was in Lhasa). I left a note at Base for George to the effect that if I don't get there before the trekkers leave, to have Bob Fleming leave me the number of a telephone contact in Kathmandu that can help me arrange transportation in Nepal.

When I returned to my tent to rest, I had a curious experience. I decided that I would change the inner boots in my climbing boots. I've been wearing some new expedition-issued Koflax double boots, which I'd acquired when the company gear arrived at Base Camp. They are lime green and, I must say, pretty classy looking. They have both regular inner boots and special aveolite inners for extreme cold.

I hadn't yet put in the aveolites. Much to my consternation, I discovered that I have two left boots and two left inners. Not only that, one of my boots is a 7½ and one is a 9½. But my unused pair of aveolites have a left and a right, both size 7½. I don't know what I am going to do. It's both a practical problem and a humiliating one. Can you imagine climbing Everest with two left feet . . . and not even noticing it?

5 P.M. I've figured out what happened. When we stayed at the cache tent last night, there was an extra pair of boots, exactly like mine, in the tent. They were lime-green Koflax with Chouinard Super-Gaiters the same color as mine. When I woke up yesterday morning, I picked up one boot that wasn't mine. I didn't recognize that it was a size and a half bigger than my right boot because my feet were numb with cold. Obviously, my mind was, too. I even adjusted the crampon for my right boot, (which I thought I'd done properly only the previous day), but I didn't dwell on it—I was too maladjusted to figure it out. I'm relieved: at least I haven't been climbing for two months with two left boots. At dinner I told the story on myself. The guys roared. It seems that Ross had left his climbing boots at the cache tent when he descended to Base.

"When you left the cache tent," Julie said, "I thought something looked funny about the way you were walking. I started to say, 'Sue, if you can't walk straight going down, you'll never be able to climb back up.' But I didn't want to make fun of you because you looked so utterly miserable." More laughter.

But for all the hilarity, this isn't a joke at all. It is exactly the kind of thing that happens to an oxygen-deprived brain at high altitude, not unlike Bob Bohus's forgetting to bring his down pants and Gore-Tex suit for our final summit days. It is a warning, Sue: you are beginning to make mistakes.

I've been resting now all afternoon. I haven't picked up anything heavier than my water bottle. I did put some more sponsor patches on my high-altitude suit. When I found out that I didn't have to actually sew them on, but that I could put them on with shoe glue, I happily pasted patches all over. I'm a walking advertisement. In my days of competitive athletics, everybody was an amateur. In tennis, for instance, we couldn't do any advertising. Here we want to do all the advertising we can for our sponsors. I may turn out to look like Mario Andretti.

The wind has blown away all the clouds. It is clear and sparkly blue, but fiercely cold and ferociously windy. It was minus 22 degrees last night. Tonight, I'll be cold, even wearing everything I have, including my down coat. My clothes and I share space in the bag with my boot inners, extra socks, one or two water bottles, my tape recorder, my flashlight, some extra batteries, and a tube of face cleanser—everything I don't want frozen. My down bag is inside a bivvy liner, which adds a windproof layer. My Makalu jacket and high-altitude suit are stretched over me. I will wear a Synchilla hat and draw the hood and collar of my bag tightly around my head and face, leaving only a tiny air passage lined up with my nose.

On this little rise above the rest of Camp III, my tent is situated perfectly to intercept the wind. Between gusts, I can hear what sounds like a freight train—the wind rushing down the cirque to find me. It gets louder and louder, then slams into my tent, causing everything to shake and rattle and roll. Then all is still again. Once in a while, when it's quiet, instead of the freight train I hear a gunshot sound piercing the night—the distinctive crack of the glacier. Occasionally a lone rock bounces down, but with everything frozen solid now, there is little rockfall. Tomorrow is October 7: sixty-seven days on the road, forty-four nights in my sleeping bag.

OCTOBER 7, 1988. Changes every day. Brian, Jim, Mack, and Carl have descended. The new plan: the Col Boys go to Interim tomorrow for a couple of days' rest. David Frawley and Rick Dare are to hold Camp IV tonight. The summit team will battle up the Col and take over Camp IV. Then we'll wait for a weather break to go to Camp V. We will do everything we can to consolidate Camp V and establish Camp VI. Brian's team will be back to IV in four days. If we have no chance for a summit attempt, perhaps Brian's team can try an alpine ascent. Time has about run out. Our yaks arrive in three days to take the first load of gear down.

Team Four looks shell-shocked, all evidencing the telltale fatigue of hypoxia. They think they can get back up one more time, even though the conditions are more than formidable. They talk in awe about the winds.

"Man, I flew fifteen feet on one gust," Jeb said. He's six-five and 200 pounds. "Answering nature's call is a real act of bravery. I had to plant my ice axe all the way in and fasten my safety belt to it. I didn't want to take off in that position."

Camp IV at 23,500 feet on top of the North Col. Cowboy footprints are discernible on the North Ridge route rising in the background. PHOTO BY CARL COY.

"We've got to restake the tents here, just as we did up there," said Brian. "Check the anchors, guys. And make sure the flys are secure. Do you see any weak seams? If there's even a small rip, the wind will shred the whole tent to pieces."

"Wind isn't our only problem," Mack told me. "There was a small avalanche over the route. We had to dig the ropes out just to get down." I must have looked worried, for he quickly added, "It's okay, Sue. The anchors are still good. If we don't have another storm tonight, you'll be going up to Camp IV tomorrow."

During our conversation Anne Stroock returned from Base Camp. I knew she would—she's tough. She came into ABC smiling, as always.

"Chuck called two days ago," she said.

"Did you talk to him? Does he know we're okay?"

"He talked to Padwa. I'm sure David told him we have been stopped by the wind. But he won't know that you're going up tomorrow."

I sent a message to David today with Doug Burbank, who will reach Base sometime tonight. I've asked David to let Chuck know that I will not be able to go out with George and that it is unlikely that I can meet him in Budapest. The best I can do now is to try to make arrangements to leave shortly after we clear the mountain to get to Kathmandu and meet him sometime thereafter. I know he's worried. It's really tough on our families, since there's no specific day on which they can sigh with relief and say, "This Everest business is over. My loved one is safe."

Today is Jim Burnett's birthday and tomorrow is Jim Robinson's, so we combined the birthdays and had a party. We ate more of the lamb that David Frawley brought and an attempt at a cake by Astrid. The guys came up with some creative decorations for the mess tent. They took a dozen surgical gloves from the medical tent and blew them all up like balloons. Hanging from the ceiling in the mess tent, the distended appendages looked like a cross between bovine teats and contraceptive devices. Indelible ink enhanced the smooth surfaces with grimacing faces and unprintable phrases. It was the best we could do at partying.

The mountain has turned mean. I understand now why so many people have died trying to reach the peak. All we have to rely on is our own inner strength, and each other, to get out of here alive.

CHAPTER XIV

Blasted

OCTOBER 8, 1988. DAWN. A second false start for the summit team. Just as we were preparing to leave, we had a radio message from the Col saying that the wind has blasted most of Camp IV. Three tents are down and need extensive repair. We don't yet know the fate of Camp V. Simultaneously we had a weather report from Penn State, relayed by David Padwa, which contained some surprisingly good news: though the winds will continue to be heavy today and tomorrow, they should diminish the day after. It could remain relatively calm for the following few days. Given the tent problems at Camp IV and the prospect of diminishing winds, the summit team will remain at ABC.

We almost lost the mess tent last night and then again this morning. We have restabilized both the mess tent and the cooking tent and put a new fly on the medical tent. The old one was ripped off by the wind. It's cold. Our water sources are completely frozen over. We now have to hike about 300 yards up the hill to a ponding area where we have dug sixteen inches through the ice to a fresh water source. Hauling the volume of water that we need for drinking and cooking is not fun. As time goes by, everything gets more difficult.

5 P.M. Camp IV is wiped out. We just received the bad news from the North Col. Everything is gone but one broken and tattered, precariously clinging tent. Our weeks of work in carrying loads to the cache tent and up the Col simply blew away on vicious, invisible streams of air. Weeks of work gone. No protection left for our climbers at the top of the Col.

We will not give up. Camp V may still be in place. Tomorrow every able-bodied climber will carry replacement tents and equipment up the Col. We will establish a new Camp IV, and on the following day, Tuesday, eight climbers will try to move to Camp V. Six will stay there Tuesday night, two will descend to Camp IV. On Wednesday, six will go to Camp VI, two will descend to V, and the four strongest will have one shot on Thursday for the summit. That's it. All of our options are reduced to Thursday, October 13.

9 P.M. Those who were at the Col have come down, just barely. Mack and Courtney went out to give them hot drinks and carry their packs into ABC.

"It looks like a bomb site," said Rick when he came in. Dr. Bob cast his eye over the crew, picked out Rick as the most needy, and began examining him. "My head is killing me." He looked wasted—sunken eyes, staggering gait, white face.

"The Walrus tent is damaged. Lost its fly, too." Brian reported. "The North Face cook tent has ripped nylon, broken poles. We had restaked and reinforced every tent, but when the winds came, everything went airborne."

"Could you salvage anything?" I asked.

"The Kelty tent is the least damaged of the five," said Rick. "David started working on the cook tent and wouldn't take my advice. I told him no matter what he did, that tent was lost. I looked down to cover my face from the next icy blast, and when I looked up again, the tent was flying. It flipped and rolled several more times."

"It collapsed on itself after the wind snapped the tent poles," said David. "Incredible—just like matchsticks. We had three hundred pounds of gear inside, including oxygen tanks and radios. I just had to save it. I ran and threw myself on it, spread-eagled. Now it had almost five hundred pounds to hold it down. That sucker just lifted up and started to fly away. I didn't want a magic carpet ride two thousand feet down the Col, so I bailed."

"At one point," said Steve, "four sleeping bags went flying thirty or forty feet above our heads. I was at the same spot on top of the Col with Lou Whitaker, when we did that *Winds of Everest* video. Nineteen

Camp IV after the winds hit. A lonely Cowboy tries to salvage the last shredded tent. PHOTO BY JEB SCHENCK.

eighty-four was mild compared with what we have now. Talk about the winds of Everest! Nobody's going above the Col. Nobody."

Camp IV now consists of two tent remnants. The other three tents were destroyed, blasted by the wind. Every tent pole is broken. Half a dozen sleeping bags have been blown off. Ditto our pads, our Therm-a-Rests, our radios, our cameras, our equipment.

"We've been trying all day to rebuild," Rick said. "By midafternoon I had to take a break. Just went to my tent—what's left of it. We left David to work on a snow cave cache." Dr. Bob had given Rick morphine for the headache and was digging out a canister of oxygen for him to sleep with. "When Quint and Bob Skinner showed up with propane for the stove—we'd run out in the morning—we finished the caches and retreated. I could barely move, let alone carry down my personal gear. My head feels as if someone is blowing up a weather balloon inside and simultaneously trying to burst it with a ball peen hammer from the outside."

"Hang in there," said Dr. Bob. "The oxygen and pills will help."

We began discussing our options, now that so much of our equipment has been lost.

"Snow caves," said David. "Our only chance above the Col is snow caves. I started one and stashed what we could salvage from Camp IV. We'll never get enough equipment back up there in time for a real chance at the summit."

We adjourned, all of us hoping desperately that the forecast for diminishing winds on Tuesday and Wednesday is correct. We can't afford to lose another day. For the last few days we have been racing to the mess tent at 9 every morning to get the weather report, as if our lives depended on it. But then, of course, they do.

CHAPTER XV

The Invisible Enemy

OCTOBER 10, 1988. CAMP IVA. 7 P.M. We are a little above 23,000 feet, on a ledge just below the lip of the North Col. The top of the cirque that forms the North Col is stepped, creating a sort of double shelf where the uppermost reaches of the glacier have pulled away from the steep cirque walls. We have established Camp IVA on the lower of the two steps. The platform where our tents sit is separated from the face by a gaping bergschrund crevasse.

This time last night I was working my way up the face of the Col. We started late, and although I felt fine, Courtney insisted that I use one of the small British oxygen tanks. Nonetheless, I was not moving fast. It was turning dark just as I started up Mack's Lead, about half-way up the face. There things got a little tricky. I had run out of both oxygen and daylight. It was 1,000 feet up to safety at Camp IVA, 1,000 feet down to safety at the cache tent. The temperature was well below zero. I had no radio. I had a light but I couldn't get to it because the terrain was too steep for me to take off my pack, anchor it, and get my headlamp out. I was afraid I'd make a mistake and my pack, with my survival gear, would rocket away from me, or alternatively, that once I took the pack off, I wouldn't have the strength to get it back on. I was tired. But if I retreated, I knew I wouldn't get another chance. I elected to keep going up.

Courtney Skinner smiles, despite the wind, the cold, and our dwindling odds of reaching the summit. PHOTO BY CARL COY.

I felt my way along the fixed line. There were several spots that made me think twice. The worst was a Z-back, where the rope, at an anchor point, headed back downhill and crossed a crevasse. It was too dark to see where (or even whether) the rope was attached on the other side of the crevasse. After sitting in the darkness, pulling my mind together for as long as I dared sit still, and being sure my eyes were used to the dark, I started across the crevasse on a narrow snow bridge and hoped I'd find a rope on the other side. When there is absolutely no room for fear, I have no trouble at all focusing on the problem at hand. After twelve to fifteen feet I reached the other side. I groped around and found the next rope.

By that time Courtney, somewhere below me on the Col, Bob Skinner at ABC, and Orion and Fred at Camp IVA, had been on the radios trying to find me. I thought Courtney had seen me above Mack's Lead before I disappeared over the top. I had to keep going up. I didn't know what time it was. I didn't know if I was cold or not. I knew I could make it to our new Camp IVA if I could keep my mind together and keep moving. I climbed mechanically: one step up with the right foot; kick in; move the jumar up the fixed line with the right hand; weight it, be sure the teeth hold; move the ice axe up with the left hand, thrust into snow; lift left leg up, kick in with the left foot. Repeat. At each anchor point, don't forget to move your waist harness safety strap to the upper rope before taking the jumar off the lower rope and reattaching it above the anchor. Check your waist harness. Whatever you do, don't drop a glove. Don't stop to rest. Don't look back.

Surely, the new camp site was near. I peered up the face. It was too dark to see anything above me. I stopped to listen for sounds. Silence. I inched along in darkness.

Suddenly, from out of nowhere I heard a voice. "Sue, are you down there?" It was Orion. They had a fix on me.

I took a deep breath and yelled back as loudly as I could, "I'm below you! By the crevasse!"

"Do you need help with your pack?"

An enormous rush of relief and pleasure swept over me. "No thanks, Orion, I'm fine." I'd done it. By myself. I was safe.

I'm glad I didn't have a radio. I later learned that Bob Skinner was trying to call me to order me down off the Col. I would have had no choice but to obey.

I topped the ropes into IVA about 9 P.M., seven hours after leaving the bottom of the Col. The four summiters who had preceded me had put up three tents. Fred and Orion were in one of the Bob Skinner–designed, Thermolite-lined, three-man tents, and Julie and Jim in another. In between, they had set up a tiny two-man Snowden tent for Courtney and me. I called out my thanks, but no one responded. They must be exhausted, too, I thought. Then I realized that I was very, very cold, particularly my hands and feet. I dropped my pack, unzipped the Snowden tent, and plunged in. I lay there trying to recuperate enough to bring in my gear. It took all my will power to get up and go back out, drag my pack to the tent, throw inside what I needed, and attach the pack to the fixed line running in front of the three tents. While outside, I glanced around at the seracs towering above our camp. I wondered whether the site was secure.

When Courtney came in about forty minutes later, I had gotten only as far as getting my bag laid out.

"How you doing, Sue?"

"Fine," I said, for both our benefits. But I was shivering uncontrollably and didn't have the strength to talk. Courtney saw the familiar signs of hypothermia. He pulled his pack up to the entry, threw his things in, and fired up two of our tiny butane stoves to prepare some hot water. He made small talk and hot drinks and a couple of rounds of hot water for bottles to help my feet get warm. I stayed in my bag and mumbled. For two hours Courtney was bringing in snow, adjusting the stoves, melting water, getting it hot, and rotating the bottles to warm my feet. I was too numb to help.

The overnight temperature was 30-below. Courtney and I both wore just about everything we owned inside our bags. It was claustrophobic in our tiny tent, but intermittently, I slept. We had periodic wind gusts that shook us like an angry parent shaking a naughty child. With each gust, spindrift from the ceiling filled the tent, and icy snow sprinkled down onto my face and sneaked into the cracks that I thought I had closed. Spindrift is exceedingly clever and has the ability to find any opening in a sleeping bag. Overnight one of the tent poles broke and the roof now descends at a rakish angle, taking a quarter of my already tiny sleeping space. Our shelter is in complete disarray.

This morning I feel decent but drained. As long as I'm in my bag, I'm okay. Moving around is tiring, and I left the tent only once today for ten minutes. What a spectacular view! The terrain at this spot is awesome. Our new camp, these three little tents, occupies the only flat spot below the Col, a shelf about the size of a tennis court. The ice cliff above us gives a margin of protection from the wind blasting across the top of the Col. There is, however, no real escape. We must secure packs and all loose items to the fixed line. Immediately above is the back of the U-shaped armchair, the final 300 vertical feet of the North Col. We are separated from its icy face by an ugly, serpentining crevasse, the dimensions of which are shrouded by jumbled snow and ice. A few steps to the east of my tent is a wind cornice, a built-up snow lip, that hides the 2,000-foot fall to the cache tent below. If you sleepwalk, you're dead.

Near the back of our tent, to the left facing the Col, are what Mack and Brian and I originally thought were bodies. Pressed into the stratified ice are remnants of old expeditions: a piece of tent protruding at one level, shreds of a jacket sleeve flapping in the wind at another. Victims of the Col. About 400 feet above our camp, to the west, a few jagged rocks, too steep to hold snow, have pierced through the ice and stand over us like sentinels. Just a few steps from our tent we can see over the cornice to the cache tent site (the tent no longer exists) and all the way down to ABC. The entire East Rongbuk Valley, through which I have climbed, wanders north into Tibet, extending to the horizon. Snaking away to the northeast, through a break in the cornice, is the fixed line I ascended last night. Today the brilliant blue sky, together with the dark rocks above me, provides a sharp contrast to this starkly white world. I am transfixed.

As beautiful as our home is, it is also dangerous. We cannot stray far from our shelf. A climber on the 1976 British expedition got up during the night to relieve himself, and fell to his death in a hidden crevasse.

Anne and Steve just radioed down. They are in the last wisp of the film tent on the ridge at our old Camp IV. Yesterday the two of them were trying to salvage and reconstruct another tent; the wind tore it away last night. We have also confirmed that the tent at Camp V has been ripped out. So with the exception of the tent that Steve and Anne and the camera gear are holding down, every single Cowboy tent above the North Col has been blown away. We still have some gear and some oxygen stored at 25,500 feet, but we have no protection left on the North Ridge at all.

Interim Camp and Camp II, we learned, have also been flattened. The shelter we worked so hard to establish on this mountain has been ravaged. The summit group, including Courtney and me, are sitting here, steps from the North Ridge, with no place to go. We have enough tents and gear to take care of ourselves here, but the issue is how to safely move climbers up the mountain. Bob Skinner and five or six other climbers from ABC will try to reach us with more supplies tomorrow. If they make it, part of Team Four will stay here with us for our final push up. Any delays and we will have to back off the mountain. We know the temperatures will continue to drop and the winds will continue to rip at forty to fifty miles per hour or more.

I stayed in bed all day. Courtney did the cooking and fixed a retort dinner. Eating sufficient food is critical to survival. If the body is to generate heat, it must have fuel to metabolize. Yet cooking in frozen, oxygen-depleted, high-altitude conditions is a thankless task. Our tiny stoves rebel against normal functioning and must be kept inside sleeping bags at night. When fired up, they seem indifferent to our needs and require continuous vigilance. A meal is often two hours in preparation. As a final insult, the product resentfully slaved over emerges as an unappealing glob—and it must be eaten.

While Courtney patiently applied his culinary talents, I brought up the Cowboys' turmoil in Lhasa.

"Court," I said, "I was worried about you in Chengdu and Lhasa; you seemed pretty strung out. Now you look to be the same Cowboy I used to know."

"I guess I was really uptight," he said. "It's taken so many years to put this all together, and toward the end there—just before we left the States—I was wondering if the whole trip made any sense. We'd alienated our families, strapped ourselves financially, and it seemed to Bob and me that out of thirty-five people on the team, we were the only ones packing boxes and returning sponsor phone calls. There were so many details, we just about went nuts.

"When I got here, though," he continued, "I could feel the energy returning to my body. I've always gathered my strength from the mountains. When I was able to travel alone some of those late evenings, I could look at the views, ponder life's destiny, and know that the work and turmoil was, indeed, worth it. I feel good now."

I nodded.

"Now," he said, breaking our silence, "all we have to worry about is paying our bills."

"Not quite all, Court. We've got a summit ahead of us."

He smiled. I swear that he and his brother thrive on this cold weather. Bob Skinner was my tentmate on last winter's training climb in Wyoming. I remember one night peering out through the tent flap and watching Bob working on some of our equipment. I looked at my thermometer. It was 16 degrees below zero and he was not even wearing gloves. I am also reminded of the story of Courtney being dropped in the Antarctic with five other men and being stranded for twenty-two days. They had volunteered to band penguins and when bad weather set in, the planes that were supposed to pick them up could not reach them. Rescue helicopters were called. After the first helicopter crashed, the rescuers couldn't get another and decided to bring in an ice breaker. The *Glacier* slowly worked its way toward the stranded men but eventually had to send a small dinghy. The dinghy wasn't big enough for six men and the equipment used during the ninety days of research. Courtney wouldn't leave all the equipment behind and persuaded them to find another helicopter. It worked. The men and equipment were plucked from the ice, deposited on the *Glacier,* and transported back to McMurdo Bay. That was part of

Camp IVA was hastily established following the destruction of Camp IV. The winds that blasted Camp IV swept much of our gear into crevasses, and the need to rescue critical equipment further drained an already exhausted team.
PHOTO BY CARL COY.

Courtney's five tours in the Antarctic under the auspices of the National Science Foundation. He spent hundreds of nights doing exactly what we are doing here on Everest, winter camping. But all the cold weather experience in the world can't make Everest any warmer.

OCTOBER 11, 1988. Fred, Orion, Jim and Julie went up the North Ridge today. I didn't feel too bad, but Courtney wanted me to help him rescue some of our gear that had flown from Camp IV into the crevasse near us. We roped up, but as soon as I started to climb, I knew that I had no physical strength. Courtney directed me toward one crevasse to retrieve a bag and pad; he would belay me, paying out rope and securing me if I fell. I didn't want to let Court down, nor did I want to admit how weak I was. I gulped and chose the safer of two evils. "Courtney, I can't do it. I don't have the strength."

"Okay," he said cheerfully. "You belay me, and I'll go into the crevasse."

"Court, are you sure you want to do this?" I didn't want him to go in. I couldn't see how deep it was or where the edges were. I couldn't tell whether the snow was solid. Maybe Courtney could tell, but I wasn't confident of that, either. There's an incalculable element about the physical and mental condition of another person on the mountain. If Courtney fell, I could probably hold him, but if he was hurt, I might not have enough strength to do a rescue. He was determined, however, to salvage our equipment. He set a rope system to help me, probed with his ice axe, found a route that satisfied him, and happily descended. I was scared. If Court got into trouble, I didn't know what I was going to do. I began reviewing pulley systems in my mind and re-enacting the crevasse rescue maneuvers that we practiced on Mount Rainier. I watched as Court, now well below me, snagged a company bag. I relaxed a little. He was doing okay. Moments later Quint and Alex popped into view. Whew. Help had arrived. I would not be solely responsible for letting the expedition leader die in a crevasse on the North Col.

At the end of our two-hour equipment-rescue operation, and for the third time since October 4, hypothermia pounced. I had unroped several yards from my tent, and was coiling one of the ropes when muscle cramps throughout my body forced me to the snow in excruciating pain. As I gasped for air, the cramping settled into both legs. After torturing me mercilessly for a brief time, as cramps do, they went away. I felt drained, as if somebody had pulled a plug and all the blood had flowed out of my body. I was numb. The overwhelming cold that first makes hands and feet useless, then totally debilitates, was again taking over. I crawled on all fours to my tent and struggled into my bag.

Tonight I am in pain. I am warm enough to know I'm cold, but too cold to get warm. I've been rubbing my feet constantly. I am coughing up blood and the vision in my left eye has started to blur, obvious evidence of oxygen deprivation. Lots of warnings, Sue. How far do you go? Lie back. Rest. Think.

I have had three incipient cases of hypothermia, any of which would have been fatal had I not had help. The first one, about a week ago at the cache tent, I was chilled to the bone, lethargic, stiff, shivering. In the morning my feet were so cold that I wore two left boots the rest of the day and never noticed. Then, two days ago, climbing up the Col, my body used up all its resources. Like spindrift into a tent, the cold seeped into my limbs. I had no ability to generate heat. Today, I wasn't even out of my tent for three hours before my body revolted and collapsed. These are all warnings. When the core body temperature drops, in addition to other system malfunctions, the muscles become stiff and rigid. Uncoordinated and clumsy movement is caused when muscles are unable to contract. Cramps and spasms occur when contracted muscles are unable to relax. Muscle problems, numb feet, expectorated blood, blurred vision, and inability to generate heat—all signs of oxygen deprivation and imminent hypothermia.

I can't go higher on that ridge in this weather. I can't expect to be taken care of. I can't take care of myself or a teammate. If I'd had the strength, I would have gone down late today, when deliveries were made from ABC. Bob Skinner arrived after Alex and Quint, and I heard other voices as a fourth tent was being pitched, but I was too weak to get up. I will go down tomorrow alone. I have come up the Col by myself and I am not worried about going down by myself, if I can just get warm enough that my arms and legs will function.

I can't say enough about the care that Courtney has provided. He cares for me between all the other chores that an expedition leader has to do. Yet every night outside our tent he himself is vomiting, hoping no one will hear him.

The radio news today is that George McCown's group got to Base last night and is leaving today. Dave Padwa, Sheri King, Ethan Goldings, and Mark Pilon, for a variety of personal reasons, have also left Base Camp. Ross Greenlee left a week or so ago. Five Cowboys are gone.

It is beastly cold and getting colder every day. Jim Burnett returned to Camp IV from the ridge because of the cold. He may have frostbitten feet. Julie, Fred, and Orion will be in soon, having been unable to get to Camp V. Tomorrow, sometime during the day, when I get warm enough and strong enough to move, I will descend to ABC. Dr. Bob is still there, so at least somebody can check up on me. On the way down I will pass Brian, Mack, Jim, Carl, Brad, and Dave Frawley coming up. They are all young and strong and I hope they can still make it, despite the wind and the cold.

As I watched the other four summiters start up the North Ridge today, I had great pangs of anguish, I wanted to be there so badly. But I promised myself, and my family, that when the time came, I would use good judgment. And Bob Bohus's words rang in my ears. As I left ABC for the Col, he stopped me and said, "Sue, I'm a physician. I know what happens to bodies at altitude. The warning apparatus of pain provides a margin of safety, but for some, the desire to succeed can override the pain. You damn well better not let that iron will of yours overcome your good judgment." Same words: good judgment. I have to exercise it before I have none left.

It makes perfect sense to me that people can tolerate altitude and extreme cold for short periods, but we have been on the mountain above 17,000 feet for seven weeks, with three weeks of foreign travel and food before that. Could I have gotten higher in late September, under our original summit schedule? I could have. I was not having trouble with the altitude. My skills are sufficiently developed. The weather was good. I could have done it. Did Stacy Allison's success in becoming the first United States woman to summit take some of the drive out of me? Perhaps. I wasn't disappointed, but a little edge gave way—I knew that to have the women summit was no longer as important to the team. And I knew that Julie and I needed everyone's help to be successful.

Lying here in bed the last couple of nights, I have listened carefully to the sounds of Everest. They're crystalline in the thin, cold air. I wonder if the sounds are directed toward me. The wind blasts through on its thundering freight train, roaring in my direction, or down a nearby gully. The glacier consolidates with its gunshot crack and I wonder whether the nearby crevasse is changing its shape. Rocks torn from their precarious perches on the jagged peak crash down, and I wonder if a rock could ricochet this far. I think of David Frawley and the 500 pounds of man and gear being swooped into flight, and I wonder if our tents are well anchored. I hear a sound that differs only slightly from a disappearing jet plane, and I wonder if another avalanche has let loose. Where is it? I see in my mind the magnificent seracs and wonder how many decades, years, or hours they will stand.

From where I am lying I peek out through the tent flap to the magnificent rock buttress above me, and off to my right, to the ropes that lead home. This is elegant, magnificent, awesome territory. I don't expect ever to be here again. Suddenly, apprehension grabs me and twists my mind. I think, "What if this is the night the North Col goes?"

It's now several hours since I decided to descend. I am tired. I am still cold. I am disappointed. I am relieved.

And I'm not going down tomorrow. I will climb the North Ridge.

CHAPTER XVI

Up the North Ridge

OCTOBER 12, 1988. Hundreds of 20,000- to 25,000-foot mountain peaks lie at my feet. I am on the North Ridge heading to Camp V. There is nothing above me but the peak of the highest land mass in our world. I have shed the valleys, the rivers, the moraine, the seracs, the ice walls. I am free of all. Free to walk the broad, inviting North Ridge . . . up.

Today I had to try one more time. "He who approaches close," wrote Noel Odell in 1924, "must ever be led on . . . oblivious to any obstacle . . ." I had to get closer to the summit. As I ascend the mountain, the plains of Tibet are on my left, viewed over the huge cornice sculpted by the winds. To the right is Nepal, and beyond, India. Pumori's 23,507-foot snow-cone peak dominates the foreground just below me. Behind is Changtse. Straight ahead, the Pinnacles mark the turn up the Northeast Ridge on our route to the top of the world. The vista is nothing short of breathtaking.

Today I climbed alone one more time—by choice. I cannot trust myself to help a teammate. I want nobody's life on the line with me. While the rest of the Cowboys at IVA worked on equipment rescue, retrieving some of the gear swept off the top of the Col into crevasses, I started my climb. "Courtney," I called. "I'll be right back." He didn't try to stop me.

Rick Dare crosses the yawning crevasse on Carl's Ladder and peers 150 feet into the icy abyss. PHOTO BY CARL COY.

First I climbed the perfectly vertical 300 feet of fixed rope to the old Camp IV site. Just below the top of the Col is Carl's Ladder, bridging the last crevasse that bars access to the North Ridge. This crevasse is a heart stopper—about 150 feet deep and twenty-five feet wide. The rope ladder that so impressed me inside the ABC mess tent is no longer such a marvel of engineering. The ladder has no hand line, and the pickets that act as rungs are not bolted. Sorry, Carl, this ladder does not come close to meeting O.S.H.A. standards. It lies at an upward pitch that makes it impossible to stand up straight and walk, yet difficult to get onto all fours and crawl. First I use the "monkey technique": all fours in contact with the ladder, crampon points straddling the picket rungs, seat in the air. That isn't comfortable. I switch to the "half-crawl," letting a knee sag to a rung when necessary for balance and to keep a low center of gravity. Going hand over hand, it is impossible not to look straight down into the crevasse. Icy blue at the top, it deepens to black at the bottom. At 20 to 30 degrees below zero, if I fall in, I will not get out before I freeze. A slightly aggressive move causes the weight in my pack to shift. The ladder sways. I pause for a moment. Steady the ladder. Steady myself. Repeat. I step off and kick my crampons into the last short, steep pitch to the top of the Col.

When I edged over the lip, I was greeted by the King of the Col, Steve Marts, who had managed to burrow in among the remaining threads of his camera tent and create a homey little spot among the twisted remains of our old Camp IV. What a pro.

Steve gave me a guided tour. He identified the famous routes on Everest: the Japanese Couloir, the Horbein Couloir, the West Ridge, the North Face, others. He pointed out the spot on the North Face where Marty Hoey stepped back, leaned against the fixed rope, and disappeared forever. My eyes traveled the path of the Khumbu Glacier on the South Col route. I could see the base camp of the Spanish expedition, attempting the West Ridge right now; despite the avalanche tragedy, they continue, drawn by this mountain that has lured so many to its flanks.

I started up the North Ridge. My physical condition was nothing short of miserable. As a final indignity, I had had bad diarrhea in the morning. There was not one ounce of ingested substance remaining in my body. My peripheral vision was fuzzy. I could take only five steps at a time. Then I had to stop, bend over, rest my hands on my knees, and breathe deeply. Then I'd rise slowly, so as not to disrupt my equilibrium. Five more steps, repeat.

When I could no longer take a step, when I'd gotten as high as I was ever going to get, I turned around to look at the view—and my heart soared. For one brief moment, I *felt* as if I were on top of the world!

With what strength I had left, I began my descent. After backing down Carl's Ladder, I came to what I thought might be an insoluble problem: after all these days, after all this climbing, I had no idea how to attach my figure-eight to the rope so that I could rappel off the top. I just couldn't get my mind to work. While I was puzzling over this problem, Steve reappeared. Gently and considerately, he called across the crevasse, giving me careful verbal instructions. I rappelled into IVA. My brain was gone.

In the now-established routine, I crawl into my bag to stay the onset of hypothermia and warm the blood going to my oxygen-starved brain. I fumble around and try to start the stoves for hot water. Courtney comes in and takes over to melt snow and fix dinner. Courtney is worried about my going down alone tomorrow. I told him I was now an old pro and reminded him that the last time up, I came through some of the toughest parts of the Col in complete darkness.

Doug Burbank at Camp V. The camera can capture the spectacular view through the clouds, but it cannot convey the fury of the winds or the danger of the cold at 25,500 feet. Camp V was blown off the mountain by the same storm that destroyed Camp IV. PHOTO BY DAVE McNALLY.

"Tomorrow," I said, "will be a piece of cake. You focus on moving our team to the top."

I had little strength to talk, but I was curious about how Courtney perceived the expedition so far and the challenge to his and Bob's leadership. Though less taciturn than brother Bob, Court is not inclined to talk a whole lot. I knew his primary goal was to get everyone out alive—a job that was not yet done. I expect that both Court and Bob are disappointed in some things, like team cohesiveness, and I suspect they feel that some climbers didn't rise to meet the demands or grow into their responsibilities. I probed along those lines but got noncommittal responses. Lacking the strength to go into a full-scale cross-examination, I sank into my own thoughts.

Even though sometimes disappointed in a decision (or more often, the lack of definite direction), our team members have been loyal to the Skinners and to the multifaceted intent of the expedition. Yes, there are things each of us would have done differently, and the responses, I think, would vary among the Cowboys as to whether they'd try Everest again with the same format or the same people. I wondered how much the near certainty of not summiting inspired criticism of the leaders.

I was interested to learn, after our return, of the leadership bashing on the eminently successful Northwest American Everest Expedition. To that team's great credit, it had successful summiters (including Stacy Allison); no fatalities or serious injuries; and several physicians who saved stricken climbers and Sherpas. Nonetheless, extensive criticism of team leader Jim Frush by team members was reported in the press upon their return home: that he hired the wrong Sherpa overseer (thereby causing the team to lose additional summit chances after the weather turned bad in early October), that he was more interested in his own summit possibilities than those of the team, that he departed early from the team's base camp by helicopter with what one team member called frostnip, and so on. Frush was reported to have accepted the criticisms rather stoically, with comments to the effect that it was impossible to satisfy so many (fourteen) diverse climbers, and that when climbers are unsuccessful in achieving their own personal goals, they tend to look for a scapegoat.

Interesting comments from both sides of a team—not totally inapplicable to the Cowboys. Criticism is easy. Individuals suffering from great privation, with body systems stressed to the max, tend to exhibit a whole range of human frailties. It is one of Everest's challenges.

I couldn't solve the issues of group dynamics, so my thoughts turned to cataloging ailments from the bottom up. *Feet.* All toes on both feet are completely numb. Some have frostnip (frozen exterior tissue), but not frostbite, so they will revive over time. I will lose some toenails. *Legs.* One of my knees, twisted on the moraine below ABC, is sore, but except when bridgecrawling, it seems to be stable. *Trunk and central body.* My tummy complained vehemently for the first time today. Diarrhea, which almost everybody has had at some point, attacked unmercifully. (Not pleasant. Especially if it's below 30 degrees, with blowing snow. I won't try to describe the problems.) My ribs are still acutely painful. My cough has graduated to a blood-letting exercise, as well as an interrupter of breathing. Almost everybody gets some kind of vaginitis or crotch itch. I've got that, too (the former). No piles, though—which I know others have. *Neck and head.* A sore throat is a constant companion because of the cold, dry air. Many people have had severe headaches. I have had one or two minor ones. Retinal hemorrhaging is not uncommon. My vision is blurred. Mental confusion, lethargy, lassitude, inability to lift a crampon—these have plagued us all. Everything I've read about the effects of oxygen deprivation is true.

This is by far my worst day physically. I'm not strong enough to try a summit attempt. I peaked many days ago. I might not have made the summit, but I felt great and I could have given it an all-out try. Now I am a basket case. Great timing, Cobb. Great timing.

I am not alone, however, in this regard. Orion has developed pulmonary edema and had to descend today. Jim Burnett's doing poorly and must go down tomorrow. That leaves eight Cowboys: Court, Fred, Julie, Mack, Brian, Brad, Carl, and David Frawley for the final challenge. Maybe, if I have a good night, I can get one more day out of my body. I'd love to go up again. But Dr. Bob, by radio, has ordered me down.

What is it that causes us to want to go higher? How does it make sense to fight minus 50 degree temperatures and winds over 100 miles per hour and face death to stand on the highest spot on earth? How did this common desire and will come to be in this widely diverse, pitifully drained, last remaining handful of climbers sleeping tonight on the edge of Everest?

OCTOBER 13, 1988. 10 A.M. The climbers are ready to go. I am not fit. Jim, too, deteriorated last night. He has signs of pulmonary edema, hypothermia, and frostbite. His deterioration was rapid and surprising. Julie is upset but will continue without Jim.

No one tried to leave in the predawn double-digit below-zero temperatures. They started filtering out of camp around 10. Julie was the last to leave, at noon. Seven Cowboys. Jim would have been the eighth. I would have been the ninth. I was too weak this morning even to help boil water. All I could do was lie in our tent, look out through the fly and watch the preparation. Every time I got up to help, I became dizzy and nauseated. While just lying still in the tent, I had another retinal hemorrhage. At least I think that's what happened. My vision suddenly closed down from the outside edges inward, like a camera shutter, but slowly. It scared me. I lay still for a long time and slowly my vision began to normalize.

My worsened condition this morning is disappointing. I slept well last night and I thought there was a chance I could go up with the summit team today. It was the first night that I had oxygen. At

Courtney's urging, I used a face mask, and I slept the best I have since arriving at ABC. No waking, thrashing, turning, or kicking. I was so quiet and still that Courtney thought I had died. He told me this morning that I'd nearly scared him to death. He stayed awake and periodically leaned over to listen to my breathing, to be sure I was still alive.

This morning as my teammates walked past my open tent to start up the ropes for what is undoubtedly the Cowboys' last chance at the summit, I held back my tears. I want so much to be with them. I want so much to try one more time. But this time, I can't. I want desperately for them to make it to the top, but more desperately, I want each of them to come back alive. I choked back my tears and called out something inane, like, "Good luck, guys—go get 'em." They each stopped by my tent as they left camp. I'm not sure who said what. Their words to me became jumbled in my mind: "Wish you were with us, Sue." "It's been great traveling with you, Sue." "Hang in there." "Sue, you're going to be with us in spirit." "See you soon." I lay back and thought about what a long way we've come since those lonely, painful carries of early September. Over and over I prayed, "God, let them all get back alive."

Jim and I prepared to descend. Courtney wouldn't let us go alone. He wanted to go down through Mack's Lead with us. I didn't think he should, because he needed to conserve his strength, too.

I couldn't even lift my water bottle the last hour we were on top of the North Col. Courtney got everything ready. He put all my gear into my pack. He checked my harness. He checked my crampons. I was trying to talk to him, but I was incoherent. The only thing that was clear to me was that I was losing my capability to think, talk, move. Court handed Jim and me each a bottle of oxygen and a mask. The oxygen helped, but I couldn't get my sentences out straight. It was as if my mind and tongue had no connection. The thoughts seemed clear to me inside my head, but when they got out I heard myself saying only a random word or two related to the thought.

"Courtney," I thought, "I want to help get my pack and gear ready to go down. You shouldn't have to do this." I even saw myself get up and go to help. But I never moved, and what my ears heard was something like: "Court, help pack down." I stopped trying to talk. Then I knew for sure that I was in trouble. Blurred vision and slurred speech occur just before a terminal coma. I thought, "You've got to get down—quickly. Keep your wits about you, Sue, for one more day."

When the three of us left, Jim took the lead, followed by me, then Courtney. Starting into the Col so weak scared me. Most climbing accidents happen on the way down, and even mildly hypothermic individuals have to expend much more energy than a healthy person to perform the same amount of work. The top part down through Mack's Lead, the steep blue ice laced with crevasses, is tricky going. If I started to fall, could I recover? Would my muscles work? I was so weak I could hardly stand up. I wondered if I had enough physical strength to rappel. This time, being frozen had nothing to do with the cold—I was scared. Of course, it was the first time I had looked down the entire Col route in daylight. I was peering straight down 2,000 vertical feet of jumbled ice and snow. I stood for a long time and silently vowed to myself that henceforth I'd do all my climbing at night, so I couldn't see what I was doing. That thought struck me as hilarious. I laughed out loud. It was the tension breaker that got me moving. I was tentative and super-cautious, going slowly and carefully, talking to myself: "Okay, Sue, concentrate . . . take a breath . . . easy now . . . concentrate . . . take a breath . . . easy does it." Gradually I began to feel comfortable and in control.

At the Z-turn before dropping down to Mack's Lead, I reached a protection point and had to change my safety line and jumar to the lower rope. My nose was almost touching the ice wall as I stood on a 12-inch ledge above a four-foot wide crevasse immediately under my heels. My body was forced right up against the vertical ice wall. It's an awkward spot, and as I bent to unfasten my safety line, the top of my pack hit the wall and threw me off balance. I began to fall backward. My right hand shot up and grabbed the jumar and I pulled hard on the fixed rope to stay upright. I didn't have enough strength to pull myself up with one arm, so I took a giant step with my left foot—back and down into thin air—and felt my crampon land firmly on the opposite side of the crevasse. What a silly position! I was in a vertical spread-eagle, straddling a bottomless crevasse above a 2,000-foot face. But I was upright and not hurt. With strength born of fear—not that I'd fall, but that Courtney or Jim would see me—I kicked off the downhill side of the crevasse, quickly fixed my gear, and continued as if nothing had happened. The incident gave me confidence. Now I knew that not only did I have strength left, I could be motivated by such a simple thing as embarrassment!

I rappelled to the bottom of Mack's Lead, made sure I was stable and hooked in, then looked up. "Oh, my God. How did I ever do that?" I said out loud. It was vertical, sheer ice, and I could see the shadowy deep blue veins of crevasses. I was astounded, just astounded, that I had actually climbed through there. And I was excited. I had done something that looked to me, in my weak and depleted state, simply impossible. I was more than excited, I was exhilarated. I know that what we gain too easily, we value too little. I stood there smiling ear to ear.

After I reached safety below Mack's Lead, Courtney started back up to Camp IVA. Jim was waiting below. I had one more maneuver on the top part of the Col that required my undivided attention: traversing a snow bridge ten yards long and six inches wide over yet another crevasse. Here one could easily fall to either side. The problem was that the sides of the six-inch snow bridge tended to crumble away beneath a climbing boot backed by 150 pounds of pressure. If one could tiptoe right down the center, where the snow was most compacted, something like mincing ten yards down a railroad tie in crampons, the bridge was pretty secure. This, of course, requires exquisite balance from a nonaddled mind. I held my breath and took baby steps. Once I was across, the descent became much easier. On the next few sections, where the grade was only 45 degrees and the snow was a little softer, I was able to fly. I attached the carabiner on the end of my safety line to the fixed rope, secured a handhold just below the 'biner, leaned out, pulled against the fixed line to create friction, and took giant, bounding downhill steps, slowed and supported by the pull against the fixed rope. I descended that portion quickly. I was tired, though, and still had to rappel the last steep pitches.

I stopped below Lunch Ledge to unrack my figure-eight and prepared to rappel down the last two pitches. Jim, who had waited for me below Mack's Lead, and who had been patiently coming along behind me to be sure I made it okay, caught up. I was pleased to be getting so close to the bottom and knew I couldn't do too much more that would be terminal.

"Thanks for the company, Jim," I said. "You know, you look lousy. You should get yourself to a doctor."

As he prepared to go ahead of me, he asked one more time (so sick and so polite!), "Are you sure you're okay?"

"Jim, I'm fine, I'm really just fine. And you know what? I hope that in twenty-eight years, when you're fifty-one, you're somewhere in the Himalayas, hanging off the face of an eight-thousand-meter mountain and you think back to this day, just as some twenty-three-year-old swings by you, leaving you in her dust." He mustered a laugh and took off on the rope.

The remaining section was not difficult. I hadn't even had to rappel on my previous descents. But it was icy now and I was tired. I needed the support of the fixed line and front points so that I wouldn't end my descent in an undignified heap at the bottom of the Col. I took another deep breath and kicked out.

Finally I reached the end of the fixed rope. Dr. Bob, Rick, Jeb, and Jim Robinson were there. Quint had already left with Burnett. I couldn't believe Rick and Jim were still here. They'd both looked like ghosts the last time I'd seen them. The guys took my load to the cache tent and gave me a Thermos of hot tea. Despite their own health—and they all looked haggard—they offered me help and kind words. I appreciated it more than they knew.

As we walked from the cache tent to ABC, we listened to the radio reports from above. Things had continued to deteriorate. Brad Werntz and Carl Coy led a valiant effort to push the route higher, with Brian McLean and Mack Ellerby on their heels. None of our climbers, however, were able to withstand the merciless wind and debilitating cold. Fred had developed severe internal bleeding and had turned back. The others were expected to return to IVA soon. There is no way to reach Camp VI tomorrow. Everybody is deteriorating so rapidly, the only reasonable thing is to get off the mountain. Being so far out on the edge puts things into perspective. We wanted the summit badly, but now it's best to get everyone out alive.

On the flank of Everest's north side, as I prayed for the return of my teammates, I had no idea what was in store for climbers remaining on the mountain. On the Nepal side that night, October 13, one Sherpa accompanying a French climber died of exposure. Between October 14 and 18, teams making their final desperate pushes to reach the summit were to lose an additional five lives. Another Sherpa died, and four Czechoslovakians, among them world-renowned climbers, never descended from their last assault. The four Czechs had already pushed themselves beyond human endurance before making their last summit attempt. Three were almost blind from the effects of altitude and dehydration, but did not descend. Their final night, they attempted a high-altitude bivouac. None made it out alive.

On our side of Everest, the radio report is that Mark and Barry, the two Everest Express climbers who started up their route last night at 10 o'clock, are now above 25,000 feet, but Barry is sinking into cerebral edema. They have radioed the Cowboys and are trying to make a traverse from their couloir onto the North Ridge to descend to our Camp IVA, where we have oxygen. Jeb, Rick, and the Canadians, John and Hank, are en route to the cache tent with hot water and lights to meet them and help get them down.

As I descended into ABC, I was woefully tired, still carrying my pack, still plugging along one step at a time: one step, stop, breathe, balance so as not to collapse; another step, stop, breathe, balance. The others had gone on ahead. Alone, again. Just a hundred yards or so above camp, I saw Quint coming up over the hill to meet me. He put his arms around me and I started to cry. I love these guys. Quint made a move to take my pack. I shook my head.

"No? Okay, then. Sit down." He took my crampons off and helped me back up. "Take my arm." I leaned on him as we covered the last rocky steps into camp.

"Sue," he said, "I just want to say congratulations on your effort. I know you tried as hard as anybody on the whole team to get up there."

I looked at him, too choked up—and too amazed—to utter a word. I didn't think anyone knew how hard I'd tried.

Finally I was back in the mess tent at ABC. Quint took my pack to my tent. As I sank into a corner, Peter Breslow hopped up and got me some hot tea. Bob Skinner had just gotten back from accompanying Orion to Camp II. With pulmonary edema, it was critical that Orion continue all the way down to Base. Bob, exhausted from the struggle back up the moraine to ABC, has a new worry: Orion hasn't gotten to Base Camp yet. We have radioed Base to send somebody up the mountain to look for him.

Of our original six designated summiters, only Julie is left. I don't know how she is tonight. Surely my teammates still on the Col have gotten tucked in by now and are warming themselves. Our radio reports are spotty, but everyone seems to be okay. They have oxygen if they need it. Two Cowboys are still out looking for Mark and Barry. Dr. Bob is watching Jim Burnett in the hospital tent. Jim's not in dangerous condition, but he's not in great condition either, with minor frostbite and evidence of pulmonary edema.

9 P.M. Orion is safely in Base Camp. They found him half an hour ago. He should recover quickly, now that he's at 17,000 feet. Bob Skinner has retired. We're monitoring the radios, but everything seems to be under control tonight.

My condition generated some debate, but Dr. Bob ended up saying I was in better shape than his other patients. My pulse was 100 when I got down. I was dehydrated, but that's not a first. I drank a lot of water and tea and had the first good meal that I have had in four days. I could not eat at 23,500 feet, much as Courtney tried to tempt me with retorts. Last night for dinner at IVA I had two dextrose pills. Tonight Astrid fixed tomato soup, rice, peas, and chocolate mousse. Chocolate mousse! It was wonderful and I started coming right back to life. Dr. Bob is concerned about my lapsing into hypothermia, though, because my body systems have obviously come close to shutting down and my core temperature drops so precipitately once I stop moving. Medical research has shown that after a body temperature drop of only 1.1 degrees F., resting individuals have a dramatic increase in oxygen consumption. Even lying quietly, such a person consumes 360 percent more oxygen than an individual in a normal state. Dr. Bob wants me to sleep with oxygen tonight and he wants someone in the tent with me.

I am inside two sleeping bags, in my down coat, and have a hot water bottle at my feet. I have had three Tylenol tablets with codeine. Dr. Bob set up the oxygen with a nose plug arrangement: two plastic hoses that go into the nostrils and supply oxygen. The O_2 helps. I will be a lot warmer tonight.

10 P.M. I hear the crunch-crunch-crunch of footsteps outside my tent.

"Sue? You awake?" It is Dr. Bob.

"What's up?"

"Since Carl's still on the Col, John Wayne is going to be your roomie." He sticks his head through the tent flap, and behind him I can see Bob Skinner.

"I'm all right, really."

"I know, but it would be best if someone's in the tent with you. Just in case you need something."

"I'm sure I won't need a thing. Besides, John Wayne needs his rest, he can't afford to sit up all night with me. I'm okay now."

"Are you sure?"

"Positive."

They close the flap and leave. Crunch-crunch-crunch.

I'm not positive, I'm not sure I'm okay. I have never been so truly exhausted, but with enough oxygen, food, and water, I hope to be strong enough to make Base Camp tomorrow. I cannot ascend and help my teammates on the Col. I don't think I can even go uphill to the cache tent. Maybe I can go downhill. In September Fred and I took nine hours to reach Base from this camp; it will surely be a longer trudge tomorrow. And since all our camps have been blown out, there's no place to stop. It'll be all or nothing.

I am anxious to get down and talk to Chuck. Courtney was kind enough to radio Base from the Col earlier tonight and ask them to be sure to call Chuck and tell him I was off the Col and safe. I also want access to a phone to see what I can do for the team on departure arrangements. I may be able to help with logistics, if Mary Skinner hasn't already arranged everything.

I received a wonderful long missive from Chuck, delivered to ABC today by the yakkies. Dated October 7, it outlines the elaborate plan he has for me to join him in Milan, Madrid, Rome, and Budapest. Unfortunately, I can't meet the dates even if I get to Base tomorrow. Somehow I will figure out how to get to Europe. The funny part is that Chuck is expecting me to go to all these embassy receptions and dinners with ministers, ambassadors, and other diplomatic types, and the only apparel I have is mountain clothes, lived in for two months. I'm 100 percent Cowboy now—and a distinctly grubby one at that.

I hope everyone on the Col is all right. Courtney is still in the same tent we had when I was there. Poor guy! Each morning we woke up covered with snow. Normally, you can slide up, without getting all the way out of your bag, and start hot water in the vestibule. But because that tent wasn't spindrift-proof, snow fell all over us every time one of us moved. It was like being in one of those glass paperweights that when shaken, create a snowstorm around the little people confined inside. We begged for hot water from our buddies, whom we visualized as being in a tropical paradise in their three-man, Skinner-made, spindrift-proof tents. It was worse for Courtney than for me, because most of the time I was in a fetal position inside my bag with my head covered. Courtney did all the work. I would never have lasted without him—or even been there without the help of the other team members. At some point, each one of the Cowboys did something to move Sue Cobb along the route toward the North Ridge.

My God, what's that? An enormous rockslide just exploded behind me. It sounded like a squadron of fighter jets zooming into the back of my tent. I scramble outside and see it veer off downhill away from our camp. I am just settling back into my bag and readjusting the O_2 system when Dr. Bob reappears. He needs the oxygen for Barry Blanchard. Barry definitely has signs of cerebral edema. Bohus figures I will survive, but the Canadian needs the oxygen.

It's cold again. The Everest sounds will not cease. The wind is trying to sneak under my tent and attack from beneath. Now I wish John Wayne were here.

CHAPTER XVII

Retreat

OCTOBER 14, 1988. ABC. I was deemed unfit for travel. Bob's judgment is correct. I am too weak. Jim Burnett is getting better and Barry is coming back from the cerebral edema scare. We'll rest here another day. The guys will stay on the Col one more night, except for Fred, who must descend today.

6 P.M. At dinner in the mess tent, a somber group of Cowboys heard Courtney Skinner radio the following message from the North Col to Base Camp:

"On Friday, October fourteenth, at sixteen-hundred hours, in the cold shadows of the north side of Mount Everest, with the temperature at minus twenty-seven degrees F. and winds of forty-two miles per hour, the decision was made to begin an orderly withdrawal from high on the mountain. Seventy-six days into the expedition and after some sixty-two days above seventeen thousand feet, after positioning for three summit attempts, the decision, although difficult, was the only wise and prudent one available.

"With sustained and tenacious effort, the Cowboys established stocked camps up to twenty-five thousand, five hundred feet. We were not turned back by climbing difficulties, as those had already been brilliantly solved (though we had the Second Step yet to go).

When the jet stream caught us in full force, valiant and heroic efforts were made to hold our high camps, but it was not to be. The deteriorating October weather and our time at high altitude sapped our strength. With sadness and relief we will begin our retreat."

The official word. It's over.

Tomorrow the group on the Col will start tossing soft goods off the top, to get some of the weight to a lower elevation without a lot of carries. Everybody at ABC who is able will help retrieve the company gear and bring it back down to ABC for the yaks to pick up.

Fred came down today looking glum and thoroughly drained. He is in pain and moves with the slow deliberateness of a man taking his first steps after surgery. Brian, the indefatigable Brian, has finally given out. Jim Burnett looks wan, with cracked lips and sunken cheeks, but says he's feeling better. I am merely saggy, draggy, and droopy, with the energy of a slug.

It gets so cold now that it doesn't take long for everyone to finish dinner and head for their sleeping bags to try to keep warm, though it's often too early to sleep. I can't read in my tent because it's too cold to have my hands out to hold a book and turn the pages. I find my companion is my recorder. Anne and I talked today about some of the goals and objectives of this expedition. Whatever our perspectives, everyone has to be pleased with the scientific research and educational achievements. The one goal with the highest media profile, the summit, we didn't reach. But our four high school teachers, two high school students, and artist have all experienced life in a different world. Our medical, geology, meteorology, and communications researchers all completed their scientific work. We return to the States with a little more knowledge to add to those disciplines and to share with our colleagues.

Tonight is my last night at ABC. The winds are back and that familiar freight train is roaring down the valley toward me, crashing into my tent. It is 30 degrees below zero. I want to go home.

OCTOBER 16, 1988. As I left ABC yesterday morning, all able-bodied persons were headed up to the Col with empty packs to bring down the gear. I can't believe some of our guys are going back up. Rick, for example. He has lost a lot of weight, and he was sick with the dry heaves this morning.

"If I could just eat something," he said, "I'd have something to throw up." I watched him head out. He stopped frequently to rest,

Tibetan prayer flags and the colors of the United States and the State of Wyoming flew proudly over Base Camp. PHOTO BY ORION SKINNER.

and when he doubled over, it appeared to me that he was retching.

The aim was to clean up the mountain of our tents, sleeping bags, propane, food, oxygen, everything we'd so laboriously carried up. The guys will attach the gear to their harnesses and drag everything to the cache site, and on to ABC, through snow drifts and blasting wind. Then the yaks will take over.

I left ABC at 10 A.M., carrying twenty-five pounds. I expected to see some traffic on the highway: Pete Breslow, Jim Burnett, and Mark and Barry of the Everest Express were all headed down. Fred started down too, but planned to pitch a tent at the Interim site. It was much colder than the last time I climbed the East Rongbuk Glacier. Before I got to Interim, I was dragging. My senses were dulled. My body was drained. I simply resolved to keep moving. I was conscious of the shifting and cracking seracs and of the rockslides all through the moraine, but the dangers seemed surprisingly ordinary, I'd been there so many times before. Progressively, I began to feel worse. I did not have a radio, because there weren't enough left for all who needed them—we'd lost so many on the Col. It didn't seem important. It is amazing how your perspective changes: I was traveling less than fifteen miles at 21,000- to 17,000-foot elevations. I recalled that 17,000 feet was a big deal when we crossed those first passes out of Lhasa.

As I passed the Camp II site, Mark and Fred were somewhere above me. When I stopped for a rest below Interim, Mark passed me. I was now the last descending climber, Fred having holed up at Interim. About half an hour later I looked at my watch. It was 6:30. I had expected to reach Base Camp before dark, but the long October shadows were now stalking the valley. It wouldn't be long before all light disappeared. No way was I going to get into Base before dark. "Okay, Sue," I said to myself, "one more goal. Before it gets dark, get through the steep hillside section just below Camp I, where a fall could do some damage." The trail, such as it is, runs parallel to the bottom of the river gorge about 200 feet above the drainage. In several places there is no trail. It has been obliterated by rockfall, landslides, and scree. A misstep there would give me and whatever rocks I kicked loose a long and unpleasant slide down to the river.

Off I went at a quickened and determined pace. But a combination of fading light and fading energy slowed me down. I was at 19,000 feet and could feel the difference in the air, but after eight hours of hiking, I was still five miles from Base. Periodically, I would lose the route. Glacial movement, rockslides, and landslides had altered its path. I picked my way down and reached our old Camp I site with, at best, a few minutes of dim light left. Would there be a moon tonight? I hurried past a gear stash and, as darkness fell, timidly embarked on the steepest section of the trail. It was pitch black—no moon. Now I slowed to a snail's pace, probing ahead with my ski pole for stable ground, for a spot where a slip in the scree wouldn't take my feet out from under me. Then I'd take a tentative step. If it felt firm, I transferred my weight and tried another baby step. If I slipped, I would not have the muscular strength to recover. I came to a small rock bench and fussed with my headlamp long enough to get it working. I descended the last steep portion of the East Rongbuk Glacier and was funneled into the gully toward Base Camp. Several hundred yards above our camp, the narrow valley opens into the broad Rongbuk Valley base camp area. Then I would cross the Rongbuk River one last time, round the drumlins, and be in Base Camp.

I had about four miles to go. The valley is narrow and well-defined with abrupt hillsides, so I could not go too far astray. My last challenge was to cover the distance in the dark without tripping and cracking my head on a rock, without falling and twisting an ankle, and without sitting too long at rest. I knew what would happen to me if the heat generated by my muscle activity ceased. If only I could radio my location. I didn't want to be stuck out all night, unable to move, waiting to see if I was alive in the morning.

It was getting late. Would someone from Base come to look for me? I thought about our call to Base for someone to climb up to meet Orion. Surely, they'd talked to Bob at ABC, or to Fred at Interim, and know I am headed down. A sickle moon appeared. The shadows played tricks on my eyes. I sat on a rock to focus down the valley and listen. No sound. "Come on, Sue. You can't sit. Keep moving. If you can get closer to the end of this gorge, someone might see your headlamp. Keep moving."

Several times I took my headlamp off and flashed it down the gorge. I hadn't given up the idea that someone would come to look for me. There was no response. Were they all sound asleep at Base Camp? Did they think I'd stopped at Camp I, where they'd left a stash? Finally I emerged from the narrow gorge into the broad Rongbuk Valley, and this time, when I flashed my headlamp, I saw a light down the valley. Was I ever happy! Finally I could sit down and rest for a moment. I sighed in relief and sank onto a rock. But the light went out and there was no further indication that anyone had seen me. The light must have been a mile away. I flashed my headlamp again, picked myself up, and started stumbling in the direction from which the light had come. I kept flashing my headlamp. Flashing. Flashing. The distant light reappeared. They'd seen me! As I sank down on the ground, the light disappeared again. Several minutes passed in which I repeatedly blinked my headlamp. No response. One more time, I picked myself up and struggled on.

Suddenly, not more than a hundred yards away, I heard a voice. "Hey!" I called out. "Ted, is that you?" There was no answer. Out of the darkness appeared two men. "Hello! It's Sue!" Even as we drew closer, I couldn't recognize them. They would be from another expedition. The Canadians, perhaps? But no, a Japanese and a Chinese. "The Cowboys," I said. "I'm trying to get to the Cowboy Base Camp."

They shook their heads—they didn't understand my words. But they did understand the situation. One shouldered my pack, and with the Japanese on my right and the Chinese on my left, each holding one arm, I crossed the Rongbuk River for the last time and limped into the Cowboy Base Camp.

10:45 P.M. I was down.

CHAPTER XVIII

Out of China

OCTOBER 16, 1988. I slept ten hours last night and awoke with a drained and sore body, but a new lease on life. I am warm and soon I will be heading home. Mary Skinner has already completed the travel arrangements for the Cowboys. There are two drivers in the valley with jeeps. So whichever way I can make arrangements, either to Lhasa or to Kathmandu, I will go. I am told that it will take two or three days and at least two nights in either direction. So far the best price I can get is $1,000 to get to Lhasa.

Other than a general overall tiredness, I am in fairly good shape, although I have lost between twenty-five and thirty pounds. At breakfast the conversation turned to our team's health and to other teams' tragedies. Everest has claimed thirteen lives this year, nine while we were on the mountain, six on our route—but no Cowboys. I am hoping everybody up above us is hanging on in good health.

8:00 P.M. I just got off the phone with Chuck. He's heading for Madrid tomorrow. The driver for the Canadian team is down to $800 to take me to Lhasa. Tomorrow I will call Bob Fleming's friend in Kat and see if I can arrange for somebody to pick me up at the Nepal-Tibet border, then see what the Canadian driver will charge to take me there. Once I get to either Lhasa or Kat, I can fly *somewhere* and catch up with Chuck.

OCTOBER 17, 1988. I finally got a call through to Kathmandu. The phone connection was very bad, but I *think* they said that they could send a car today to the Tibet-Nepal border, but not tomorrow or the next day, because of the Dasain festival in Kathmandu, the country's most celebrated holiday. I walked to the Canadian camp, to see if their Tibetan driver would take me to the Nepal border. After lengthy negotiations we settled on 1,800 yuan (or about $450) for the 450 miles from Base Camp to the border. Then I was told that an interpreter must accompany every driver. The Chinese manage to add extra costs to everything. My tab ended up being around $600 to the border, where I will presumably meet the car from Kathmandu, which will be another $150. I need to be ready to leave in an hour.

I gave Ted Handwerk my gray Koflax double-lined mountain boots to give to Norbu, to replace his tennis shoes. Wool socks were another item that were popular with the yak herders, so I left all I had. And by now, one of the yakkies is probably strutting around in Toby's Brooks Brothers suit.

At the last minute, David Frawley decided to go with me. We raced around to say our good-byes, to thank everyone. Those who become friends at 350 millimeters of mercury will be friends for life. I wanted to say goodbye to Julie; she will climb whatever Everest that comes into her path, but Julie, Court, and Bob were not yet at Base. I guess I'm glad. It would have brought me to tears to say good-bye to Court and Bob, we've come so far together. David and I both feel bad about leaving, but at least we know all the Cowboys are safe and headed down.

David and I pulled out of Base Camp in a Nissan wagon with a Tibetan driver and a Chinese interpreter who calls himself Sampson. We had to detour through Xegar, over two hours out of our way, to drop off a sick Japanese climber. David and I were both quiet, pensive, as we retraced the Rongbuk Valley road. We barely spoke until we reached Xegar. We had dinner at the old Dogtown hotel, where we had spent a week in early August, waiting for our trucks to arrive and trying to circumvent the washed-out bridge. It brought back floods of memories, most of them bad.

Our cranky Nissan driver wanted to stay overnight at the Xegar Hotel and leave the next day. We said absolutely not — *Keep driving.* As we left the hotel compound, the driver was stopped at the gate. We learned through the interpreter that when we get to the border in five or six hours it will be closed. "We must stay here tonight," Sampson said.

In my firmest lawyerly tone I said, "Tell the driver to drive on. Now." Turning to David, I said, "I don't know about you, but there's *no way* I'm staying one more night in Dogtown. I don't know if there's a car waiting or where we will stay if there's not, but let's go for it." Being as ignorant of the border topography as I was, David readily agreed. Reluctantly, our Nissan captain started back the now familiar Friendship Highway, passed the turnoff to the Rongbuk Valley and headed southwest toward Nepal.

9 P.M. We are somewhere on top of the Tibetan Plateau, heading for the Nepal border and uncertainty. Crossing the Nepal-Tibet border, we were told as we left, is always unpredictable. Due to the past monsoon seasons, the road is severely damaged. The border area is steep and subject to landslides, some mammoth. We were told to be prepared to hike ten miles or more with several thousand feet of altitude change. According to the trekker grapevine, there is danger from falling rock, precipitous cliffs, and raging rivers. It is not done at night. Perhaps there are some unexpected adventures ahead, but the greatest of all, the Everest climb, is fading into the distance behind us.

OCTOBER 18, 1988. 2 A.M. I just crawled into a bed. We drove as far as we could, to a monster landslide that has washed away the road and everything around it. At midnight, we abandoned the Nissan. Our driver had been obstinate and not too pleasant a fellow, so we weren't sorry to say good-bye to him. Sampson accompanied us, even though he didn't know where we were going, either. The three of us set out on foot. It was pitch black. We crossed a tumultuous river on slippery rocks and climbed up out of an enormous deep ravine. We skirted the cascading waterfalls of the headwaters of the river and stumbled our way along an ill-defined trail through water, mud, and darkness. Descending the steep incline, we didn't know where the trail was going. What an ignominious end for two stalwart mountain climbers, if we failed to negotiate this section. Sampson had been told that if we crossed the gorge through this massive washout, and de-scended several thousand feet, we would come to a little village where we could find a place to sleep. We worked our way to the other side of the slide. There was, indeed, a village. Along the switchback dirt road we were descending were lean-tos made of pieces of weathered canvas. Tiny "house" after "house" of canvas lined the path. Tied in front were donkeys and goats. Dogs rummaged around, or lay with one eye watching us. All these canvas houses opened to our path. Inside, human forms were lying on what appeared to be grass mats. Even though it was now 1 in the morning, people would rise up on an elbow and speak to us in Tibetan, Nepalese, and Chinese. When did they sleep, I wondered?

Farther down were some good-sized wooden structures, clinging precariously to the side of the mountain, one of which was the Zhangmu Hotel. With Sampson's help, we checked ourselves in. Before giving us our keys, though, the Chinese owner tried to add an additional amount to the stated room rate. "Why?" we asked. "Because we are coming in after midnight," Sampson said. David erupted. On principle he would take no more last-minute price increases. He said he'd sleep on the floor in the lobby. "Gee," I said to myself, "this means I have to support my buddy and sleep in the lobby, too." I didn't want to do that, because for the first night since early August, I was tantalizingly close to a real bed. We negotiated. David and Sampson ended up sharing a room. I got a room. For the first night in eight weeks I am not in a sleeping bag. The bed is not quite like home, but I don't have to unzip it to get out. In the morning we head for Kathmandu, though I have yet to see any cars.

7 A.M. The terrain last night was obscured when darkness descended on the Tibetan plateau. In the dead of night we stumbled into the Zhangmu Valley. My mind retained a snapshot of the stark and austere dry brown plains at the foot of Everest. When I opened the curtain this morning, it was as if the set had changed while I was out for intermission. Below me was the archetypical brush painting of the misty mountains of China, with lush green vegetation and frame houses tacked to the side of the hill, supported on the steep downhill side by long wooden stilts. The Sun Kosi River, on its way to the Gangetic Plain of India, runs beneath the stilts. People and animals bask in the warmth of the sun. But it is the vegetation that amazes me. Trees, foliage, growth—everything is green!

Now it's time to get out of China. Sampson walked with us in the direction of the border station. When it was in sight, he started the return climb to the top of the washout to find the Nissan. David and I proceeded to the control point. There, as the Chinese officials took our passports to check us out of their country, a flurry of conversation erupted. "Oh my God," I thought, "they're not going to let us out."

PHOTO BY DAVID FRAWLEY

David ran to the door to hail Sampson, so that he could explain what problem had arisen. Sampson was gone. We had no idea what was going on. Moments later a young woman in a Chinese army uniform handed me a crumpled piece of paper. I unfolded it and almost fell over, laughing with joy. David grabbed it from my hand and read aloud: "Mrs. Cobb, your car is waiting at the bridge. Please proceed."

Grabbing our bags, David and I took off in the direction of the Friendship Bridge, two miles and another 2,000 feet below us. We walked, ran, slid, jumped, and raced all the way downhill into Nepal.

Riding in the car to Kathmandu, I breathe the clear, oxygen-rich air rushing in the windows. I lean back against the seat in 78-degree warmth and think of the ice and snow on the North Col. Nothing grows on the North Col. Now everything around me is alive. I'm alive and I'm going home.

EPILOGUE

On the evening of October 20, Chuck and I had a happy reunion on the Spanish Steps in Rome. We traveled the next day to Hungary for a convention at which Chuck was to speak. There I got an unexpected bonus. By coincidence, the speaker sharing the platform with my husband in Budapest was none other than Sir Edmund Hillary. I spent the morning with this remarkable pioneer. Today, as New Zealand's representative in India, Nepal, and Bhutan, Hillary maintains close ties to the Nepalese Sherpa community and to the mountain with whose name his is inextricably linked.

Within a week, I returned to Miami to see my boys. We celebrated with a family excursion, boating across Biscayne Bay to Elliott Key. We anchored for the night, sat on the fantail, and Chris barbecued some snapper and fresh lobster that Toby brought up from the sea. I felt the soft, warm trade winds brush my skin, and my eyes traveled out over the bay to the sailboats rocking gently in the emerald and turquoise waters. As we watched one of the most glorious sunsets imaginable, a brilliant red-orange sun falling off the edge of the world, I marveled at the contrasts in our universe. Ten days before I had been standing on a glacier, almost on top of the world, surrounded only by snow and ice, with no vegetation within thousands and thousands of feet, trying desperately to protect myself from hypothermia. I know now what a fine line I was walking between living and dying. I recognize now how depleted my body was. I realize how dependent I was on my teammates. I feel fortunate to be alive.

The contrasts remain startling in my mind. Friends ask "How long will you feel the vividness? How long will you appreciate it?" I hope forever, because so few people have been where I have been. I am asked, "What stands out most since you returned?" That's easy. The greatest experience of all was that of humanity: the fellowship on our team, and the friendship and support that flowed in from around the world for the Cowboys, for my family, and for me.

I'm often asked if I would go back. I remember that while on the edge of Everest, I said unequivocally no. Yet time has a way of healing wounds. It is not the loneliness and the pain that I remember, it is my teammates' good will, it is the small triumphs, it is the sheer joy of climbing on the mountain that is the symbol of mankind's highest aspirations.

Sometimes at night, despite all that transpired, I hear again the sounds of Everest, softer now . . . a gentle siren song. "Come on back, Sue," it beckons to me. And I listen. Still, the overriding sound that echoes in my ears is not the siren song, but the sounds that came to me out of the sky, from the Indian Ocean satellite, "Come home, sweetheart, please come home."

THE COWBOYS

Courtney Skinner, 52, wilderness outfitter, Pinedale, Wyoming: expedition leader

Robert Skinner, 58, wilderness outfitter, Pinedale, Wyoming: director of mountaineering

SUMMIT TEAMS

Fred Riedman, 30, credit manager, Salt Lake City: deputy leader

Orion Skinner, 31, geologist, Parker, Colorado

Sue Cobb, 50, attorney, Miami

Robert Bohus, 35, physician, Sheridan, Wyoming

Julie Cheney, 31, climbing guide, Eau Claire, Wisconsin

Jim Burnett, 22, student and logger, Kemmerer, Wyoming

TEAM ONE—BASE CAMP AND MEDIA

Dan Pryor, 27, real estate, Williston, Vermont: Base Camp manager

Sheri King, 33, physician, Pueblo, Colorado: Base Camp physician

David Padwa, 56, lawyer and professor, Boulder, Colorado: research and development, communications

Jim Clayton, 33, artist, Denver: cook, photographer, artist

Matt Ellenthal, 25, account representative, Old Greenwich, Connecticut: photographer, communications

Anne Stroock, 29, television, Casper, Wyoming: filmmaker, publicity, press

Steve Marts, 49, photographer, Seattle: filmmaker

Peter Breslow, 37, broadcasting, Washington, D.C.: communications, radio

TEAM TWO—RESEARCH AND SUPPORT
Ted Handwerk, 33, building contractor, Boulder, Colorado
Dave McNally, 34, artist, Jackson, Wyoming
Alexandra Hildebrandt, 35, venture consultant, New York
Mark Pilon, 32, software engineer, Golden, Colorado
Doug Burbank, 36, geology professor, Los Angeles
Steve Gardiner, 34, scholarship educator, Jackson, Wyoming

TEAM THREE—HIGH-ALTITUDE SUPPORT
Jeb Schenck, 38, teacher and photographer, Thermopolis, Wyoming
Ethan Goldings, 28, student, Stanford, California
Quintin Barney, 29, printer, Salt Lake City
Rick Dare, 34, teacher, Wright, Wyoming
Sibylle Hechtel, 37, translator, Boulder, Colorado
David Frawley, 43, business manager, Lowell, Massachusetts

TEAM FOUR—HIGH-ALTITUDE SUPPORT
Brian McLean, 34, materials engineer, Littleton, Colorado
Brad Werntz, 22, student, Evanston, Illinois
Mack Ellerby, 36, fence contractor, Denver
Ross Greenlee, 31, physician, Salt Lake City
Carl Coy, 33, teacher, Gillette, Wyoming
Jim Robinson, 25, broker, Dallas

SUPPORT MEMBERS
Luke Omohundro
Brian Shoemaker
Kang Jian Cheng
Michael Jauregui
Fred Riedman, Sr.

THE EVEREST FOOD PLAN

Thirty-five people. Three months. Over ten thousand pounds of food. Six camps. The nearly overwhelming responsibility of the Cowboys' food supplies was successfully undertaken by Ted Handwerk. Ted's job, feeding an Everest expedition in China, was extremely complex. Logistics and cost had to be considered, as well as the special nutritional requirements of climbers, who need palatable, high-calorie, nutritionally balanced meals that can be easily packed and prepared with minimum effort.

For the Wyoming Centennial Everest Expedition, Ted prepared a 41-page computerized plan, separated into high-altitude and low-altitude foods, and based on a 65 percent carbohydrate, 22 percent fat, and 13 percent protein ratio. The low-altitude food plan entailed providing meals for all the residents from Base Camp (16,700 feet) up to and including Advanced Base Camp (21,120). Meals in Camp IV (23,500 feet) and above fell under the high-altitude plan. The higher the camp for which meals were intended, the lighter in weight and easier to prepare the food was.

At high altitudes, anorexia (loss of appetite) is a major problem. Climbers burn 5,000 to 6,000 calories per day on the mountain, yet most have difficulty consuming more than 4,000 calories per day. Without adequate calorie intake, a climber rapidly loses strength. It is therefore important that climbers have a variety of high-calorie foods from which to choose. This encourages consumption not only at high altitudes, but also at lower camps where climbers are resting.

Prior to departure from the United States, cases of food were unpacked, sorted, weighed, and repacked into man-day needs for each camp. The reorganized food was then loaded into lightweight, durable, watertight boxes weighing 60 to 70 pounds each for shipment to China. The containers were sealed and marked with a code that identified their destination on the mountain, with each camp having a different code. This procedure minimized the work load of the climbers and allowed careful control of supplies.

Low-altitude foods that required cooking, such as noodles, rice, and potatoes, were shipped in bulk. Cooks were assigned to prepare meals at Base Camp and Advanced Base Camp. These prepared meals limited the freedom of climbers to choose their own food, but they were, in general, superior to what tired climbers would have made for themselves. Lunch and snack foods were stored in designated areas at both Base Camp and Advanced Base Camp and were available 24 hours each day so that climbers suffering from loss of appetite would have food continuously available, thereby encouraging them to increase their calorie consumption.

The high-altitude food plan was more complex. Climbers at altitude have higher caloric requirements, but less energy and less comfortable conditions for food preparation. High-altitude foods were specifically chosen to minimize the mental and physical effort exerted by climbers at and above the North Col. Each package contained two meals and the label identified both the type of meal (breakfast, lunch, dinner) and the destination of the package (Camp IV, V, VI). At high altitudes, the food plan provided two to two and a half pounds of food per man-day, compared with the three pounds per man-day at Base Camp.

The prepackaged meals did not require cooking. Retorts (foil-packed entrees) had been precooked and could be heated or eaten cold. As always, special attention was given to make these meals nutritionally balanced as well as interesting and palatable. A sample breakfast at a high-altitude camp could include instant hot cereal, granola bars or cookies, and hot chocolate, tea, or coffee. Lunch might be peanut butter and jam sandwiches on Rubschlager bread, beef jerky, cookies, hard candy, gorp, and Kool-Aid. A retort of sliced pork with gravy, noodles, soup, crackers, hot Jell-O, and hot chocolate or tea would be a sample dinner.

A summary of the Handwerk plan for high-altitude dinner foods is shown below.

SUMMARY OF HIGH-ALTITUDE DINNER FOODS

	Days	Folks	Each Portion	Number of Portions	Total Quantity	Unit Weight	Total Weight	Man Days
Assorted retorts	32	12	1 package	1	384	7 ounces	168 pounds	384
Potato flakes	6.4	12	1 cup, dry	1	77	2 ounces	10	77
Rice	6.4	12	1 pouch	2	154	1.4 ounce	14	77
Noodles	6.4	12	1 pouch	2	154	1.4 ounce	14	77
Stove Top stuffing	6.4	12	1 ounce	3	231	1 ounce	15	77
Couscous	6.4	12	1 ounce	3	231	1 ounce	15	77
Cup-A-Soup	32	12	1 package	1	384	.7 ounce	17	384
Ramen soup	12.8	12	1 package	1	154	3 ounces	29	154
Crackers	21.3	12	.125 box	1	32	10 ounces	20	256
Rubschlager bread	10.5	12	1 package	1	127	8 ounces	63	127
Sharp cheddar	16	12	.125 pound	1	24	1 pound	24	192
Colby	8	12	.125 pound	1	12	1 pound	12	96
Monterey Jack	8	12	.125 pound	1	12	1 pound	12	96
Milk powder	32	12	–		26	5 ounces	8	384
Tea	32	12	1 bag	1	384	.166 ounce	4	384
Hot chocolate	32	12	1 package	1	384	1 ounce	24	384
Hot Jell-O	12.8	12	.25 quart	1	38	3 ounces	7	154
Hot cider	12.8	12	.25 quart	1	38	3 ounces	7	154
Hot orange	6.4	12	.25 quart	1	20	3 ounces	4	77
Vivonex tens	10.5	12	.378 quart	1	47	4 ounces	12	127
Butter	32	12	–		8.5	1 pound	8.5	384
Cookies	21	12	.125 box	1	32	1 pound	32	254
Cheese cake	5.3	12	.25 box	1	16	11 ounces	11	64
Coconut cream pie	2.7	12	.25 box	1	8	9.5 ounces	5	32
Chocolate mousse pie	2.7	12	.25 box	1	8	9.5 ounces	5	32

TOTAL   540.5

211

SUE COBB'S EXPEDITION GEAR

MOUNTAIN CLOTHING
medium-weight down parka
    with hood
extra-large anorak
Gore-Tex pants (2)
wind shirt
wind pants
Wyoming Woolens pile suit
Patagonia Synchilla sweaters (2)
polypro vest
down vest
cotton turtlenecks (3)
cotton scarves (3)
poncho
lightweight down mittens
Gore-Tex −30° gloves
leather gloves
Gore-Tex shell overmitts
    (2 pairs)
fleece liners (2 pairs)
Thermax liners (2 pairs)
polypro liners (2 pairs)
polypro hats (2)
polypro neckwarmers (2)
silk balaclava
wool balaclava

longjohns (2 pairs)
Capilene underwear (2 sets)
polypro socks (5 pairs)
wool socks (5 pairs)
neoprene socks (2 pairs)
vapor-barrier liner socks
    (2 pairs)

CLIMBING GEAR
Chouinard 75 cm ice axe
Chouinard body harness with
    gear rack
Wild Country harness with
    gear rack
MSR helmet
rigid snap-on crampons
ultralight crampons
lightweight gaiters
insulated gaiters
Equipe Solitaire suit
Makalu high-altitude parka
North Face bib
Dana oxygen pack
oversized mitts
pile suit

Clog ascenders
carabiners
ice screws
figure eight descender
ski poles
altimeter
compass
avalanche beeper
neoprene face protector
space blanket
Dana high-altitude pack
maps
repair tape
headlamp
bulbs
crampon parts
lithium batteries
disposable lighters
whistle

FOOTWEAR
Koflax climbing boots
Koflax Ultra Extreme boots
aveolite liner
Asolo 101 boots
Gore-Tex hiking boots
Sorels
tennis shoes
down booties
overboots

EYEWEAR
glacier glasses (2)
prescription goggles (2)
regular plastic glasses

TENT GEAR
48-inch RidgeRest
extra long Therm-a-Rest

¾-length Therm-a-Rest
pillow case
down pillow
Feathered Friends Snow Goose
 −40° sleeping bag
Gore-Tex reflective bivy bag
groundcloth
water bottles (2)
water bottle insulator
pee bottle
pee bottle funnel
flashlights (2)
small Swiss army knife
large Swiss army knife
Leatherman tool
brush for boots
plastic garbage bags
sealable plastic ditty bags
toilet paper
mug
spoons
mesh ditty bags (5)
pack towels (2)

COSMETIC
small towel
mirror
toothbrush
toothpaste
cleanser and soap
comb
dental floss
Gladstein Pik
lip balm
sunscreen
dry shampoo
tissues and Freshettes
hand lotion

continued

MEDICAL
aspirin
athletic tape
Spenco Second Skin
moleskin
ace bandages
adhesive bandages
water tablets
throat lozenges
cough drops
vitamins A, B6, B12, C, E
iron and folic acid
sun blister medication
mild sleeping aid
codeine
Motrin
zinc oxide

PERSONAL
sewing kit
passport carrier
Walkman and tapes
stereo case
insulated bags for tapes
camera and film
recorders (2)
waterproof notebook
pencils and pens
pencil sharpener
oxygen information
WCEE postcards
mailing labels
books
flags and pins